THE

PENETRALIA;

BEING

HARMONIAL ANSWERS

TO

IMPORTANT QUESTIONS.

BY ANDREW JACKSON DAVIS,

AUTHOR OF SEVERAL VOLUMES ON THE HARMONIAL PHILOSOPHY.

The power to put a question presupposes and guarantees the power no less to answer it.
See page 14.

BOSTON:
WILLIAM WHITE & COMPANY,
158 WASHINGTON STREET.
NEW YORK:
BANNER OF LIGHT BRANCH OFFICE, 544 BROADWAY.
1868.

SAVAGE & McCREA, STEREOTYPERS,
13 Chambers Street, N. Y.

PREFACE.

FROM time to time, during the past three years, the Author has been interrogated on almost every topic; frequently by letter, sometimes orally, and naturally by the subjects themselves while undergoing examination.

This volume is designed and fraternally submitted as a *responsum*, or reply, to such questions as have appeared most important and serviceable to Mankind.

"PENETRALIA" is a Latin term, signifying the inmost or "secret recesses" of a palace, temple, idea, or principle.

Accordant with the spirit of this word, the Author has *penetrated* the hidden and sequestered parts of numerous questions, of the most momentous import to every human mind.

From the spiritual interior—from the *penetralia* of the imperishable Univercœlum—the essence of each answer was derived. Nevertheless, the method is familiar as the ordinary deductions of the intellect.

The Author does not presume to believe that his replies will be either final or gratifying to those who occupy different positions in regard to the several subjects considered. And yet, his spirit is animated with the hope that, to such minds, the following pages may *suggest* even more than they express, of high thoughts and saving principles.

The motive that actuates the spirit of this "PENETRALIA" is, to cause a *diviner faith to shine in the heart of huma nature.*

In order to accomplish this glorious result, it states the questions in a variety of forms, and answers them in plain words and familiar illustrations:

It probes the various departments of human existence, and considers both the ordinary and extraordinary, the sensuous and celestial:

It reaches down to the very foundation of Nature's trifold Temple, and conducts the philosophical reader through pleasurable labyrinths innumerable:

It sweeps the chords of creation, sings the sweet anthemnal song of Eternal Harmony, and awakens aspirations toward Love, Wisdom, and Liberty.

A. J. D

NEW YORK, *June* 12, 1856.

CONTENTS.

THE

PHILOSOPHY OF QUESTIONS AND ANSWERS.

POLITICALLY and theologically, the human mind is in bondage; but constitutionally and spiritually, it is free as Deity. Its thoughts, regardless of the barriers of time and space, fly on swiftest pinions everywhere. Everlasting mountains, though piled up and lost in clouds, are but play-grounds. Thoughts, in good minds, are angels. The mind, fearfully and wonderfully made, composes itself in harmony; and, like a demi-god, commissions its Thoughts to do the out-door work. By sober reflection, who can trace the rovings of Thought? Thoughts, the mind's children, play in Nature's fields. On eager wing, they fly down the long ages gone, perch themselves on the beginnings of life, and answer questions as by the breathings of intuition. The varied journeyings of these angels are hard to trace. Like birds of another sphere, endowed with functions of fleetest motion, men's Thoughts revel amid stars, and play fearlessly with shining hosts, where, one would say, only highest seraphs dare to tread. Meanwhile the mind, clothed with the physical vesture, sits in judgment upon the tales of Thought — pronouncing them "good" or "evil" by an inward law of Justice eternal. In great and good minds, all thoughts are harmonious and meek; but the thoughts of small minds fret and strut, like puppets in a showman's box.

Taking the risk of shocking your experience, I begin with the affirmation, that the human mind is possessed of no power or function whereby to conceive or suppose *things* and *ideas* which do not essentially exist. I do not believe that man can fancy impossibilities. Every human thought begins in the essence of truth. And yet, on either side of this mighty river of currental truth, you will find the noxious weeds of diminution or of exaggeration. In all inferior stages of human growth, you will observe persons born with proclivities either for *diminishing* or else for *exaggerating things*, which produce ideas. Diminishers are called skeptics; the exaggerators, idealists. The former dwell in facts; the latter in principles. Those unjustly termed "skeptics" believe only in the *Finite*—in things cognizable by means of the senses; while believers are skeptics in matters of fact, and concern themselves only with the *Infinite*—in ideas of the illimitable and boundless. Error so called is to be found, in large or infinitessimal proportions, on these two sides of Life. Each mind starts from the central depôt, and rides to directly opposite extremities of the Universe.

What men term "Imagination," I deem the mind's power "to body forth (prophetically) the forms of *things* unknown"—things, which live inherently in the constitution of the soul, but which may not have met their corresponding symbols in the external world. The *idealist* entertains primarily the church and the state in his mind. Picture and statue existed first in the artist's mind. In the mechanic's mind, the first railroad was laid, the first steam-engine built. There was, therefore, a time when church and state, statue and picture, railroads and locomotives, were simple unsymbolized Ideas. The skeptics (the men of the finite or facts) stigmatized them "Imaginations." Many a merchant mourned, with contemptuous pity, over the *steamboat* fancies of John Fitch and Robert Fulton! The first steamboat was built and launched and propelled up and down the broad rivers of Reflection in John Fitch's, and more particularly in Fulton's mind. Time was when this steam-phantom excited the ridicule of sensuous minds. But do you say this phantom has not come into practical life? If so, I reply that the most extravagant imaginations of Fulton are surpassed by the commonest engines of the workshops.

You must not accuse me of *skepticism*, but rather look within, and condemn yourselves. I doubt what the world believes, in many things, because I behold so much which I can not doubt.

If I were to classify the three departments of human thought, I should say that Man is an *Indefinite* world, situated between the *Finite* and the *Infinite*—or that there are *three* worlds in which his thoughts may eternally roam and be gratified. Man is to himself the *Indefinite* sphere; and thus "all our knowledge is ourselves to know." This is the only knowledge that can humble the mind; it is the knowing to a certainty that we are ignorant. Thus, before self-knowledge we reverently bow; as in the presence of some God both strange and undefinable. But pride comes in with the outward, *finite* sciences. Give a man to feel that he knows the science of the stars, Astronomy, and forthwith he straightens his spine when before his fellow-men. Give him to know the science of the earth, Geology; or the science of quantities, Mathematics; or the science of qualities, Chemistry; or the science of solids and surfaces, Geometry; and straightway he becomes the child of Vanity and Ambition. Especially is this true in minds which only know the fragmentary facts of these sciences—a sort of "smattering" information—such as floats upon the surface of modern newspapers and periodic literature; but, mingle with these sciences the fundamental principles of self-knowledge, and you humble the mind in reverence before the God of its being, and a true humility is inevitable. We may ask, "Why does self-knowledge or wisdom so alter the current of man's feelings?" Because it opens to the soul two great overwhelming worlds of being, not visible in the Finite sphere, viz., the *Indefinite*, which is himself, and the *Infinite*, to which he feels himself instinctively and eternally related—the private wonder of each mind.

Let the curtain be but partially raised which has so long hung between his present and his future, and Man sees himself as an unsolved problem. And here begins an infinite series of *questions and answers*. Man stands, before his brother man, with questions. Each one discovers in himself a desire to know; hence the hundreds of thousands of millions of billions of trillions of questions which swarm the fields of human experience. The mind asks questions, orally and in silence, because it is itself a world of interrogation; but, when we tell all, it is found to be no less a world of answers at once simple, fearful, wonderful, satisfying.

The questions of man, in regard to his *Infinite* relations, have built monuments of useless theology. Poems and precepts and bibles have been written to answer these ever-rising questions. Cathedrals and churches have arisen, to sound the replies in hundreds of ears at once. The infinite has been interrogated; but lesser worlds have alone returned answers.

And so methinks it will ever be. The Infinite will never answer the finite; except through its never-changing channels of consciousness. If a man can ask a profound question, there is a power latent in his nature not less able to reply; that is to say, the ability rightly to put a question presupposes the ability rightly to answer it—even as all spiritual desires are inward assurances of ultimate satisfaction.

When faithful memory shows me the feeble lineaments of my early experience, as an interior being, I quickly recall the kind words and questions that were pronounced in my awakened ear. My soul had slept in childish ignorance till then. Questions only of the common sort—such as people use in plainest modes of thought—were familiar to my ear and tongue. But what wondrous words came to my lips, in answer, when I heard—"Jackson! what do you see?" The high unfolding of Infinite truth seemed to flash athwart the horizon of my awakened perceptions. No sunbeams of spirtual light ever gilded the heavenly hills more tenderly, than did these truths irradiate my mental sky. But I realized nothing till I heard the question. No power was given me to answer then. But from that day to this, I have labored to tell the outer world what the inner world tells me!

And now, if I may be permitted still to speak of myself, I affirm, that whether I am a *benefit* or a penalty to you remains with you to decide. In you lies the power to determine the question of profit or loss. Steam and stars are valuable, or not, as you learn the art of putting to them the right questions, and procuring from them the best practical replies. You may ask steam, "What can you do?" It answers, "Clothe me in an armor of steel and iron, give me a boat to push, a mill to drive, or a train to draw, with a skilful hand to hold my reins, and I will show what I can do!"

Bnt how long did steam go unquestioned? For millions of years it played, in the foolishness of imbecility, before the dreamy eyes of men—never answering a question, because a question was never put to it. Ask the stars, "What can you tell us, or do?" And they answer, "Study us, and we will tell you of the immeasurable magnitude of God's own glorious temple! Ask us truly, and we will tell you of gravitation, and the laws of tides, of light and heat, of the seasons, of prosperity, of summer and winter, and seed-time and harvest; all of which you may write down in your almanacs, and sell them to the poor in purse and in spirit, who can find neither time nor comprehension to study at our school."

What I desire is, to impress you with the *law of questions*, so that evermore you will treat everything as if it could curse or bless, in *accordance* with the use made of it. 'Tis said, "The commonest mind is full of thoughts, some worthy of the rarest; and could it see them fairly writ, would wonder at its wealth." Yon tree says nothing, unless questioned. It imparts its best truths when best interrogated. To the dog it is only an object which, in running across the garden, he must avoid. To the intelligent botanist it tells great chapters of secrets. To the untutored Indian, it is good, or "no good," according to the fruit it bears. To the poet, it prophesies of beauty and truth. It is to him a beguiling bower of deep feeling, like a pure woman's heart; the type of joys to come, and the harbinger of sorrows too deep for words.

I may say that it is the main purpose of existence to tempt forth, by pure and appropriate questions, the great thoughts that lie buried in the mental essence. Every system of education, not based on this principle, is irksome to youth, because it is essentially erroneous and fundamentally unadapted. A child is never ready for knowledge till its soul is moved to put questions; then comes the period to try the teacher, for only he is fit to teach who answers like a child, and can put fresh questions to tempt forth the child's intuition and expand its native endowments.

It is impossible to teach all children by the same methods. Souls are blessings, or not, as we conform our methods to the temperaments in which we find them. The multiplication table delights your son; but your daughter is made to fancy a mental oath, when it comes her turn to learn it. But the right questions open her soul to itself. What a charmed world it is! In a moment, her soul leaps over whole years of being; her eyes are opened, and she feels wise as the fabled Eve. Nor is this self-knowledge an evil. It will tell us where we are naked—destitute of wisdom and harmony—and inform us of the methods of life, which bring the soul's true Eden.

Among the Jews it was a custom, derived from Egyptian jurisprudence, that every child should be taught the Jewish history and laws. In conformity with this method, the son of Joseph and Mary was taken to the *temple* of law, physic, and divinity. It is said that he was then only twelve years of age. He went to have his name enrolled among the males of the nation. It was also the custom in those days that the lawyers, ministers of justice, Sunday school teachers, and doctors of divinity should ask the young boys certain historical, legal, and religious questions in order to make sure of patriotism and orthodoxy.

Joshua* seemed to satisfy all the professors save the "doctors of divinity" who were astonished and confounded by the profundity of his answers! He manifested the dialect of intuition—a fact, as much owing to the effect of being questioned as to the hidden excellence which sustained the responses. Yea, it is said that the catechumen and doctors were astonished at the answers which they elicited from Joshua! And modern teachers think that only a God-sent and a God-inspired being could do it. One can not but regret the omission, on the part of historians, of questions put and replies received. Because, if doctors of divinity in the days of Joshua were no better enlightened

* Jesus is the Greek for the Hebrew word "Joshua."

concerning spiritual principles than the same class of our century, we can not but conclude that the "doctors" were greatly astonished a long time before the "profound" was reached.

I think they must have been astounded, and, perhaps, instructed, by the courageous announcement of his reformatory disposition and spiritual mission; not less by his utterance of inbred wisdom and intuitive knowledge, entirely natural to his organization, but far in advance of boys of his age and limited education. In the meantime let us not forget, that it was all elicited by the putting of appropriate questions.

Questions do not always imply a moving of the lips, and a sound upon the ear. Every MAN is a mark of interrogation! His existence summons thought.

In the Harmonia you will find this motto—"Spontaneous and profound questions are living representatives of internal desires; but to obtain and enjoy those pure and beautiful responses, which are intrinsically elevating and eternal, the inquirer must consult, not superficial and popular authorities, but the everlasting and unchangeable teachings of Nature, Reason, and Intuition." When I first wrote this, I did not comprehend it. But I now see that every part of a human being *is a question.* It asks, "Whence?" "What?" "Whither?" "What our origin?" "What are we?" "What destination?" The bibles and churches are yet monopolizing these questions, and patenting the answers. But we are not to consult superficial authority; we must find the answers in the sphere where the questions originated. And yet we can not work for ourselves, except by proxy. No man can answer himself, though he can satisfy his brother. On this principle, "shoemaker's wives and blacksmith's horses go unshod." Physicians, when sick, need physicians. It will not always be thus. Men will be more self-containing when better cultivated; or, when they know how to USE *things and ideas*, without the discount of *diminutions* and *exaggerations*—wherein we find error, so called, and the superficialities of our pilgrimage.

If you will read the circumstance of the world-renowned

"Sermon on the Mount," you will observe that the preacher "opened his mouth, and taught," as if he was answering questions. The multitude followed him. They were asking for his replies to thoughts in themselves. Each man was a question; an organic interrogatory! Had they been so many sheep or cows, do you suppose that his soul would have felt questioned. His best words are responses to questions put to him.

The most important question, in all the record, was put by *Pilate*. After interrogating Jesus on the subject of his kingship, &c., Pilate asked—"What is Truth?" The account stated, that, "when he had said this, he went out." Therefore, it has ever since remained an open question! We must regret, for the sake of mankind, that *Pilate* did not procure a reply. What a vast world of dogmatism it would have prevented! Catholic and protestant priests have patent replies, fixed as words of Fate. What a mass of theological conjecture rests upon this omission on the part of Pilate! And besides, the world is left in skepticism as to *the kind* of truth the Ruler referred to: legal? historical? geological? or theological? Since the question was not answered by Jesus, every soul should then consider itself questioned, and reply as best it can.

Great mountains of gold are far less valuable to mankind, than the discovery, that the power to put a question presupposes and guarantees the power no less to answer it. I affirm that Pilate possessed the power to answer his own interrogatory. But, as it is a law of Nature that the acorn shall precede the oak, even so, and by virtue of the same law, do questions oft-times long *precede* their answers. If a soul can summon no power to satisfy its questionings to-day, or during this generation, nor yet in the next hundred years, the time will none the less surely come when it may do so with ease—and not only so, but realize an ability to ask for greater knowledge and higher wisdom; to find which, the mind will consume the hours of eternity as they roll round the wheel, and continue thus its happy progression toward the unattainable *Infinite*.

"What is Truth?" asked Pilate. Now it depends entirely on his meaning as to whether he could himself answer in one hour, in one year, in five years, or in a million! If he meant *all Truth*—scientific, philosophical, theological, and spiritual—he then, through the centrality of his own individual consciousness, presented his question to the *Infinite*, and will be able to reply, item by item, stratum by stratum, as he ascends the unfolding spheres of the illimitable Future.

Because, if he meant *all truth*, he then had asked an eternal question; and the answer, through his own soul, could come in a period no less interminable. And yet, as, from his undeveloped state, he could not have meant *all* truth, (for only a God could intelligently put a question so profound,) therefore, I affirm that he will find many answers—each of which, at the time, may seem to his soul to be the *ultimatum* of satisfaction—at which he will rest a brief period, enjoying the answers; but presently the ability comes to put questions yet more profound, in other directions of being; and thus it is, by a method of spontaneous inward propulsion, his soul, ever unfolding in the grace of life, progresses through interminable series of degrees of Wisdom and Knowledge!

For myself I say that the reverence of my soul is deeply affected by questions put to Jesus—for I doubt whether anything else could have so impressively tempted forth the rich excess of spiritual beauty which characterized his responses. Plato felt questioned by all mankind. And so he answers, "All things are for the sake of the good; and the good is the cause of everything beautiful." And the world, in some cultured parts, felt so charmed with the Greek's Wisdom, it returned a compliment—"If Jove should descend to the earth, he would speak in the style of Plato."

Plato felt the world's needs, felt its questions, and gave his life to render the service thus demanded of his opulent nature. It hath been said, "he kindled a fire so truly in the centre of life, that we see the sphere illuminated, and can distinguish poles, equator, and lines of latitude, every arc and node; a theory so averaged, so modulated, that you would say, the winds had swept through this rhythmic-structure, and not that it was the brief extempore blotting of one short-lived scribe." The purity and truth of an answer depends upon the quality of the question. "A soft answer turneth away wrath" it is true; but a soft reply can be made only by souls who feel their charity questioned.

Each man is capable of rendering high service to humanity; but whether humanity gets it from him, or the reverse, will ever remain for the world to decide. Man is able to work. But he must be made to see the occupation which is *good for all;* or being born for *action* of some sort, he will perform the inharmonious part. Enslave a man, and, by virtue of his degradation, he will in return enslave you. Do injustice, and you will suffer it; for questions and answers, like cause and effect, essentially correspond.

Now here am I, acting faithfully in accordance with my personalities and its boundaries. If you know how to use me, as my nature prescribes, I shall then yield you a permanent benefit. But, if in your ignorance of yourself (and, therefore, of me), you do not put me *to the best service*, you will soon feel the penalty. This penalty, nevertheless, is a benefit, though of a negative character. It will not teach you a truth, but of an error committed; and teach the method of escape. The tree is true to itself; and I to myself. If I know enough of myself to put the best questions to that tree, it will yield me the best lessons of benefit—lessons, which the woodman does not get, nor the bird that sings upon its boughs, neither the squirrel that feeds upon its fruit. Yet there remains to the woodman, to the bird, and to the squirrel, *other* benefits in the tree—to obtain which I have neither the disposition nor the power. Thus, the same tree, when tempted forth, will serve and benefit a hundred individualities, a hundred forms of matter; the earth, the water, the atmosphere, bird, quadruped, and mankind. Its power to do this, however, lies not so much in itself as in its interrogators.

"I will go into the desert and dwell among ruins," said Volney; "and will *interrogate* ancient monuments on the wisdom of past times." He asked the past for its history of evil in the world; and it answered him.

If you perceive not my meaning—because of the new dress my thoughts may have assumed—you will nevertheless get something. What I mean to mean you may not see, but you are very likely to see what I do not; and you might impart to me, in the next hour, that which I have now no power to communicate. The pathway to one Truth, perhaps, I can now show you. But, while on this path myself, in the service of pointing out the road to you, I may suddenly learn *a new truth*, admonishing that this is not the road for me to travel. Or, I may behold additional reasons why I should not fail to pursue it, and reasons, also, why you should not. I define, to your minds, my position. But if you can not see my reasons, nor the legitimacy of my position, in you lie the power and the liberty to go on without me. And as the new path breaks upon you, and you fail not to best employ all you have and meet, even so may you obtain *bread* from what, in the distance, appeared to me to be *stones;* and health, also, from what I called poison and disease. The cicuta-plant yields *honey* to the bee, who instinctively knows how to question it; to man it would yield bitterness and death. The bee questions the flower, and man the bee; which answers through geometrical avenues—bleeding forth at every pore the life-elements of sweetness.

Let each, therefore, be himself; but if he would help his condition, he must use his neighbor well; for, at most, we can help ourselves only by proxy. The web of life is to be spun. And man, like the spider and silk-worm, must work from within! *The benefits of Individualism*, so manifold, so complicate, escape the consciousness of those who depend, too constantly, upon *externals* for sympathy and support. That we are benefited by everything, without and within, in proportion to the *justice* with which we treat it, is not yet practically recognised on earth. I say, justice; because *it is superior* to all the humanities—to sympathy, benevolence, philanthropy; for Justice comprehends all—and is, therefore, the highest manifestation of true Religion!

Yon aged oak—solitary, stalwart, and grand—has not yet declared itself to the world; because, simply, the world has not known how to question it. Opulent with great quantities and qualities of matter—self-defended against storm and tempest by *its own* strength and armor—it stands a stranger yet to man. It is a stranger to itself not less! Who knows what else it can do, beside making ships, sideboards, or kindling the cottager's fire! It remains yet to be questioned. Where is the man, who knows enough of himself, to do it?

What there is hidden in the recesses of my being, I have no power as yet to divulge. I yearn for the right man to come, from any degree of life, to put to my soul the right questions. For then I shall answer him with thought and articulation, at once so profound and beautiful, so truthful and elevating, I know not when I could recover from self-astonishment. But in all this arcanum of "questions and answers," there are truths in man which *only* a woman can elicit; and powers in woman that come forth only at the mandate of masculinity.

Innumerable are the persons from whom ascends the mournful cry—"Alas! not one can understand me—by no congenial spirit am I comprehended!" This insupportable agony, this ungratified desire for appreciation, in sensitive and cultured natures, attains unto speech. They spend precious moments in inward acts of self-commiseration. They weep when relief is nigh; but, sometimes, the feeling becomes too deep for tears; then silence, like the drapery of night, throws its mantle over, and folds in, the soul—saying, "Peace, be still." They sing the saddest songs. They write poetry, pervaded with an *indefinite* grief. But persevering in expression, they gain at last a result, of all ends the most important, but which the mind, in its ignorance of nature and adaptations, knew not how or where to seek. For thus it is that the sorrows of the "Five Points" have arisen into literature. The degradations of imbruted men, and the execrations of abandoned women, have been translated into the English language. And the plaintive cry of "Hot Corn" is heard in fashionable parlors—uttered by pet-lambs in magnificent folds, whose shepherds are Wall-street bankers, perhaps, and South-street commercialists. Thus the heretofore unappreciated see the pathway leading at last to justice and satisfaction—obtaining a literary notoriety which promises *popularity* in the fullness of days.

Self-comprehension, however, though always to be aimed after, will ever remain above the capacity of the *comprehend-*

ing faculty. Even so, Reason can not tell what Reason is; but what *it is not*, that it can easily decide. What men call *Conscience*—the summary conclusion of all the functions of Mind—I term JUSTICE. But what justice IS, no man's mind can determine; but an injustice, this the faculty quickly decides. "What God is," says a German thinker, "I know not; but what *he is not*, that I know." For ever will this fact in man's nature—this power of positives to determine only negatives—keep his soul folded in more or less of mystery. Man is the *Indefinite* world; because subsisting between *things* and *ideas*, between the finite and the infinite.

Many philosophers, becoming wearied with the ever-recurring contradictions and paradoxes of human nature—acting foolishly when wisdom was appropriate, manifesting insufferable weakness when strength was demanded—have allowed themselves to grow cynical and sarcastic. The human world disgusts them; and so, like Diogenes, they spend their days in petulant misanthropy. Mr. Emerson says—"I knew a philosopher, who was accustomed to sum up his experience of human nature, in saying—'Mankind is a damned rascal.'" Perhaps, it was a gush of this impatience of human paradoxes which caused the Nazarene to whip the "money-changers;" not less to denounce many as "serpents" and "vipers" worthy only of Gehennal damnation.

Man is ever the *indefinite*—but he must be questioned. No sooner do we suppose ourselves *fully* analyzed and *finally* classified by some new phrenology or anthropology, than we suddenly break out in a fresh spot—provoking ourselves and our dogmatizers equally—with new mental exhibitions; with new characteristics, for which no science, no religion, no bible, has provided laws and adequate explanations. And so, in spite of all arbitrary restrictions and canonical injunctions against self-reliance, we are peremptorily thrown back upon *our own centre*—to begin another series of questions and answers toward self-comprehension. Of course, one may say, the history of man remains the same, in substance, from age to age: that no new law is developed from him; but there is, I think, one thing in which mankind continue homogeneous—

viz.: in the immutability of their changeability. It is this law of Unity, in Variety, which we yearn to understand.

But the great end to gain is, the converting of everything into a benefit. On yonder mountain's side, you behold the joyous brook leaping down to nestle in the lap of the valley — like a fleet, happy child, hastening to play with the grasses and flowers on the plains beneath! Was it made for play only? Can it do nothing more? Yea. The thirsting cattle may drink great draughts of strength from its rippling bosom; and the meadow-lark, seeing itself reflected, may sing all the sweeter to the children of men. And is that all? Can no one bring out of it a still greater service? Verily, it can accommodate man deeply, if man knows how to help it to bestow accommodation. The mill can be driven by that stream; it can work and play at the same moment; suffering no impoverishment thereby. But it knows not its own power; it waits for interrogation.

The Blackstone river, beginning in Massachusetts and flowing through a portion of Rhode Island, hastened along, babbling and silent by turns, for thousands of centuries. How long it flowed in solitude! But the red man's canoe rode on its surface; yet the aborigine knew not the river. At last, the white man came, who knew how to put the idle tide to service. He built an obstruction across its course. As the human mind stops at an interrogation, so did this strong *dam* arrest the waters. As a sequence, the tide set back, spreading over adjacent margins; and then, with the power of accumulated weight, ran vigorously through the new channel made for it, against an intercepting wheel, which, turning steadily upon its axis, imparted motion to the mechanism of a Cotton Mill. Did that river know before its power to bless? Could it set itself to the work? What it was, it knew not. Its power was concealed from itself, and rolled and flowed indolently. But now, this playful, musical, beautiful stream supports no less than *one hundred and thirty* great cotton, woollen, and other factories! It gives drink to the thirsty cattle no less; it waters the meadows no less; it talks and dashes along as light and free as it did centuries ago; is as beautiful to the eye as when but "sweet sixteen;" gambols as cheerfully over rocky terraces; leaps as fearlessly from height to depth as ever it did; and yet, because it has been appropriately questioned, it turns something like two million spools and spindles between Worcester and Providence — comprising about fifty miles only of its original play-ground.* While in idleness, it had no intelligent admirers; for such, by nature's law, is the fate of all drones. But now, it is the chief delight of hundreds of working men and working women, who, though they may not stop the haste of labor to gratefully remember the service by the river rendered, yet derive their sustenance from year to year, by waiting obediently upon wheels and spindles which buzz and whirl at the gentle, but imperious, pressure of its ever-flowing tides.

Does it suffer loss? Does the sun lose light by painting daguerreotypes? Does the soul lose life by thinking?

Nay! The stream flows on and widens into the greater river, bearing up ships and steamers, and still onward to the ocean. Thence it ascends in vapor, forms numberless fleecy clouds, fills the artist's soul with love and lessons, and, in the fresh forms of beauty, returns, perhaps, to its original source. It may thus live over and over again its useful and beautiful life. And so, it works in its waywardness — and plays with powers it knew not — bright as the birthday of flowers, threading its way through the feathered grasses and along vernal, verdant plains; boisterous in places as the Delaware; in spots as beautiful as the Hudson; and almost more industrious than the famous Merrimack!

So, too, is man idle — till the world interrogates his nature. By putting the right questions at the right time, and in the right manner, a human mind may be measurably revealed to itself. In this art lie all true methods of education.

"Know thyself," said Pope, "presume not God to scan." There is rich wisdom in such counsel. Because, to be intelli-

* "So great have been the improvements effected in spinning-machinery, that one man can attend to 1,088 spindles, each spinning three hanks, or 3,264 hanks per day; so that, as compared with the operations of the most expert spinner in Hindustan, the American operator can perform the work of 300 men."

gently introduced to one's own soul is to go reverently into the presence of all the God the soul can ever realize. Than this there is no deeper, no wider, no higher revelation. But the soul can not question itself! Man must put his questions to Nature; he must be free to do this; and free, not less, to answer questions which Nature puts to him. No trammeled and bigoted sectarian, heathen or Christian, can be free to do either; and so such offend the law and take the penalty of injustice; causing meanwhile world-wide suffering through the ties of inseparable sympathies.

All past catechisms contain questions put by the world, while yet in its teens, and may therefore be pardoned by this maturer era.

But what questions now appear? Who shall ask? Who shall answer? We must have no more dogmatism! Come, then, ye children of experience, let us hear your words: speak! and the world will accept all the truth ye can give. Let the right voice sound, and lo! like the musical throbbings of the peacefully rolling sea, our spiritual enjoyments will swell—extend and expand, waving and surging forward—till angels in higher worlds receive refreshment and grow more beautiful, even as we drink from wells which spring out of the dark and dreary earth.

The law of questions and answers regulates the world. In all things we behold a law of association: what does it mean? Insect, bird, and quadruped, progressively recreate each other—forming, in their conjunctions, a brotherhood: why do they exist? What bible answers? Where shall we go for wisdom? Sanguinary wars, separating souls from the bodies of men, scourging families and nations: why do they exist? What and where is God? What are his laws? Are we immortal? If so, what for? If not, why not? Who shall answer?

"Eureka!" *Man must both desire and learn to answer every question he finds the power to ask!* Herein lies the *cause* of all progressive development.

Hunger asks man, "Do you know how to satisfy me?" and man tills the ground. *Fatigue* asks man, "Do you know the means of rest?" and man invents beds and furniture. *Love* asks him a question: and he seeks companions. *Wisdom* asks: and man looks toward the *Infinite*. SCIENCE asks: and man studies the *Finite*. PHILOSOPHY asks: and man searches the *Indefinite*. REASON asks: and man seeks to familiarize himself with himself — to harmonize the other two worlds. HUMANITY asks: and Humanity, ever hopeful, ever promising, replies, "BE JOYFUL, O YE DWELLERS OF EARTH, FOR THERE SHALL BE AN ERA OF UNIVERSAL PEACE AND UNITY!"

THE

ASSEMBLY'S SHORTER CATECHISM,

REVISED AND CORRECTED.

Every century that rolls over the earth adds another volume to the world's Library. Each page presents a kind of daguerreotype impression of some event, accident, circumstance, or development. And each person is certain to write something; the high and the low, alike, are authors. Every individual thing also—the tree, the bird, the flower, the animal, the fountain, the sun, the star—is a faithful contributor to the pages of this mystic cohesive Record. We transfer ourselves to the life of Posterity, physically and spiritually, as hillside streamlets flow onward to create the Ocean. Hence, every person has an immortal influence; even in this, the embryological sphere of human existence. On turning over and perusing the recently-written pages of this century—especially those contributed by the advancing portions of our race—I observe the frequent recurrence of important questions, physical, social, moral, scientific, spiritual. These questions conclusively prove that the earth's inhabitants experience dissatisfaction with the answers given by revered sources of instruction. Theological monopolies, if out of time, antagonize individual progress; scientific discoveries should not outnumber advancements in theology and religion; an opinion which, within five years, has acquired prodigious strength and unparalleled popularity. En couraged, therefore, by the kind reception which several great improvements in the Arts and Sciences have met with among able and fearless classes, and believing such minds will welcome theological improvements not less hospitably, I proceed to introduce *a revised and corrected edition* of the world-renowned Assembly's Shorter Catechism; and it is sincerely hoped that the alterations and emendations here presented, although similar to the Westminster method of asking questions and giving answers, will not be adjudged uncharitably, nor pronounced by any theologico-monopolist to be an actionable infringement upon its predecessor. Beginning, then, with the best and most peaceful understandings between the past and the present, I venture the presentation of responses, to Important Questions—in accordance, of course, with my conception of teachings evolved by the Harmonial Philosophy.

What is the chief end of man?

Man's chief end, in shortest speech, is endless progression; to do good, be happy, get wisdom, and aspire calmly toward perfection; to become harmonious even as his Father-God and Mother-Nature are harmonious.

What rule have Father-God and Mother-Nature given to direct us how we may obtain these ends?

Our Heavenly Parents have given us a rule in the spiritual constitution of our being; also, in the conformations of man's outer form; and on a still broader scale, in the constitution and lyrical harmony of the surrounding Universe.

What is this rule called?

By Sensualists—Pleasure; by Religionists—Scripture; by Harmonialists—Progression.

Who are most correct?

Those who, regardless of outward authority, seek Progression.

Why do you think them most correct?

Because sensualists or materialists aspire after *Pleasure* as an *end;* Religionists aspire after *Truth*, as it is in favorite creeds and formularies; Harmonialists aspire after eternal life and endless improvement; of which Pleasure and Truth are the *incidental* developments and ever-healing concomitants.

How many persons are there in the Godhead?

There are in the Godhead and Godbody (that is to say, in the imperishable Mansions of Father-God and Mother-Nature) all the persons that were ever developed on any star in the firmament or on the earth beneath; all men, all spirits, all angels, all archangels and seraphs, which people the immeasurable spheres of life and animation; for we live and move and have our being in the Divine Existence, "whose body Nature is, and God the soul."

What are the decrees of God?

The decrees of God are the eternal laws of his vital system; written upon the constitution of Man; and republished whenever a Child is born.

What are they called?

According to recent discoveries we term them Association, Progression, Development.

Do these decrees — the laws of Association, Progression, and Development — apply to Individual Man?

Yes, but only in that stupendous application of ideas which recognises man as *a microcosmical part* of the Universal System.

What, then, are those decrees of God which concern the immediate government and salvation of man?

All animated beings, especially mankind, are regulated by fixed laws—*physical*, *organic*, *spiritual*—the first determines the relation of the body to every other object, its temperature, its elasticity, density, &c.; the second determines the relation of the organic or *vital* requirements of the body, and regulates the supply to the demand; the third determines the relation of the soul in its friendships and sympathies for things both seen and unseen, temporal and eternal; and, as implied by this admirable code of decrees, the happiness or misery of individual man is proportionate always and everywhere, before as well as after death, to his obedience to, or transgression of, these divine mandates.

How can we ascertain these laws?

By the employment of our intellectual and social and spiritual faculties. Each law, and its positive requirements, can be perceived only by those parts or faculties or functions which it (the law) is designed to govern and harmonize with the system of creation without.

What do you mean by this?

I mean that the body, by means of its *sympathetic nerve*, is itself qualified to perceive the relation subsisting between it and all other objects and bodies; that the intellectual faculties, by treasuring up such observations, create a science of gravitation, juxtaposition, &c.; on this principle, of like seeing and comprehending like, the *organic and vital* functions perceive the chemistry of foods, fluids, odors, flavors, sounds, sights, colors, and the like; the *social and affectional* principles apprehend the nature and valuation of friendship, childhood, conjugialism, and universal identification and unity of human interests and attractions; and lastly, the *spiritual faculties* on the upper brain put forth their marvellous far-comprehending powers toward those stupendous, beautiful, vast, attractive, sublime, divine, celestial, and supernal *Realities* which exist rudimentally on earth but fully bloomed and blossomed out in the higher Homes of the Soul. Human beings, therefore, may be physically happy and socially miserable, or *visa versa*, may enjoy the spiritual and suffer in the organal department of existence, according as they conform to or transgress the law which is designed to control and govern such department. Thus, each part of man's nature hath its own immutable regulating principle, which is of necessity the source of beautiful *benefits* or of painful *penalties*, a cause of happiness or of misery, just as the possessor may by his life decide.

How does God execute his decrees?

By living in accordance with the unchangeable principles of his own physical and mental being; by universalizing his spirit, and making the humblest things examples of his love and wisdom.

What is the work of creation?

There is no creation; but formation perpetual.

How did God create man?

God did not create man. Man came from Nature's matrix as a child from its mother's womb; a Product of Nature; and, like a child, looks to her for all sustenance, entertainment, and instruction.

What are God's works of providence?

All things in the universe; nothing is especially designed; everything comes forth in its natural order and discreet degree; according to laws which are without variableness.

Did our first parents continue in the state wherein they were created?

Our first parents, when they discovered that they were endowed with intellectual perceptions and physical necessities, began to bestir themselves in accordance with instincts of dis covery and self-preservation. They began to learn, to suffer, to subdue. Marriage and mechanism were found to be insep arable; as with the little birds which are compelled to learn how to build nests for their young. On this principle, though upon an exceedingly low scale of existence, our first parents slowly advanced from a state of ignorance to comparative enlightenment; yet they were the veriest barbarians when compared with any portion of the Anglo-Saxon race.

Did our first parents never fall from innocence?

They could not, because they never stood erect. They began physically and mentally in the lowest part of the valley of human existence; hence, as there was no "deeper depth," a fall was impossible. Yet they have *stumbled* often in ascending the hill of progressive development.

How can you prove this assertion?

By the blessed and even infallible scriptures.

What scriptures do you refer to?

The scriptures which the true eternal God has written. The whole universe consists of sentient beings, each of whom is an express word of the Supreme Being. Nature is a book whose every sentence proves the ascension of man from a small point of life; the first productions of Nature are inferior to her every subsequent unfolding.

What is sin?

Sin is a name for excess; a mark missed by man in his development; a ditch, into which, when with ignorance or passion blind, we stumble for a season.

What is the sequence?

We get pervaded, perhaps saturated, with its pollutions.

The deeper we plunge, the more polluted; so exceedingly soiled at last, that we dread to find ourselves in daylight. We therefore (mentally) go into outer darkness; shirking the sun and gaze of honest eyes, because of our debasement.

Did all mankind fall in the first transgression?

Nature, through all her parts, is regulated by the same changeless principles—one being the law of progressive improvement; hence, descending from the primal races by ordinary generation, posterity is *benefited*, not injured, by primitive misdirections; for so great and powerful and just is the Divine Spirit, that all evil is overcome by good, and one of the original mistakes of our remotest ancestors has proved more valuable as a means of victorious achievement in righteousness than a million acts of passive rectitude or negative goodness. Because such acts, like man's primitive misdirections, are not the result of voluntary affection or intelligent choice, based on adequate experience—but mistakes and acts, on the contrary, stumbled upon and kicked out of the sands of Progress, even as the precious diamond was thrown up into open day and proverbial celebrity by the undesigning toe of a wandering savage—in which there exists neither merit nor demerit, but *discovery* nevertheless and benefits innumerable.

Into what state did the fall bring all mankind?

What is theologically called a "fall" was in truth the greatest benefit to mankind; it developed physical industry, beautified the soil, and improved the climate, exercised the intellectual faculties, evoked the sentiment of association, and awakened the spiritual affinities; in short, according to this oriental myth, it drove the Aristocratic Family from velvet lawns, from paths luxuriously ornamented with flowery carpets, from the presence of ceaseless perfumery, from rustic chairs not the product of pleasurable invention and victorious toil, from natural-tufted sofas 'neath the graceful arches of magnificent trees never planted or treated by human hands, from the lascivious pleasing of the lute-like song of paradisaical birds, from the flowing of rivers whose indolent powers had never pressed the ponderous wheel of a cotton-factory or the pioneer's saw and grist mill; therefore, the fall was in fact the first step up that hill which leads to manly enterprise and womanly independence — the democratic road to useful Knowledge.

Wherein consists the sinfulness of that state whereinto man entered?

The sinfulness of that original revolution in the habits and manners of the Adamic Aristocracy, consists in the fact that, according to the account, the act was not a result of pre-determination, but of mere "idle curiosity" to taste, *ad libitum*, all fruit indigenous to that sunny soil; in a word, the sin (or pity) consists in the *procrastination*, in the lack of industry and self-sustaining effort, which characterized the reputed first pair, and which they have transmitted to all labor-dishonoring portions of mankind.

What is the misery of that state whereinto man entered?

The misery to idlers and aristocrats consists in the discovery that all true success and permament distinction depend upon sincere active individual Enterprise; regulated by principles of justice, truth, love to man, reverence of Father-God, and temperance in all things — a misery familiar only to those who desire to live on "the labor of others," who desire riches and authority even at the expense of the Poor, who love Notoriety and Popularity devotionally, and not Truth for its own sake.

Did God leave all mankind to perish in this state?

Blasphemous question! How can an omnipresent and unchangeable God withdraw his spirit from man, whose every drop of soul-life is derived from the eternal Fountain!

Did God elect some to everlasting life, and others to endless destruction?

God is the Father of the spirits of All men. Hence all men *have their entire existence* in the one omnipresent Spirit of Deity. Think you that the Whole can be happy when many of its *parts* are miserable? Human souls are detached individualized personifications of the Deific Nature and Essence; and the imperfection or destruction of a single detachment would, like the loss of a wheel from a perfect watch, impair the goodness and derange the infinite precision of the Universal Mechanism.

Who is the Redeemer of Man?

If by the word "redemption" you mean *improvement* in all things natural and spiritual, then man's redeemer is WISDOM — the beautiful Son of a holy nuptial blending of Love and Knowledge; the soul's "Christ-principle" — a natural prophet, a prince of peace, a spiritual priest, a God-inspired king of that kingdom which is within you.

How can Wisdom, being the sum of human attributes, save man?

By opening the soul to a perception of things spiritual, angelic, celestial, and heavenly. Like a peach which treasures up the perfections of the entire tree which produced it, so Wisdom attracts together all the beauties of the affections of both Love and Knowledge (as explained in 4th vol. of Great Harmonia), and thus opens the soul's portals to Infinite Love, to Eternal Truth, to Father-God, to Mother-Nature.

What benefits do believers receive from Wisdom at their death?

Pure Wisdom, having opened to the soul a glorious consciousness of the existence of a better and less rudimental world Beyond, brings a great peace into the mind and surrounds the believer's bed with many spirits and angels.

What benefits do believers receive from Wisdom at the resurrection?

At the resurrection, believers, being raised up immediately after the heart ceases to throb on earth, shall be acknowledged in the Spirit-Land by welcoming hosts of friends, and thus, unlike disbelievers, be made direct partakers of that full enjoyment which the harmonious only know.

What is the duty which God requires of man?

The one true eternal Father-God requires of man faithfulness to the dictates of his highest attractions. (See questions on "Life.") To do right from a sense of duty, or obligation, or fear, as most people permit themselves to do, is far below that exalted motive which prompts noble natures to do good and speak the truth to gratify their attractions.

What are man's highest attractions?

Man's best and highest attractions take their rise in the superior part of the brain called the wisdom-region; that is, in the organs of benevolence, veneration, conscientiousness, firmness, self-respect, hope, sublimity, ideality, marvellousness, and love of Truth.

What did God at first reveal to man for the rule of his obedience?

God, by living in man's soul from the very beginning, revealed to his religious or wisdom faculties this law—"to be carnally-minded is death; to be spiritually-minded is life and peace."

How did God reveal this law?

God revealed this law, first, in the common relations subsisting between man and man; second, in the "still small voice" of integral perception of justice, called Intuition; third, by the various spirits and angels who presided and still continue to watch lovingly over the earth, and who sometimes spoke in visions to young men, in dreams to women, and through commandments to religious chieftains.

Where is the moral law summarily comprehended?

The moral law, which signifies the immutable principle of JUSTICE everywhere manifested in the superlative Constitution of Father-God and Mother-Nature, is summed up and most beautifully expressed in the body and soul of Man.

Where is the moral law truly visible?

The moral law is fully and practically exhibited and fulfilled wherever a human being has attained entire Harmony—to the fullness of the stature of a perfect Man in Love and wisdom—by obedience to his own divinely-originated and supernally-authenticated *twelve* commandments

What is the sum of the twelve commandments?

The sum of the twelve commandments is, to do good and harmonious works, for the redemption and ennoblement of your fellow-men. Such works to be purely "good" must be wrought regardless of age, sex, complexion, belief, or reputation; because the Human Race is but One Family—all members of one body—in which there is neither Jew nor Gentile, Nazarene nor Greek, Ethiopian nor Anglo-Saxon

What is the preface to the twelve commandments?

The preface to the twelve commandments is in these words: "Write me as one who loves his fellow-men."

What does the preface to the twelve commandments teach us?

The preface to the twelve commandments teacheth us, that because man did not originate himself, but came into existence involuntarily as the Child of Father-God and Mother-Nature, therefore to love and improve and render happy the pathway of human beings is the best and highest and most acceptable homage the soul can pay to the "Great First Cause," which was before all things and in which all things exist.

What is the first commandment?

The first commandment is: "Obey the normal requirement of Self-Love;" which is the Central principle of man's exist ence.

What is required in the first commandment?

The first commandment requireth us to know and acknowl edge the wisdom of Father-God by perceiving this law of Self Love to be *the foundation* of all individual rights and liberties.

What is forbidden in the first commandment?

The first commandment forbiddeth both the extreme and the inverted practice of this central Affection; the penalty of disobedience being both immediate and remote, and, while persisted in, never detached from the transgressor.

What is extreme and inverted practice?

Extreme Self-Love goes time-serving, fortune-hunting—full of baseness, being at once egotistical, illiberal, mercenary; while inverted, it produces opposite effects—not nobleness and magnanimity, but self-abnegation, lukewarm carelessness, and personal filthiness, as explained in the Great Harmonia.

What is the second commandment?

The second commandment is: "Obey the law of Conjugal Love with all thy heart and with all thy mind;" for out of the operations of this principle springeth the myriad generations of men, spirits, and angels.

What is required in the second commandment?

The second commandment requireth the receiving and the keeping of all pure and spiritualizing conceptions of the true marriage relation; the *central* conception being, that Man and Woman are the twofold manifestation of One existence, each acting in the other as a *Messiah* throughout eternal worlds.

What is forbidden in the second commandment?

The second commandment forbiddeth the *prostitutions* of Extremism and the *pollutions* of Inversionism; also the telling of all anecdotes, and the reading of unclean books, which tend to breed unchaste emotions in the soul.

What are the causes of conjugal misfortune?

The causes are, first, ignorance of the use and holiness of marriage; second, a lack of spiritual culture among those who, in other respects, are intelligent and exemplary persons; third, a transitional fact incident to the slow growth of the ages.

What is the third commandment?

The third commandment is: "Obey the law of Parental Love with a pure and reverent devotion;" for the foundation of the world is Childhood; and the happiness of future spheres bubbles out of terrestrial fountains.

What is required in the third commandment?

The third commandment requireth that parents should respect the *rights* of the babe before birth by abstaining from all blood-love indulgence; also, after its introduction to objective life, that parents and guardians open many *liberties* to offspring, and teach the awakening faculties quietly and only as they ask questions; until the season has arrived when physical industry and mental discipline become both natural and necessary; then the Harmonial Institution should go on with the requisite process of harmonizing the body and mind of the young.

What is forbidden in the third commandment?

The third commandment forbiddeth all inharmonious examples by parents in the presence of the young: such as intemperance, the use of tobacco, the excessive use of meat, the habitual drinking of tea or coffee, vulgar habits, profane words, lack of punctuality in promises, deceptive or evasive answers, expressions of prejudices against neighbors, reiteration of slanders, opposition to persons who differ on religious questions; also every species of irreverence which could generate laxity of moral principle or blindness to the Divine Existence.

What is the fourth commandment?

The fourth commandment is: "Obey the law of Fraternal Love with all thy soul and with all thy understanding;" for this is that principle which binds man to man in the vast brotherhood of races and nations.

What is required in the fourth commandment?

The fourth commandment requireth the exercise of that ennobling sentiment of fraternal "charity, which thinketh no evil;" as in thine own household so also in the habitations of thy neighbor; because, to the truly gifted in Wisdom, there is nothing unclean nor unrighteous absolutely, except in the sense of mis-adaptation or substitution of laws and conditions; such, for example, as a man adapting himself to habits of body which are just only to some animal, or substituting for the government of civilized races despotic and warful laws which belong in justice only to savage and barbaric generations.

What is forbidden in the fourth commandment?

The fourth commandment forbiddeth all transgressions of the principle of Fraternal Love. Therefore, all theological distinctions are forbidden.

What examples can be given of mischievous theological distinctions?

There are many such examples in ecclesiastical history; and yet more in the blood-stained history of bewildered humanity. The Old Testament recognises Masters and Slaves. Kings and Subjects are presented in bold distinction. I hear insulting and unfraternal words concerning plebeians and patricians. I hear merciless sermons concerning the *good* and the *evil*, the *sheep* and the *goats*, the *elect* and the *reprobated*, still resounding from pulpits as cardinal portions of the gospel. The *genius* of this doctrine is utterly opposed to the fraternal welfare and peaceful progress of mankind. The fraternal interests of the world are divided by it; every man against his neighbor. The unity of history is marred by its promulgation. It retards the growth of the universal sentiment—"Ye are all brethren." All human history must be regarded as the growth of a Tree—first, the little germ; then, its subsoil expansion; then, the going forth of diverse roots from the germinal point; then, the ascension of a tufted column from the centre; then, the appearance of thorns on this body, and sometimes unsightly excrescences; then, the reproduction of the underground roots, with all their beautiful eccentricities, in the form of overground branches; then, an infinite reduplication of these in the shape of twigs starting out of branches; and lastly, buds of promise break forth on each extremity—prophesying and proclaiming the approach of blossoms, and from blossoms, FRUIT. So should the history of mankind be studied; no complaint of evil, no pulpit scolding, no canonical profanity. One time the Race brings forth only thorns, at other times dry limbs without beauty, then beauty without energy, but all in proper season; and, in due course of this progression, the whole is begemmed with an infinite fruition—all pure, all noble, all HARMONIAL!

What is the fifth commandment?

The fifth commandment is: "Obey the law of Filial Love with all the spontaneousness of thy grateful spirit;" for it is this beautiful principle which links inferior to superior, animals to the human world, and mankind to the interior and spiritual.

What is required by the fifth commandment?

The fifth commandment requireth the honoring of "thy father and thy mother" because they were instrumental in giving you an eternal individualized existence! Gratitude is next to generosity. But this Filial law does not require a child to obey a foolish or intemperate parent; nor slaves to yield themselves blindly to the *dictum* of self-constituted masters, who appropriate rights and assign only duties to those who serve them; for no human being is obligated by any natural (or divine) law to sacrifice individual "rights" in order to perform "duties" imposed by those arbitrarily vested with authority.

What is forbidden in the fifth commandment?

The fifth commandment forbiddeth the neglecting of this Filial homage which is due to every person, idea, or truth, that giveth evidence of superiority and innate righteousness. All contemptuous treatment of a human being—all scorning of those who live in poverty; all supercilious mannerisms toward those who labor in field, workshop, or kitchen; all trampling upon the rights of others; all mocking and jeering and hissing and hooting at that which (without due investigation) is pronounced prejudicial to morals and religion; all irreverence and politico-sectarianism manifested toward the inhabitants of foreign countries and principalities, either in thought or speech; finally, and in short, all voluntary transgressions of this Filial Principle in reference to man on earth, to spirits in the heavens, to angels in the spheres, to seraphs in the constellations, or to Father-God in the nuptial embrace of Mother-Nature—is positively forbidden now and for ever.

What results will follow obedience to the fifth commandment?

The results of obedience will flow like crystal waters through the garden of the soul. The effects are beautiful and saving like deathless flowers shedding immortal fragrance o'er the path of life — Gratitude, Generosity, Patience, Devotion, Moderation, Justice! — these are the jewels which beautify the true child of Nature, having the power to bring long life and prosperity.

What is the sixth commandment?

The sixth commandment is: "Obey the law of Universal Love with the total ingenuousness of thy inmost nature;" for it is this uncircumscribed principle which circulates and throbs through all the veins and arteries of Humanity.

What is required by the sixth commandment?

The sixth commandment requireth each individual to identify his peace and prosperity and happiness with that of every other. Isolated being and unaided doing are not compatible with true humanity and permanent progression. Universal Love is founded in the vivifying essence of universal existence, and should regulate the highest and noblest impulses operating in the broad domain of Human Nature.

What is forbidden in the sixth commandment?

The sixth commandment forbiddeth all selfishness and all isolated strife for wealth and power. Monopolistic enterprises and competitive industry are forbidden by virtue of this principle. By a philosophical analysis of the origin and nature of what are termed *man's vices and passions*, I discover that, with few exceptions, the worst and most discordant manifestations of character, are engendered and fortified in the strong entrenchments of political, ecclesiastical, and social Institutions.

How did these institutions originate?

These tyrannical arbitrary institutions (which despotize mankind and develop subversive effects) originated from man's *ignorance*, and not from man's depravity; although ignorance gives rise to a multitude of ungovernable propensities which Wisdom alone can calm and beautify. It should be steadily remembered that Man (and the whole race also) is a progressive Being. His life and deeds at different periods of the world, like hands on a dial, indicate the order and degree of his progression. And "regeneration" is a perpetual phenomenon of human existence. The elevation and expansion of man's affections into Universal Love, is the perfect fruition of the tree of Life; the result of no miraculous "change of heart," but of perennial growth in love and wisdom. When this commandment is obeyed, the various races will shake hands through mutual organizations of interests, and a stupendous harmonial temple will overarch the world.

What is the seventh commandment?

The seventh commandment is: "Obey the gospel of USE"—for this is the first manifestation of the principle of Wisdom.

What is required by the seventh commandment?

The seventh commandment requireth us *to use all things* which minister to the growth, ennoblement and happiness of our physical and mental being. There is not a blade of grass, nor a grain of sand, but may be set in accord with the key-note of man's needs. Subjective wisdom seeks objective existence; giving the artist an intelligent impulse toward the appropriation of colors, and the beauty-lover a desire to embellish his habitation with picturesque results. The man of uses, whose mind is devoted thereto, is a man of effects and details; the exact sciences and constructive arts are outworks of this law. When we render useful any element in nature—when we work to fill a useful position in the living world, when we convert a misfortune into a means of success, when we set in serviceable operation a physical or intellectual gift, when we triumph over a fault by compelling it to wield a good influence, when we stand god-like over the volcano of rash and uncontrollable affection and roll back the burning tide of consuming passion at the very moment when the fire and smoke of prostitution and profanation overshadow the citadel of inward purity—then do we obey the seventh commandment.

What is forbidden in the seventh commandment?

The seventh commandment forbiddeth the desecration of any natural object by misapplication; also the profanation of any function or faculty by misemployment. For example, using a cow or a horse, a woman or a man, to do work in harness which electro-magnetic forces and steam or caloric could dc quicker and better; employing the hand to strike a brother; using the tongue to moisten tobacco or to give free expression to inelegant words; using the lips to pray to God or to imprint the betrayer's kiss; using memory as a trunk for that unculled and wasteful rubbish which may accumulate in the journey of life; using the knowing faculties to outwit and overreach neighbor; employing the poetic impulses as angels of light to engulf a fellow-being in conjugal abandonment; using the powers of clairvoyance for selfish ends and mercenary enterprises; all this, and infinitely more, is forbidden in the seventh commandment.

What is the eighth commandment?

The eighth commandment is: "Obey the gospel of JUSTICE"—which is the second manifestation of the principle of Wisdom.

What is required in the eighth commandment?

The eighth commandment requireth of us the "lawful procuring and furthering of the wealth and outward estate of ourselves and others;" also requireth every one to seek to establish an equilibrium of interest and duty, so that no one will be called to do that which is not in accord with the highest justice. For example, the lawyer is mostly interested in human misunderstandings, the physician in human sicknesses, the clergyman in human subjection to outward institutional authority; while, at the same time, the lawyer's duty is for peace on earth, the physician's for health on earth, and the clergyman's for individual harmony and self-legislative sovereignty. Hence our present social relations generate every species of *injustice;* which, while perpetuated from necessity, is by all acknowledged to be unwelcome.

What is forbidden in the eighth commandment?

The eighth commandment forbiddeth whatsoever may infringe upon the *rights* and *liberties* of others. O Earth! thrice beautiful thou, and fit for the young spirit's early unfolding, *when men love justice and live it.* Justice! the highest form of true Religion, enriched with angel harmonies, with sleepless universal penetrative eyes, looking straight into the soul of human motives, seeing the thought before the deed, the substance through the shadow, rending the false and flimsy veil that men secretly hang between themselves and the world without! Upon the now unconscious leaves of the eternal tree of Life within, this majestic principle writes down every thought, word, deed, of the undying spirit.

What is the ninth commandment?

The ninth commandment is: "Obey the gospel of Power"—which is the third manifestation of the principle of Wisdom.

What is required in the ninth commandment?

The ninth commandment requireth the energetic employment of both body and mind, for human good and happiness. What Socrates did in the market; what Plato taught in his regal robes to metaphysical students; what Aristotle witnessed of atom, world, time, space, eternity, infinity; whatever else was seen or said or prophesied of by the succession of royal Thinkers—by the Lockes, Humes, Kants, Bacons, Newtons, Cuviers, Goethes, Spinosas, Fouriers, Humboldts, Parkers, Emersons—is possible to thee, yes, *to thee*, incredulous Reader! Even greater works than these shall ye do! Human life is eternal; and power, to accomplish the loftiest flight, is in thee hidden; therefore, believe now and be saved.

What is forbidden in the ninth commandment?

The ninth commandment forbiddeth physical idleness, mental debility, and disproportionate development of the heart and head; also it condemneth continued over-exertion for the gratification and enrichment of aristocrats.

What is the tenth commandment?

The tenth commandment is: "Obey the whisperings of the spirit of true Beauty"—which is the fourth manifestation of the principle of Wisdom.

What is required in the tenth commandment?

The tenth commandment requireth us to harmonize our loves and mental desires throughout; and thus create that Beauty, full of symmetry and regular conformation, which will prove a joy eternal.

What is Beauty?

Objective beauty is that which acts through the eye upon, and excites pleasure in, the spiritual temperament. (See 4th vol. of Great Harmonia.) We need not roam through vast domains of rich grandeur, nor fathom the deep mines of essences bodiless or abstractions metaphysical, to solve this simple question. True beauty is that, without or within, which yields pleasure and awakens gratitude.

What did the ancients say of Beauty?

It is said that Socrates called Beauty a short-lived tyranny; Plato, a privilege of nature; Theophrastus, a silent cheat; Theocritus, a delightful prejudice; Carneades, a solitary kingdom; Domitian said, that nothing was more grateful; Aristotle, that Beauty was better than all the letters of recommendation in the world; Homer, that it was a glorious gift of Nature; Ovid calls it a favor bestowed by the gods; Emerson, that Beauty is the mark God sets on virtue; and a French proverb, that Beauty, unaccompanied by virtue, is as a flower without perfume.

What definition can you give of Beauty?

I define Beauty to be the incarnation of three active principles—Use, Justice, Power—the coronation of whatsoever is serviceable, harmonious, energetic. He who would be truly beautiful must not be deformed with ostentation.

What is forbidden in the tenth commandment?

The tenth commandment forbiddeth all physical habits which might impair the most agreeable proportion of form or feature; and much more, every mental disposition that could deface the richer Beauty with which Father-God hath adorned the inner life. "In deeds and in motives untold by the tongue—by chisel uncarved, by poets unsung—the Beautiful lives in the depths of the soul."

What is particularly forbidden in this commandment?

The tenth commandment forbiddeth* all turbulency of spirit which in a few years wrinkles the beautiful brow; also, all animality which destroys grace of bone, gives prominence to the

* The reader will pardon this dictatorial word on the ground that it is employed in conformity to the Shorter Catechism, and not in any sectarian sense so repugnant to the author.

joints, and dissipates the freshness of youth from the teeth, eyes, hair, and skin (see 4th vol. of Great Harmonia); all discontentment with conditions which are incidental to an embryo existence, "envying or grieving at the good of our neighbor, and all inordinate affections for anything that is his." But Nature allots to no man more than is sufficient for a subsistence and guaranty against the intrusions of Poverty, physical and mental; all else, though strictly lawful according to existing constructions of individual rights, is nothing less than an appropriation of our neighbor's property and depriving a brother of the means of happiness.

What are we to conclude from this?

We are to conclude and resolve at once, that in this tenth commandment is forbidden all social or civil laws that infringe upon the Beauty of Universal Justice. Furthermore, all religions which make a virtue of crucifying the organ of Ideality and the normal requirements of the spiritual temperament. Beautiful external objects—pictures, statuary, flowers, ornaments; beautiful external odors—delicate perfumes, violet, mignionette, geranium, cascarilla; beautiful external sounds—songs, musical instrumentation, words of love, bells of liberty, the rounding cadences of Wisdom's words; beautiful external tastes—all berries and fruit which grow in sunlight and please the tongue; and thus, through all the vast, profound, and mystic simplicities of every day's sensuous existence, the tenth commandment forbiddeth every civil circumstance or religious obligation which could mar the symmetrical development of that Inner Beauty, which is mighty as Truth and essential to happiness as heaven itself.

What is the eleventh commandment?

The eleventh commandment is: "Obey the gospel of Aspiration"—which is the fifth manifestation of the principle of Wisdom.

What is required in the eleventh commandment?

The eleventh commandment requireth us to acknowledge, in our daily walk and conversation, our grateful consciousness of whatsoever is interior and supernal—our relation thereto and dependence thereon—which is at once a source of imperishable pleasure and a cause of growth in rich domains of glorious meditation; vaster far than fields of intellectual culture, deeper than oceans of theologic lore, sweeter than a thousand gardens of paradisaical flowers, diviner than the songs of the flowing Mornia, pure as the perfect Love.

What is Aspiration?

Aspiration, as the word implies, is a spiritual reaching upward—a prayer for providential aid, a longing after things and truths superior—an attraction toward that which is in store for the soul.

What is forbidden in the eleventh commandment?

The eleventh commandment forbiddeth all ingratitude; all habits of negligence in the wisdom faculties. Also, all irreverence toward that which is truly useful, just, energetic, beautiful—not merely in the sight of the body and its senses, but toward whatsoever administereth lovingly and wisely to the highest faculties; all abuse of that which thus lendeth wings to imagination, and expandeth the capabilities of the inmost understanding.

What is the twelfth commandment?

The twelfth commandment is: "Obey the gospel of Harmony"—which is the sixth manifestation of the Wisdom principle.

What is required in the twelfth commandment?

The twelfth commandment, which is the sum of all Wisdom, requireth us to be and do that which will render our fellow men the best service and the longest happiness.

What is forbidden in the twelfth commandment?

The twelfth commandment forbiddeth every system of government and all religions, which retard mankind's progress toward HARMONIAL UNITY.

Is any man able perfectly to keep the commandments of God?

No man alone and unbefriended, unsupported by the counsel and magnetism of personages superior, can keep all these commandments; but a firm desire, a sincere aspiration, to do so, will bring to his aid the friendship of angels, and help to centerize his personal capabilities.

Is angelic aid the principal and most needful thing?

No; the principal condition, favorable to individual progress, is external harmony; not only in bodily health, but in the several relations demanded by the several loves. A married woman, to be happy, aside from her own natural peacefulness, requireth a good and intelligent companion. No parlor is harmonious with discord in the kitchen. Spiritual righteousness and happiness are impossible while the outward conditions of man's social life antagonize. Oh, that churchmen could see more of Time in their benevolent enterprises! The affairs of eternal worlds can be more easily comprehended and controlled by their inhabitants. Man's works of salvation and redemption should be adapted to this world.

What explanation can you give for the absence of social harmony among Christians?

It is of the utmost importance that we understand the *true theory of reform;* at the same time, also, the reason why the Church system does not succeed. The Church professes to be adequately armed to battle with sin, and provided with *all the true instruments* of social Reform. It professes to have the stupendous "Word" on its side—not only so, but the Almighty with it. In fact, all the persons of the God-head are claimed as both prime movers and co-laborers in the vast field of human redemption.

What result does this church association bring forward?

The whole supernatural system has been well nigh two thousand years converting fifty millions of Protestants into religious Sectarians. But these fifty millions are, after all, far from being reformed and harmonized. Many of them still own slaves, sustain the Fugitive Slave Law, and go strong against the dethronement of King Superstition. These church members and church supporters make no better merchants; as tradesmen they are not a particle more honest than an honest Doubter; they make no kinder or wiser "Bosses" to journeymen and apprentices; they are no better than, and ofttimes not so good as, the so-called skeptical and unregenerated

How do you explain this fact?

It is because the whole church theory of Reform is unnatural; it is logical from a mythological foundation; and overlooks time in its aims for eternity. All Christians candidly confess that it is very *unnatural* to man's natural heart to be a bible Christian. Hence a foreign or supernatural aid is invoked. At length they suppose they obtain such aid, then they become "Christians"—that is to say, they become *unnatural*—but, perhaps, not a particle more pure, more honest, more humane. It would be a curious circumstance, should the affidavits of one hundred apprentices be taken, fifty with church members as bosses, and fifty whose masters make no profession of faith in any form of sectarian religion. The question is: "Which class is the most cheerful, kind, honest, humane?" I am fully satisfied that we should get the most favorable report from the so-called unregenerated. It is, alas! too well known, by many a poor boy and orphan-girl, how insupportably severe is the domestic discipline of church Deacons and praying Laymen. They make the most tyrannical masters; the most invincible slaveholders; the most cruel parents; the most ignorant foes to science; the stoutest friends of bigotry; and the abettors of narrow-mindedness.

Why does the Christian church fail?

The church fails, because it looks to a *wrong Source* for its aid. It expects to reform the world by preaching the Love—and the Hate—of an omnipotent Jehovah; with the necessity of faith in the virtue of that blood tragedy called "Jesus Christ and him crucified." The world can be *restrained* thus, but not reformed. The sectarian harness may be worn by thousands; they may work in the traces of duty, as kindly and docile as horses used to the gearing; but at the end of life, what are they? Are they unfolded in Love and Wisdom? Are they attractive representatives of the divine Life? Nay: they terminate their earthly voyage ofttimes as much in bondage—as little developed—as when they began. The greatest temporal achievement of a protestant Christian is, to triumph over the fear of dying—an accomplishment which the warrior, the Hindoo, the Turk, the Roman Catholic, possesses to an eminent degree, reposing upon his bed of death with a serene resignation.

Is love the best cause of reform?

Human love, by itself, is no source of Harmony; yet, in Love do we find that which is good and perfect. Your warm heart may be overflowing with Love, but are you, therefore, a harmonial man? No: the most loving and enthusiastic person, not regulated by intelligence, is perhaps the most impulsive and discordant. Wisdom must throw his temporizing influence o'er Love before the soul can become self-poised and upright in character.

What shall be said of modern church-religion?

A correspondent of the Southern Literary Herald, after attending service in Dr. Hawks' church, in New York, very aptly replies: "The luxurious pews, everywhere filled with well-dressed and comfortably-looking people, were little suggestive of the trials and sufferings of the Christians of an earlier day, who met upon the open downs, or beneath the leafless oaks of the wintry forest, to lift up their voices of praise and supplication to God. . . We could not help thinking that the minds of very many of the congregation were upon the next day's operations in Wall street, rather than upon the service, and that the *liturgy* would have been responded to with greater unction, if among its deprecatory clauses there had been this little petition—*From all losses by land or by water, from broken banks and bad investments, from false policies and a fall in flour*, GOOD LORD DELIVER US!" Modern *Religion* is courted so long as she resides in costly temples, gets a scholastic presentation, and is fashionable.

Are all transgressions of the twelve commandments equally heinous?

Some transgressions in themselves, and by reason of several external aggravations, are more injurious than others.

What are the lesser evils?

The lesser evils are those not accomplished by voluntary yielding to temptation; but which the spirit suffers as incidental or inevitable to surrounding circumstances.

What does every sin deserve?

Every sin deserves immediate and total destruction.

What does the victim or sinner deserve?

The sinner deserves the love and blessing of God ineffably

more than the self-sustaining and well-developed; for the wise and happy need not a physician, but those only who are sick and unfortunate.

What does God require of us, that we may escape his wrath and curse due to us for sin?

The Bible-god, who is not the eternal Companion of Mother-Nature, requireth of us faith in Jesus Christ.

What is faith in Jesus Christ?

This will be answered, *in extenso*, in another chapter of important questions.

What is repentance unto life?

Repentance unto life is a resolution taken in the Wisdom faculties, renouncing a personal evil habit, before the whole angel-world, whose aid you invoke; a resolution carried out practically in every subsequent act of your life.

What are the outward and ordinary means whereby Christ communicates to us the benefits of redemption?

The outward and ordinary means are, the charitable and wise efforts to ameliorate the condition of Mankind—efforts to instruct youth, to elevate the downtrodden, to ennoble intellect, to promote genius, to harmonize national interests, to create equitable industrial relations between the different classes, to purge existing governments, to reform creed-born religions, to abolish servitude, to bring the Harmony of Heaven on the whole Earth.

How is the "Word" made effectual to salvation?

If by "the word" you mean the twelve living commandments written by Father-God and Mother-Nature in the eternal substance of every human being, then it is made effectual only by virtue of a reasonable understanding of its positive teachings and conforming thereto with a stern love of perpetual personal righteousness.

What is meant by personal righteousness?

By personal righteousness is meant the doing of whatsoever is RIGHT in the light of your own moral intuitions; the opposite of that which you believe to be wrong.

How is the "Word" to be read and heard, that it may become effectual to salvation?

If by "salvation" you mean the rescue of man from Ignorance and its misfortunes, then the "word" (meaning the body and soul) may be read and heard effectually when selfishness shall be magnanimous enough to bring on earth, a HARMONIAL BROTHERHOOD; because the highest selfishness is identical with universal benevolence, "honesty is the best policy," and that which renders happiness permanently to one individual is a steadfast blessing to the whole race.

What is true religion?

True religion is universal Justice—which begins at the centre of the individual and widens outwardly, wave-like and as the ocean swells, till All are clasped in one pure embrace of Love—predicating, thus, the Happiness of all upon the Harmony of each.

What are the sacraments of this religion?

The sacraments of this religion are: first, personal cleanliness and chastity; second, a heart full of warm devotional Love to man and to Deity; third, a head full of serene, strong, steady Wisdom; fourth, reverence for the marriage relation; fifth, the regeneration of the world as far as possible through little children; sixth, and every humanitarian institution which promotes the welfare of the several working classes.

What are the sacraments of the New Testament?

If by the "New Testament" you mean the New Dispensation, then the sacraments are: first, the Immortality of the spirits of all men; second, the immediate resurrection of the soul (retaining the shape of the body) at death into a purer progressive world; third, the enjoyment of intercourse with the departed through several mediations.

What is baptism?

Baptism is a sacrament of the new dispensation, signifying a bathing in the rivers of Infinite Truth, which flow unobstructed through the boundless gardens of existence—through the vast territories of Mind and Matter—the imperishable Home of Father-God and Mother-Nature, through whose sacred labyrinths the feet of men may tread with steadiness, in whose depths of translucent waters the earthly pilgrim may bathe his weary soul, and receive strength to ascend higher mountains of contemplative intelligence.

To whom is baptism to be administered?

Baptism is not to be administered to any that are not asking for New Truths—that is, no one can receive the bath of progressive Ideas unless his soul seeketh to know Mother-Nature and to wed his life-work with her All-Wise Companion.

What is the Lord's supper?

The Lord's supper is any hospitable and philanthropic feast, either physical or spiritual, which neither profanes the body nor brutifies the soul, but yieldeth enjoyment and awakeneth gratitude.

What is prayer?

Prayer is a spontaneous act of Filial Love; the soul's involuntary yearning for perpetual aid; an intuitive acknowledgment to the supernal for the fact of existence; a desire for additional benefits and continued happiness.

What is the origin of prayer?

The habit of formal praying originated among the religious sects of Egypt; a plan for placating the vengeance of angry gods, and for soliciting aid from supernatural beings; to avert impending calamities, cure disease, and secure local prosperities.

Does prayer influence Father-God?

All human history returns a negative answer; all experiences, termed special providences, yield to a different explanation. (See 2d vol. of the Great Harmonia.)

What is the legitimate effect of prayer?

The effect of too much reliance upon the invisible for aid, is, to beget weak-mindedness and unfitness for any great work; no man can accomplish much who doubts his personal capabilities and shirks individual responsibility.

Is there no good effect in prayer?

Yes; the normal effect in prayer is twofold—first, to open and prepare the soul for spiritual influx and illumination—second, to attract a portion of the angel-world into harmony with our interior necessities.

How would you further define prayer?

I would further define prayer by affirming it to be natural to all theological infants, and strictly spontaneous with those who, being children in the sentiment of religion, feel inward demands which only prayer can fully supply and stimulate.

Should we pray orally?

True spirit-prayer, like the glory of morning dew, ascends noiselessly. The answer? *that* comes, welcome as the fall of rain, when the soul most needs nutrition.

Is the habit of daily prayer beneficial?

That is not beneficial which increaseth your dependency; which impaireth the symmetrical unfolding of a beautiful self-containing Manhood. Nevertheless, there are times of ineffable trial—when the stoutest heart, having struggled and battled against some terrific enemy to life and happiness, is forced to go beyond objective Nature in prayer to the Supernatural.

Is true prayer a voluntary act?

Voluntary prayer is suggested by a consciousness of ungratified desires; but, on the other hand, when *needs* (more imperative than wants) announce themselves at the court of Reason, then the heart wells up and overflows its banks in spontaneous acknowledgments to the hidden Source of Infinite Goodness—"God of my Fathers! holy, just, and good! My God! my Father! my unfailing Hope! . . . . . . Whom have I in the heavens but Thee alone? On earth, but Thee; whom should I praise? whom love?"

Should little children practise prayer?

Little children should be taught that Father-God is a spirit, and they that worship him must worship him *in spirit* and *in truth;* that is to say, children should not think of a position of the body, nor of words, but of living good lives and doing good for goodness' sake. The daily recollection and exercise of this aspiration is a prayer "in spirit;" while resisting temptation, speaking the truth, living peacefully, washing the body, learning wisdom, and doing good toward other children—this is a prayer "in truth;" and the Father seeketh such to worship him.

Can a discordant person pray?

Yes; there is no need of prayer where there is no temptation—no discord; the good man's life is a prayer perpetual.

Are words natural to prayerful gratitude?

Hannah More hath well answered:—

"Fountain of Mercy! Whose pervading eye
Can look within and read what passes there,
Accept *my thoughts* for thanks: *I have no words.*
My soul o'er-fraught with Gratitude, *rejects*
The aid of Language — Lord! behold my heart."

When we pray should we think of a Personified-God?

True prayer is the result of no intellectual perception of persons, relations, effects, or principles; it bursts suddenly forth like a shout of joy, a cry of fear, a word of praise, a note of music, a shriek for help; hence all scholastic lip-service in churches, like a blessing hurriedly spoken by hungry mouths over a feast of fat things, is an inevitable profanation. Oh, how I love that brother and that sister — the spontaneous child of Father-God and Mother-Nature — who asketh for spiritual aid, the gratification of unselfish desire—

"For light and strength to bear
Our portion of the weight of care
That crushes into *dumb* despair
One half the human race!"

You have frequently used the terms "Father-God and Mother-Nature," what do you mean?

By the term *Father-God* is meant the living Fountain of all Causation; by *Mother-Nature* is meant the Fountain of all Effectuation.

Are these principles masculine and feminine?

Yes; and the Harmonial marriage of these co-essential and co-eternal Principles, half personified and wholly unalterable, was followed by prolifications innumerable — children, men, spirits, angels, in infinite orders and degrees of perfection — which people the countless worlds around, and the spirit Lands beyond; whose unfading groves never feel the blasts of adverse winds, whose endless avenues never lead through uncultured wilds, whose landscapes never weary the eye, nor exhaust the soul that loves the pilgrimage of Eternity!

How would you further define the offspring of this most holy marriage?

I would further define them by affirming them to be, first, all shapes and degrees and relations of Matter: and second, all forms and unfoldings and effects of Mind. This is the broadest general definition of Nature's works.

If human beings and invisible spirits are legitimate children, do they not resemble their progenitors?

Yes; man's body is a physiological representation of the physical universe, and the spiritual universe is psychologically revealed in man's mind; therefore, the harmonial body bears the features of Mother-Nature, and the best mental organization presents the image and likeness of Father-God.

What is true morality?

True morality is the living-out of *your own ideas* and sentiments of true religion. That man is truly and gloriously moral whose acts spring from the affection of Universal Justice; whose deeds owe their birth to a love of human good and happiness.

What is fidelity?

Fidelity is the integrity of your soul to itself — obedience to the angel of God within — to your best and highest Attractions.

What is infidelity?

Infidelity is the wilful violation of that within you which you believe to be Truth, Justice, Righteousness.

What is Truth?

Truth is that divine and eternal principle which "fills, bounds, connects, and equals all" — the Cause and the Effect of infinite Harmony — everywhere cohesive and at all times consistent — as in the *material* so also in the *spiritual* realms of Existence.

Who is the wisest man?

He is the wisest man who comprehendeth the boundaries of his own Ignorance, and knoweth the art of destroying them.

Who is the most successful man?

He is the most successful man who seeth the secret victory that ever dwelleth within any defeat which may follow an honest effort.

Who is the mightiest man?

He is the mightiest man who can, at all times and amid all circumstances, control the impulsions of Love by the voice of Wisdom.

Who is the greatest philanthropist?

He is the greatest philanthropist who does Good to some and harm to none.

Who is the most holy man?

He is most holy who never acts contrary to his highest perception of Right.

Who is the best neighbor?

He is the best neighbor who regulates his private affections and public deeds by the principle of Distributive Justice.

Who is the best husband?

He is the best husband who, when you examine him by your highest attractions, hath the cleanest body and the purest spirit.

Who is the most excellent father?

He is the most excellent father who begets his offspring through the attractions of pure unadulterated conjugal affection; and who, when blest with the presence of childhood, is at once a friend, brother, playmate, and teacher.

Who is the best wife?

She is the best wife who, when you examine her by the intuitions of your highest temperament, is the sweetest girl, the truest friend, the gentlest sister, the most attractive woman.

What is the law of personal progression?

The law of personal progression is to be found only in conscientious action for the benefit of others. The soul's strongest cardinal law is Action. When rightly directed, it tendeth, like a gently-flowing river, toward self-ennoblement and self-perfection: in deeds of good to mankind.

What is a humbug?

This scornful term is very promptly applied to any person, association, political party, or institution, which advertises to perform a certain feat or produce some special result, but does not accomplish it; yet dogmatically persists, nevertheless, in affirming entire fulfilment of promises publicly made or pledges privately circulated. The word "Humbug" is usually given to a pretender, to a mountebank, or counterfeiter; and sometimes, to that which is neither of these, but is thoughtlessly prefixed to a matter because it is "new" and opposed to the established routine of law, physic, and divinity.

Have we any examples?

Yes; many political schemes and some ecclesiastical institutions have never redeemed promises which they have from time to time published in their bulletins and programmes. The popular evangelical system of reforming mankind by means of religious ordinances and canonical rituals, has not performed a tenth part of what centuries ago their progenitors advertised to accomplish long before the present era.

What is Man?

Man is a product of all the Universe. Physiologically—of all orders and degrees of matter: psychologically—of all essenses and properties of Mind.

How should man be studied?

Man should be studied as the Epitome of Father-God and Mother-Nature. He may ask of his existence through science, through art, through music, through the emblems of visible creation, through anatomy, through physiology, through psychology, through theology, through philosophy, through imagination, through conscience, through all the elements of his heart-love, and through all the attributes of his Wisdom.

What is Science?

Science is an intellectual perception and systematic classification of Facts.

What is Art?

Art is the temporary beautification of ordinary objects by the skill of human nature; the transformation of lower substance into human uses and available benefits.

What is Music?

Music is the normal translation of mute sentiments into expressive sounds; the best revelation of the celestial subtilties which animate the human soul; the only language of the angel-world when discoursing of the Harmonies of Nature.

What is anatomy?

Anatomy is a knowledge of forms and structures.

What is physiology?

Physiology is a knowledge of organs and functions.

What is psychology?

Psychology is a knowledge of the mental principle; based upon a perception and classification of its phenomena.

What is theology?

Theology is an intellectual inquiry, a conjectural speculation, concerning the personality and government of a being called "God." Modern theology is ancient mythology gone to seed; a product of the poets and semi-philosophers of Egypt, Greece, and Rome.

What is philosophy?

Philosophy is a term which may be applied to all legitimate exercises of Reason and Intuition. (See 2d vol. of Great Harmonia.) I would apply this word to an intellectual perception of Facts, to a moral apprehension of Truths, to an intuitive comprehension of Principles; embracing thus, all science, all theology, all religion.

What is the reason-principle?

The reason-principle is the totality of love, spirituality, intellect. Reason is the flower of the spirit. A law of truth, regulating the entire existence of a man—physically, socially, intellectually, morally, spiritually—another word for "Wisdom," the soul's eventual Savior.

What is imagination?

Imagination is the subjective mirror of the emblems and images of objective Nature; the authorized forerunner of the intellect; the chief interpreter of the sentiments; the poet-laureate of the spiritual faculties; the Argus-eyed clairvoyant of the whole interior nature.

What is the true office of imagination?

The true office of imagination is to probe the metaphysics of creation; to give substance to shadows; to discriminate between this and that, and luxuriate in the presence of finely-drawn distinctions; to shape essences otherwise bodiless; to give solidity and representation to invisible thoughts; to symbolize the quality of an act; to individualize and give immortality to an adjective; to explore mystic fields, and break the forbidden seals of man's life-book; to sing of the good and the true, of the pure and free, in words at once sweetly human and majestically divine; lastly, imagination is designed to officiate evermore in transforming the stony-facts of sleepless science into bread of life, in moulding the surface-truths of dignified philosophy into every conceivable form of beauty, glory, sublimity, and magnificence; and, deeper still, to discover in all things the presence of truth, in each man a thought of God, in every form the Beautiful.

What are human thoughts?

Human thoughts are the effects of organized cerebral motion; the waves of the waters of life; the children of organal sensation; the signs of intelligence.

What are fixed ideas?

Human ideas, when fixed, are the patriarchs of the thinking faculties; very fond of control, mostly masculine, and uniformly overbearing; the bench of bishops who first render theological mysteries canonical, and then forbid investigation.

What are conceptions?

Conceptions are the beautiful first-born of the imagination; in disposition feminine, in effect tranquillizing and exalting; they act upon the conscience.

What is the conscience?

Conscience is a spiritual sensibility with a dual capacity, having a twofold origin—first, innate and eternal; second, ed ucational and temporary. The latter, an artificial product of the circumstances of our existence, is youngest and most active; natural conscience on the contrary, is first in the soul, is inmost, deepest, absolute, and less clamorous. You here see the difference between tuition and intuition; and the reason why persons with opposite religions, are equally devoted and ready to persecute; why a Christian's outer conscience can justify the present Ishmaelitish system of trade and commerce.

Why do we not see more of this natural conscience?

The undying conscience is now obstructed in its efforts to gain the soul's attention. It is the declaration of the principle of Justice—the clear voice of Father-God in the garden—concerning whatsoever is Right to itself and just to all men. Oh, how glorious to own a *natural* conscience! Yet, as the world goes, how extremely painful and inconvenient! Its demands upon its possessor are at once imperative and unpopular; its judgments are neither time-serving nor transient; its rewards are unperishable; its golden words are engraved, *ambrotyped*, by Imagination on the Book of Life; and the voice of its words reverberates through the labyrinths of hidden experience, denying to the discordant and sinful soul a moment's silence, till each private evil is manfully overcome and its place occupied by whatsoever is truly just and fadelessly beautiful.

Is the imagination deceptive?

Yes; when the understanding is weak or undeveloped, or when the *natural* conscience is overrun or temporarily superseded by the world's standards of right and wrong, then it is that Imagination becomes pregnant with crude forms and hurtful fancies.

What is the result in the mind?

The subjective result is that these forms and fancies—although not essentially false in the adaptation which is possible to them under the ministrations of enlightened reason—beset the mind with innumerable tricks and troublesome extravagances; hence we meet persons who, with a fruitful imagination and little conscience, seem to delight even themselves in recounting tales and adventures in which they were the heroes and victors.

Does intellect impair imagination?

Far from it; on the contrary, intelligence and a healthy conscience, combined, add consummate grace and facilities immense to this prophetic faculty; they unlock its mystic clairvoyance, inspire its pinions with herculean strength, and render it at once the most bewitching guest and the best philosopher.

Why does philosophical education destroy superstition?

Because superstition is the product of Imagination, during that faculty's childish years, prior to its cultivation and manhood; hence the more wild and undisciplined a people (like the ancient Chinese, Egyptians, Persians, and Jews), the more crude their reports of God—the more supernatural and extravagant their conceptions of religion.

Are religion and philosophy incompatible?

Religion and philosophy are sister and brother; no twins of Father-God and Mother-Nature were ever more of one accord!

How, then, will you explain the conflicts which frequently occur between them?

There is no conflict between the religion of Nature and pure philosophy. Philosophy is a universal harmonizer, and interferes with religion only when its fruitful superstitions and consequent exaggerations contradict the soul's highest affirmations —a just and wholesome interference which, resembling a wise parent checking a child's impetuosity and untruthfulness, does no injury, but, instead, strengthens and beautifies and intensifies yet more and more the native glory of all true Religion and pure Humanity.

QUESTIONS ON LIFE, LOCAL AND UNIVERSAL

WHAT is Life?

Life is felt by countless myriads; bringing to each a variable value and a different significance. Hence many and various words, embodying dissimilar postulates, are summoned to the work of definition. There are at this moment nearly a thousand millions of human beings on this globe; therefore, to the problem of Life, there are nearly a thousand millions of solutions. Man's conception of the answer will correspond to two conditions—first, the *circumstances* of his body—second, the *centerstances* of his spirit; and, however antagonistic the responses emanating from those in opposite states of flesh and spirit, yet, on the final analysis and synthetic judgment, all answers will be pronounced essentially homogeneous, and consistent every way, with the doctrine of a universal Brotherhood.

What is life to childhood?

A crown of thanks! dear reader, for asking me this question; the scene which it unrolls before my spirit is sweet-perfumed and bursting-full of promise. To a well-born and happy Childhood, Life is one with silently-creeping grasses, with emerald landscapes, with laughing lapping streamlets, with the nervous joy of humming bees, with swelling buds and blooming violets; one with flowering and fruiting trees, with the fragrance of apple-orchards, with picking clover and sweet grass in the meadow, with cuffing the brooklet that goes purling below the willows; one with boat-sailing on the glittering pond at the bottom of the field; one with leaf-clad grape-vines climbing aspiringly and lovingly over garden grottoes, with blushing strawberries beneath clefts and upon the rock-wrinkled hillside; one with the fairy dwellers of shady nooks, with the sun-ray among inhaling roses, with the diversal singing of trees swept by the wind-spirit of the mystic west; one with the cheery chirp of wren and robin; one with the evening dream of prairie fields of fresh-mown hay, with the luxurious beauty of landscapes beyond the sunrise; one with the rushing gayety of the morn ing light, with the early dance of squirrels on the old stone wall; one with the young colt, and the yet trembling calf, and the turkey in the pasture, and the timid lamb on the rolling lawn; one with the silvered splendors of midsummer hues, with the stillness of a July noon; one with the fall of rain, with the ascending moisture, with the melting bow just now arching the far-off horizon; one with the angel of sleep, with the angel of dreams, with the gods of the seasons; one with the undefinable romance of new faces that visit at the house, who eat at the table, who smile with the baby, and tell innocent stories of lands and cities yet to be seen; one with the ephemeral fascination of novel sports, with the painful trouble of finding the misplaced plaything; with the half-sad excitement when bounding impulses are checked by the interposing voice or strong hand of maternal watchfulness; lastly, and in short — Life to the best childhood is the negation of solid happiness, the blush of anticipation without the pleasure of participation, the perception of being without the luxury of understanding it, an innocence which has never felt the joy of resisted temptation; identical with initial bewitchments and glittering joys innumerable, which surround the citadel of undisciplined sensibilities, and which plant, in the rapidly-unfolding imagination, the seeds of ideas which rival the Siren Isles in beauty, and the realities of this globe as well; hence childhood, to all poets, is a holy foreshadowing of pleasures common to the spirit-Lands, a kind of *avant courier* to the facts of an existence superior to the present; a table of contents to the book of the coming ages; a daguerreotype, so to speak, of the world beyond, painted on earth by the Infinite Sun of the Univercœlum.

What is life to unhappy childhood?

Life to unhappy childhood is the breathing curse of unchaste and discordant progenitors; an organic struggle, panting between smiles and tears; a whipping-post, for the expression of domestic discontent and parental brutality; a receptacle for crude and cramped ideas of God and humanity; the fountain of several diseases to be transmitted in coming years to a consequent posterity. Oh, most unwelcome scene!

What is life to youth?

Youth is readily magnetized by the diversified phenomena of Life. It narcotizes him so gently, more and more day by day, till every object, natural as well as artificial, thrills his senses with seductive power—saying, "Behold! I'm but the type of what you may possess—the merest shadow of to-morrow's *substance!* Press on!! On!!!"

What is life to manhood?

Life to manhood is an ethereal flame breathed out from the mouth of God; given not to dissolve the world, but to purge its dross away, and to beautify all honorable relations.

What is life to ripened years?

The dreams of childhood are faded, but earliest joys come back with attractiveness renewed; youthful resolutions unkept, and participations that never filled the measure of desire, visit the old man, whose bark rides in the trough of that mountain-wave which will quickly cast him, beyond the region of danger, high upon the bosom of the Infinite. "Life is short," says Jean Paul Richter. "Man has two minutes and a half to live—one to smile, one to sigh, and a half to love—for, in the middle of this he dies; but the grave is not deep—it is the shining tread of an angel that seeks us. When the unknown hand throws the fatal dart at the end of man, then boweth he his head and the dart only lifts the crown of thorns from his wounds."

What is life to the religious man?

Life, to the orthodox believer, is God's transcendentally-mysterious and unutterably-uncertain gift; that man, through his own free agency and knowledge of moral laws, may fix, while in this world, his character and condition for eternal ages.

Is this opinion truthful?

Truthful opinions never impeach the plans of divine effort; neither do they afflict human souls with dismal ideas of the vast Beyond.

What do you mean?

I mean, in short, that believers of popular dogmas are tormented with tyrannic fear, and dare not think in freedom, "lest God should overhear their doubt—for God is thought to be always eavesdropping, and ever on the watch at the keyhole of human consciousness, hearkening for the footfall of a wandering thought—when he will stab at and run them through, and then impale them on his thunderbolt fixed in eternal flame." Hence, the religious man entertains an idea of God which impeaches at once the majesty of divine Wisdom and the universality of divine Love.

What, then, is life to the man of wisdom?

It is the harbinger of those benefits which Time's sickle can not mow down, nor the chemistry of death impair; of lessons which, whether heeded and treasured up or not in our early years, are the primal causes and necessary rudiments of an eternal education. The wise man thinketh that the life of this world, like a golden harp of infinite magnitude, yieldeth to the use made of it; music floats out from its vibrating wires, or discord goes rolling and winding through the tissues of being, just as we play upon it. John G. Whittier hath well said:—

"We shape, ourselves, our joy or fear
Of which the coming life is made,
And fill our future's atmosphere
With sunshine or with shade,

"The tissue of the life to be
We weave with colors all our own,
And in the field of destiny
We reap as we have sown.

"Still shall the soul around it call
The shadows which it gathered there:
And, painted on the eternal wall,
The past shall reappear!—

> "For there we live our life again:
> Or warmly touched or coldly dim
> The pictures of the past remain —
> Man's work shall follow him!"

What is life to the author of books?

William Hazlitt, both thoughtful and imaginative, is ready with his reply; he who never wrote a shallow, dull, or flat-bottomed sentence; yet whose position, being half-spiritual and wholly rational, may not afford the required response.

It is no easy task that a writer, even in so humble a class as myself, takes upon him; he is scouted and ridiculed if he fails; and if he succeeds, the enmity and cavils and malice with which he is assailed, are just in proportion to his success. The coldness and jealousy of his friends not unfrequently keep pace with the rancor of his enemies. They do not like you a bit the better for fulfilling the good opinion they always entertained of you. They would wish you to be always promising a great deal, and doing nothing, that they may answer for the performance. That shows their sagacity, and does not hurt their vanity. An author wastes his time in painful study and obscure researches, to gain a little breath of popularity, meets with nothing but vexation and disappointment in ninety-nine instances out of a hundred; or when he thinks to grasp the luckless prize, finds it not worth the trouble — the perfume of a minute, fleeting as a shadow, hollow as a sound: "as often got without merit as lost without deserving." He thinks that the attainment of acknowledged excellence will secure him the expression of those feelings in others, which the image and hope of it had excited in his own breast, but instead of that he meets with nothing (or scarcely nothing) but squint-eyed suspicion, idiot wonder, and grinning scorn. It seems hardly worth while to have taken all the pains he has been at for this!

In youth we borrow patience from our future years: the spring of hope gives us courage to act and suffer. A cloud is upon our onward path, and we fancy that all is sunshine beyond it. The prospect seems endless, because we do not know the end of it. We think that life is long, and that, because we have much to do, it is well worth doing: or that no exertions can be too great, no sacrifices too painful, to overcome difficulties. Life is a continued struggle to be what we are not, and to do what we can not. But as we approach the goal, we draw in the reins; the impulse is less, and we have not so far to go; as we see objects nearer, we become less sanguine in the pursuit; it is not the despair of not attaining, so much as knowing that there is nothing worth obtaining, and the fear of having nothing left even to wish for, that damps our ardor and relaxes our efforts. We stagger on the few remaining paces to the end of our journey; make, perhaps, one final effort; and are glad when our task is done!

What is life poetically considered?

Poetically considered, "the web of our life is of a mingled yarn, good and ill together. Our virtues would be proud, if our faults whipped them not; and our crimes would despair, were they not cherished by our virtues." These are the words of that world's writer, Shakspere, who, in one short paragraph, supplies the language of Thought, adequate, in fertile souls, to the production of twenty essays and fifty sermons on the mysteriousness of Life and its benefits.

If life was all pleasure, could man yield his love of it, and yearn for eternal existence beyond the grave?

It is most obvious that Letitia E. Landon's spirit-garden was cultured by unseen hands. But while, from the flowery slopes thereof heavenly incense rose, full of sweetness and spiritual gratitude, meanwhile there floated world-ward this low, deep sigh:—

"Oh, love and life are mysteries, both blessing and both blest,
And yet, how much they teach the heart of trial and unrest!"

Also, the Offering of Sympathy—published some years since—contains a good reply to your interrogation:—

"Why, when all is bright and happy, should a gloom
Be spread around us? Oh! blind and thoughtless soul!
'Tis the same power that reigns, and the same love,
Is traced alike, in sunshine and in shade:
The cloud that bears the thunder in its folds
Comes on the errand of good will to man!
Oh! we should cling too close to earth, and love
Too well its pleasures and delight,
Were there no shadows on its scenes of light,
No sorrow mingled with its cup of joy.

If sweet fulfilment followed all our hopes,
Like the unfoldings of a spring-flower bud,
We should not seek a better world than this;
Where then would be the reachings of the soul
For higher pleasures, and those purer joys
That have no other dwelling-place but Heaven!"

What is life to the chemist?

Chemically considered, Life is at once an effect and a concomitant of combustion; a force evolved, collated, and centred by the decomposition of certain elements, inorganic and imponderable. Chemico-physiologists find the temperature of the human body to be in all parts of the world about ninety-eight degrees. Heat is life, says the physiologist, and cold is death. Human food contains carbon and hydrogen. "These exist in the chyle. . . . The oxygen of the inspired air enters the capillary vessels of the lungs, mingles with the blood, with which it is carried to the heart, and thence to the nutrient capillary vessels of every part of the system. In these vessels the oxygen of the arterial blood unites with the carbon and hydrogen of the waste atoms, and carbonic acid and water are formed. This change among the particles of bodies is attended with the disengagement of HEAT." Such is the chemical idea of Life.

What is life physiologically considered?

Physiologically considered, and in accord with the materialism of the popular Christian schools of physiological teaching, "Life" is the *vis vitæ* of organized bodies—a power of animation and recuperation, recognised by its varied phenomena, known by a variety of Latin names; "vis insita," or a power in the animal muscle which sometimes acts independently of volition; "vis nervea," or a similar phenomenon of the muscle, but produced by the nerves instead of external irritation; "vis medicatrix naturæ," or that inherent power of animated beings which, in case of disease or accident, proceeds directly to counract, repair damages, and restore the system to primal healthfulness.

What is life harmonially considered?

My answer is—that, viewed from our scientific position, it is the first development of Motion, and the second prophetic manifestation, in the vegetable and animal, of that Intelligence which eventually buds and blossoms out in the human sensorium. Life is the spirit of all warm blood. It beats eternally through the vascular system of immensity—celestially healthful, spontaneously beautiful, and all-animating—fresh out-flowing from the Centre Heart of the united revolving Heavens. Contemplated from our poetic position, Life is the *soul-love* of all Nature. Theologically viewed, it is the *vital-essence* of the Infinite mind. When *morally* viewed, we say, with Longfellow:—

"Life is real! life is earnest,
  And the grave is not its goal:
'Dust thou art—to dust returnest'
  Was not spoken of the soul!

Not enjoyment, and not sorrow,
  Is our destined end and way;
But to act that each to-morrow
  Find us *farther* than to-day.

Trust no Future—howe'er pleasant!
  Let the dead Past bury its dead!
Act—act in the living Present—
  Heart within, and God o'erhead.

Lives of true men all remind us
  We can make our lives sublime,
And, departing, leave behind us
  Footprints on the sands of Time—

Footprints which perhaps another,
  Sailing o'er Life's troubled main,
A forlorn, a shipwrecked brother,
  Seeing, shall take heart again!

Let us, then, be up and doing,
  With a heart for any fate—
Still achieving, still pursuing,
  Learn to labor and to wait."

What is life socially considered?

It is a charmed circle of ceaseless friendships; an ebbless river of blessed sympathies; the fountain and mainspring of heart-born joys and loving kindnesses; of the sweetest delicacies—gentleness, tenderness, loveliness, happiness.

What is life to the politician?

A platform of action, ambition, disappointment; not regulated by Principles, but by policies, and expediencies suited to popularities and necessities of the day; more adapted to govern than to improve, more certain to shackle than to liberate. From the misfortunes of political strifes and unprincipled gladiators in the area of government; from the terrors of the god of aristocracy whose name is "Mammon;" from all temporary losses, by death, of liberty-loving natures, and, by election, from the reckless legislation of undeveloped minds — Good Lord deliver us!

What is life to the spiritually-minded?

According to the record left of Jesus's utterances by the mediumized son of Zebedee and Salome, we learn, that when absorbing and incorporating and identifying himself with the Principle of Love (or the Christ-principle), the Blessed Moral Reformer said: "I am the bread of Life — he that cometh to me shall never hunger — and he that believeth on me shall never thirst. . . Whoso eateth my flesh, and drinketh my blood, hath eternal Life; . . . the water that I shall give him shall be in him a well of water springing up into everlasting Life." But Paul's words, while more explicit and beautiful, may be accepted as not less salutary in sentiment: "To be carnally minded, is death — to be spiritually minded, is *life* and peace."

What is meant by spiritual-mindedness?

Each man of sectarian inclinations, with his intellect stored by self-constrained renderings of the Christian Scriptures, hath an answer of his own — an expression of *his* intellectual perception of what was taught by the Old Masters in spiritual contemplation; but, standing upon the platform of an equal liberty and not to assume vaster latitudes of spiritual meditation, I reply — that, he is spiritually-minded who considers absolute purity of heart and life to be the richest human possession, and that perfect obedience to the highest faculties and attributes (or attractions) of the soul is the only means of its attainment.

If such be spiritual-minded, who is the truest teacher of Morals and Religion?

Listen! the reply cometh — resounding in the firmament over the pulpits — from Theodore Parker, the fearless iconoclast of Christendom: The Teacher of Religion must seek to make all men noble. He is not to make any one after the likeness of another — in the image of Beecher or Channing, Calvin, Luther, Peter, Paul, or Jesus, Moses or Mohammed, but to quicken, to guide, and help each man gain the highest form of human nature that he is capable of attaining to; to help each to become a man, feeling, thinking, willing, living on his own account, faithful to his special individuality of soul. I wish men understood this, that their individuality is as sacred before God as that of Jesus or of Moses; and you are no more to sacrifice your manhood to them than they theirs to you. Respect for your manhood or womanhood, how small soever your gifts may be, is the first of all duties. As I defend my body against all outward attacks, and keep whole my limbs, so must I cherish the integrity of my spirit, take no man's mind or conscience, heart or soul, for my master — the helpful all for helps, for despots none. I am more important to myself than Moses, Jesus, all men, can be to me. Holiness, the fidelity to my own consciousness, is the first of manly and womanly duties; that kept, all others follow sure.*

What, then, is the truest Life?

No man ever gave a better reply than the author of Festus:—

> "We live in deeds not years; in thoughts not breaths,
> In feelings, not in figures on a dial;
> We should count time by heart-throbs. He most lives
> Who thinks most, feels the noblest, acts the best."

Who best comprehends the drift of Life?

That far-seeing, comprehensive, intellectual visionist, who, aided by an intuitive consciousness of everlasting principles invisible to outward sense, grasps that universal, gigantic law which uttereth speech from every order and decree of life — *Interior attractions are absolute prophecies of exterior destinies;* or, in other words, that each radical human *Desire* is a promissory Note, drawn up and endorsed by the Eternal God, payable at the ever-solvent Bank of Ultimate Satisfaction. This, in very truth, is the glad tidings of great joy which shall

* See Discourse by Theodore Parker, "On the Function of a Teacher of Religion in these Times."

be unto all people: a message delivered to willing minds, by the omnipotent and loving Spirit of universal Nature.

What is life to the man of silence?

It is that mysterious mood which envelops "the unknown God"—a magnificent scheme of infinite sadness—the only natural sequence to pre-existent Sorrows unutterable.

What do you mean?

I mean that of "Silence" there are two kinds—that which results from over-thought or over-feeling, and that which is created and compelled by the absence of them. The first evokes Silence as the only true expression of love, worship, gratitude, devotion; the second is overwhelmed by itself, as a desert of hot sand by its own oppressive barrenness and isolated desolation. Carlyle speaks from exalted silence: "When I gaze into the stars, they look down upon me with pity from their serene and silent spaces, like eyes glistening with tears, over the lot of man. Thousands of generations, all as noisy as our own, have been swallowed up by time, and there remains no record of them any more; yet Arcturus and Orion, Sirius, and the Pleiades, are still shining in their courses, clear and young as when the shepherd first noticed them in the plains of Shinah!"

What is true silence?

True silence is the handmaid of meditation; she is a good and faithful friend to him who prays in secret.

What is meditation?

Meditation is a beautiful angel-queen, clad in the white attire of spiritual purity, throned within the crystal palace of eternal Truth, within the "House not built with hands"—the Home of God, whose countless Mansions—heated with Love, lighted with Wisdom, ventilated with freedom, furnished with peace—bedeck the fields of Infinitude; each House with many doors; each door opening upon a new path in the pilgrimage of progression; and each new way leading the traveller into a different department of Father-God and Mother-Nature!

What is life to the merchant?

Life to the merchant hath three distinct phases. Remember these words—Meditation is the door which opens upon the divine

Presence—and I will answer the question. Fatigued with an excess of externalism, with his will all overlaid and regulated by the irresistible logic of a prodigious necessity, and although lost, as one might suppose, to every interior thought, yet have I seen a certain man, though a merchant, become temporarily a wooer of the blessednesses of meditation. 'Twas a strange spectacle! His senses firmly locked, shut up within the world-proof intrenchments of a conscious individuality, substituting day-books and ledgers for the book of life, his best customers denied admission, his whole aspect saying—"*Closed, to take an account of stock.*" Yes, distinctly I saw him, that merchant, calculating the results of his contact with his fellows—the profit and loss—how much happiness he owns, and how much misery—and seeing himself, butterfly-like, flitting away his existence up and down the fatal ledger-leaf, he writes, at the end of his retrospection—"It don't pay." Brief words these, but frightfully full of meaning. Behold! how the spirit of the age—half-fanatical with the inward flames of a bold constructive enterprise—arouses and re-energizes that merchant. "It don't pay" to be lost in vague abstractions—therefore, "thankful for past favors, resolved to merit a continuance of public patronage," he unbars the doors and decorates his windows: solemnly pledges himself, mind and might, to the graceless gods of this world; predetermines to live, like his neighbors, and equally well with the best of them, by feeding the heartless wants and feverish fashion of the fleeting hours; becomes recreant to his inner weal, an apostate to personal righteousness, sears and searches the goods and glories of conscience—alas! what do I see?—Bülletins, swinging out at each corner of his soul, saying—"Damaged goods at a bargain."

And yet, blinded by the blushes of occasional success, he pushes forward. His soul's hidden merchandise and all his habits are popular; but he would sell for "less than cost." Push off the injured stocks, so damaged by the *fire* of an offended conscience; the clerks, his thoughts, are ordered to sell them; they do so—and the merchant fancies himself victorious—the world is purchased by his spiritual devotion to it; but, after all, there remaineth a frightful residuum, a mass of ruined goods in the secret closets of his soul, on which is written, as by an angel's mighty hand—"Mene, Mene, Tekel."

And the merchant weeps! Defeat has walked by his side day and night, like a wolf in borrowed garb, dressed in the manner of victory. Ah! he has driven too oft from his soul the spirit of Meditation—has refused to enter in at the strait gate; from day to day he has allowed his business to master his manhood, has violated the laws of body and mind; and, offending still his yet surviving perception of the *Rights of Man*, he is prostrated helpless on his self-made bed of death. An angel of deathless friendship—weeping, speechless, powerful—stands yet by his side. And hung out over each door of the fast-decaying store, the material temple of the spiritual occupant, is the flag of death, the auctioneer, saying—"Assignee's sale; no postponement on account of weather."

From all the foregoing perceptions of Life, what rules shall we adopt to subserve individual harmony and social happiness?

My whole answer is concentrated in the following directions for establishing the HARMONIAL DISPENSATION:—

"THY KINGDOM COME."—*How to bring it.*—1. In the Morning arise—resolved to do nothing against, but everything for, the Kingdom of Heaven on Earth. 2. Happiness for all being the object, let every action during the Day spring from such well-conceived and well-developed thoughts as lead to its attainment. 3. In the Evening retire—at Peace with yourself—at Peace with the divine principles of universal Love and Wisdom.

"THY WILL BE DONE."—*How to do it.*—1. Be instructed by the Past, and by all it has brought you. 2. Be thankful for the Present, and for all its blessings. 3. Be hopeful for the Future, and for all it promises to bring you.

Observe these Rules, and the Harmonies of the kingdom of God will be with you, and Peace on Earth and good will toward Man be realized.

QUESTIONS ON THEO-PHYSIOLOGY.

WHAT is Nature?

Nature is the sevenfold manifestation of the Great Positive Mind.

What is the Great Positive Mind?

The Great Positive Mind is the crystalization of all Essences—the focalization of all Principles—to an extent wholly incomprehensible.

Is Nature separate from this Mind?

No; what we term Nature is the eternal associate of Deity—one living in and through the other, "all in all"—as the mutual dependence of Cause and Effect.

What are Principles?

Principles are the changeless *methods* whereby all essences are regulated in their ascension from primates to ultimates—from simplicity to diversification—from a state of merely abstract vitality to orderly embodiment and permanent organization.

Is God confined to a centre or focus in space?

The spirit of God is an omnipresent spiritual principle—animating and regulating the universal whole—being himself governed by the involuntary necessities of His own constitution.

Does God know all events eternal years before they transpire.

God knows only through the ever-awakening intelligences of his universal existence.

Can God do all things?

God is not sufficiently powerful to accomplish self-destruction. There are, therefore, necessities to omnipotence.

Is God a progressive being?

There is no increase of the quantities of mind or matter; but of progress in qualities and permutations there is no limitation.

Is the universe boundless?

Boundlessness is a comparative term applicable only to *infinity*, not to the organic or inorganic contents thereof; what men term Infinity, is that shoreless extent of space in which the universe revolves.

Are the contents of infinity eternally fixed?

Eternal fixedness can be predicated only of Principles.

Are not essences also immutable?

Immutability is true of essences only when applied to their endlessly diversified and ceaseless mutations. That is to say, all vitalic and energizing elements are strictly immutable in their changeability.

Do essences exist for ever?

There is no non-existence. Infinity is something containing something. Boundless space is at all moments occupied with unimaginable fields of matter and motion—elementary principles these, on their way up the dizzy acclivities of immensity, reaching forward progressively after expression through living organizations.

Is there no department of infinity unemployed?

No; there is no space unoccupied—no vacuum hospitable to that which should be destroyed. There is nothing existing without embodying divine ideas and subserving eternal uses. Whatsoever is good and useful can not be destroyed, and inasmuch as there is nothing but what is animated by the one spirit of goodness and utility, so is there nothing capable of annihilation in all the realms of Infinitude.

Is man's individuality lost in future spheres?

No; never! Because man's *spiritual entity*, unlike that of any inferior being, is a product of an indissoluble alliance matrimonial, between all atoms of matter and all principles of mind; the ultimate form of all forces, the *fruit* of the universal tree, and retaineth the image and inheriteth the immortality of his divine progenitors.

What is the most important question?

The most important question to this age is, that kind of interrogation which looketh into the origin of the human species; to man's improvement from the very beginning.

How can this be accomplished?

Healthy and well-constituted offspring can be brought into existence by means of just, chaste, and harmonial marriages of men and women; through obedience to the twelve commandments.

How can such marriages be secured?

True marriages may be secured by parents teaching their sons and daughters the *uses* of such relations; and then, by instructing them in a knowledge of the *central* temperaments, let them go forth and make choice upon their own responsibility. (See 4th vol. of Great Harmonia, and Marriage and Parentage by H. C. Wright.)

But how shall we comprehend your philosophy of the central temperaments?

By observation and intuitional study, as you obtain, a reliable knowledge of any subject, either scientific or religious.

Can you not give more details containing the temperaments?

Not yet; the "Reformer" was written to quicken the world in the direction of matrimonial progress; and thus, by stirring the waters of life, develop *questions* which some other day will answer; that day has not yet dawned upon the world.

Would such marriages be more fruitful?

No; true nuptial relations, consummated on the harmonial basis, while yielding vast harvests of golden joys for the world to sow and reap, would be less prolific in the multiplication of children.

How do you explain this lack of productiveness?

The explanation is, that none but the intellectual and spiritual in *motive* can conceive of and enter upon a high order of marriage; and such, being superior to extremism, and consequently deficient in the germinal properties of mere blood-love, must of necessity bring into existence fewer children, but *better* far in every organic essential.

What is the invisible spiritual principle in man?

The spiritual principle is a term employed in this Philosophy to designate that affectional and intelligent dynamical influence by which the human organization is animated and governed.

But you say on page 103 of the Great Harmonia, vol. i., that "Disease is a want of equilibrium in the circulation of the *spiritual principle.*" Now if this principle be organized, having form and solidity as you affirm, how can it *circulate* in the physical structure?

The explanation is complete when I add four words to the proposition, thus—disease is a want of equilibrium in the circulation of the *superficial elements of the* spiritual principle. This spiritual principle, being compounded of essences infinitely refined, and cherishing affinities more or less powerful for the several imponderable elements from which in part it derived its substance and individuality, is *subject* to their positive and negative action; that is to say, the superficial elements pervading the spiritual principle, may be *heated* or expanded, and *cooled* or contracted, by the action of magnetic atmospheres or electric agents, which at all times and everywhere surround the body of the human soul. In this manner the spiritual principle may be contracted or expanded (in its superficial departments) by the presence of heat or cold, as is proved by common experience, and thus be made to lose its healthy balance or equilibrium; in which case the individual is attacked with one of two conditions—a *fever*, or a *chill*—the one produced by a positive or magnetic state, the other by its opposite, the negative or electrical.

How does *sensation* (partly existing on the exterior of the physical body) which circulates through the sensitive nerves, transmit itself from its *own* vessels to other more interior and unnatural receptacles, as the mucous membranes?

The answer is simple. Although the invisible spiritual principle is an organized and indestructible substance, yet it is clothed by a transitory medium, *sensation*, capable of being influenced by heat and cold, repelled or attracted, as already explained. In further illustration let me remark, that "sensation" is a term used in the Harmonial Philosophy with two significations.

What are these two significations?

The first, that sensation is an ingredient or *elementary* principle of the immortal mind; the second, that sensation is a pervading *attribute* of the spiritual body, dwelling ordinarily on the external surfaces. Now, inasmuch as this attribute is *exposed* (because dwelling on the serous membranes and surfacial nerves) to the *action* of elements in the outer world, so is it (sensation) liable to be thrown into different phases of operation, caused, as before said, by the presence and influence of different degrees of temperature.

Can you illustrate this proposition?

Yes; common atmospheric electricity, for example, is capable simultaneously of diminishing surface sensation and of increasing the sensibility of the interior portions; while, on the other hand, atmospheric magnetism is adequate to the production of effects precisely opposite.

Can a *part*, which goes to form a perfect organization, be displaced thus and transposed, without producing disorganization?

Yes; all this, that is a change of action among the atoms of blood and a change of temperature in the subtler fluids, may occur without in any degree disturbing or deranging or displacing the deific substances of which the spiritual inmost is composed, even though such changes might be prolonged and sufficient to destroy the physiological functions and liberate the immortal mind. You perceive, then, that Sensation—not as an elementary principle of the organized soul, but only when in the capacity of an *attribute* or medium—is subject to diversal transpositions. These, I denominate "a loss of equilibrium"—the beginning of all diseases—the initial type being Fever and Ague.

What shall we do to make others unhappy?

You may be efficient in the production of unhappiness to others, first, by having a lust of control and benevolence *sufficiently small* to constantly fret at and get angry with those (quite as good as yourself), whose ruling temperaments naturally differ with your own; second, by living practically upon the extreme or inverted planes of Self-Love; or, third, by violating any one of the twelve commandments, as set forth in the present publication and in the second volume of the Great Harmonia.

When we travel for pleasure how shall we contrive to be miserable?

You may accomplish this result in various ways—first, by mentally carrying all your business along, or the perplexities of your housekeeping establishment; second, by packing up without system, and taking with you seventy-five per cent. more baggage than you will absolutely require; third, by cultivating feelings of hostility to the least inconvenience, and by combating the delays at passenger stations; fourth, by eating a large quantity of food, and by drinking stimulating fluids or water, when not really thirsting; fifth, by perseveringly avoiding every attempt at ventilation, and by wearing more garments than the temperature demands; lastly, by indulging your inverted fraternal love in thinking over the faults, plotting the downfall, or envying the good fortune, of some acquaintance, present or absent.

How shall children be made nervous, fretful, and sick, while travelling?

There are a multitude of rules, but none more correct than the following: Give the child a little piece of something to eat every fifteen or twenty minutes throughout the journey—besides, forbid its talking fast; forbid its crying even when too long restrained; forbid its desire to run about, and keep its mouth half smothered in the nurse's bosom.

Can you not give some plan whereby to fulfil this prescription, and thus make the child's unhappiness and sickness a matter of certainty?

Yes! The surest plan, one which has been "tried over and over again" and proved most successful, is this: Before setting out on a day's trip by the cars, provide your pockets and carpet-bags with the requisite variety and quantity of colored toys and confectionary substances. For example: After the first ten miles' entertainment has wearied your child's senses—after witnessing the phantom phenomenon of fields, fences, trees, villages, moving rapidly toward the place you left behind—when your child begins to ask questions, "When will we be home?" exhibiting symptoms of coming restlessness—wants to change its seat, &c., &c., then fumble in one of your pockets, and, finding, give it a stick of peppermint candy; that gone, give next *the half of an apple with its core;* next, as the child grows still more restless, *about two cents' worth of peanuts;*

these will do very well for half an hour's entertainment, when the little eyelids will close in a dreamful sleep of fifteen minutes' duration; then, as its mouth begins the exercises well known as preparatory to a half-angry and nervo-pathetic cry, put a stop to this by means of *a sandwich* you had the presence of mind to prepare before starting; next give it *a baker's sweet-cake*, or—which will do as well—some homemade jumbles; but as the hours wear slowly away, and your child's unhappiness and nervousness continue to increase, *give it a dose of medicine*, according to directions on the outside of the bottle; when its thirst becomes unbearable (after eating the sandwich), give it *a drink of lukewarm water*, which may be found at the end of the ladies' car; and now, as the cherub face looks comparatively happy once more, try to increase it by placing in the dimpled hand *a fine sweet orange*—☞ don't take off the skin, nor remove the seeds; but inasmuch as, while eating the orange, the busy head unwillingly bumped itself on the corner of the adjoining seat, and as the otherwise well-behaved child is suddenly attacked with a fretful fever and headache, therefore now is the time to give *the other half of the apple* aforesaid; this should be followed by a regular attempt to feed the empty (!) stomach, which, owing doubtless to the blow on the head, is without desire for the substantial articles; nevertheless, don't be discouraged, even if the appetite is gone and the fever does heat the brow, but give a piece of cocoanut candy or a stick of licorice-root, so very simple; as this will be quickly disposed of (a part having fallen in a pool of tobacco juice which *a gentleman* has caused to flow beneath), return to your peppermints and peanuts, to your almost-forgotten crackers and cheese, to your remaining oranges and apples; and finally, as soon as you get out of the cars, take the quickest conveyance home, with the sick child in your arms, giving it innumerable promises of new shoes, of beautiful rocking-horses, of a bran new article of clothing, &c., &c.; when arrived, despatch word to the most respectable physician, get him in your house, and say: "Doctor! do something quick for our child. Wife and I (not having any paregoric with us) have made unwearied efforts during the whole journey to keep the little darling still. About mid-day we noticed its little forehead was feverish. No appetite since morning—couldn't eat any lunch with us—and hasn't been able to take any nourishment! Oh! dear—do something for the child! What have we done to be so visited and afflicted by Providence? Doctor! what is the matter?" To which that gentleman gravely replies: "Pulse indicative of a high fever—gastric irritation—threatened with convulsions—a dangerous diarrhœa—with inflammation of the bowels—scarlet fever—prospective water on the brain—I can tell better to-morrow morning."

If our child should die, what shall we have preached at its funeral?

You should send for your physician's most distinguished friend and co-laborer, namely, the most respectable pastor in town. In his prayer, let him inform the Supernatural that we recognise this event, the plucking of this rose from its parent stock, as another warning (to those remaining) to believe on the Lord Jesus, and in his death for sinners' sake. In the sermon he should dwell, with touching eloquence and tears in his eyes, on the mysterious ways of Providence, on the incomprehensibility of God's ways to man, on the doctrine that God gives and God takes away; the whole to conclude with a pathetic prayer, touching upon the doctrine that the young spirit has gone "to the bourne whence no traveller returns," gone to the regions of the incomprehensible, gone to the mysterious un-get-at-able world, except through "faith" in the recognised standards of evangelical truth!

How shall a child be made quiet and happy while travelling?

By adopting a course diametrically unlike the foregoing. The excitement of changing and moving about, and not the labor of doing it, is the cause of a *fictitious* desire to eat. Children and adults alike require but little nourishment while travelling—taken as near as possible to the accustomed hours while at home. Preserve your balance thus, and your journey, even if half round the world, will be cheerful and comparatively without fatigue.

What is the eye?

The eye is the portal through which the soul looks out upon the universe: the light of the body; it is the Master Artist in the picturesque Academy of intellectual Design; it is the image of a principle.

What offices are there assigned to the visual organs?

Assigned to the visual organization are *three* offices — first, to paint the exact shadow of external objects upon that invisible and all-embracing canvass, called Imagination — second, to establish and regulate Memory by illuminating and expanding the understanding — third, to discover in the wilderness of human experiences the ever-pleasant and ever-attractive Paths of Pure Wisdom — paths beginning in the lowest valley, even at the foot of the cradle of life, winding all the way round the immense base of rudimental existence, and thence, with an imperceptible transition, continuing their unbroken lead spirally onward through an endless galaxy of golden homes in firmaments eternal.

Is the philosophy of vision comprehended?

No; the philosophy of human vision is as yet but little understood. If the beautiful structure of the globe of the eye was said to be a faithful representative of the *three* grand Laws of Nature, physicians would smile; yet what is more familiar to the occulist than the scientific classification of the visual membranes and humors — as the following:—

THE COATS.	THE HUMORS.
1st. The sclerotic and cornea.	1st. The aqueous or watery.
2d. The choroid and ciliary.	2d. The crystalline (lens).
3d. The retina, or inmost membrane.	3d. The vitreous or glassy.

Here are indicated the presence and action of a trinity of living Laws, which flow out into corresponding organizations.

Is the ear similarly constructed?

Yes; and every organ to be found in the animal or mental empire. The ear, for example, is composed of *three* anatomical parts, thus: 1st, the furrowed cartilage, or external ear; 2d, the tympanum, or middle ear; 3d, the labyrinth, or internal ear. So, also, by scientific classification, we learn that the labyrinthal part of the ear is composed of a *three*-cornered cavity, called the *vestibule*, the *cochlea*, and the *semi-circular* canals. Behold, herein, the action of triune laws.

What is the tongue?

The tongue is a standard of judgment to the combined digestive organization; besides which, it is the soul's chief and truest interpreter.

How is the tongue a source of judgment?

Through its sensational capacities. Owing to the admirable accuracy of its impressible nerves, the tongue is capable of deciding both in sickness and in health, what foods and beverages will best subserve the offices of the stomach; in this judgment it is wiser than all the inferential dietetic systems either of chemists or physiologists, and when *strictly* confided in and obeyed, will save the whole body from all extremes and physical discordance. Hence every tongue must be its own judge.

If this be true, why do persons who "indulge their appetites," complain of illness and propagate disease?

Because they violated, in the days of youthful rashness, that standard of taste which is supreme in the tongue. Alcohol and opium and tobacco were originally forced into the mouth, contrary to the repeated remonstrances of the lingual sensibilities, until violence and insult have established the reign of temporary silence over both tongue and conscience, but the "ills" of days' or months' or years' continuance do utter the language of condemnation, and urge the paralyzed WILL to begin the work of self-reform.

What are the uses of the tongue?

The office of this inestimable instrument is fourfold—first, to report to the physician's eye the secret condition of the sympathetic nerves and the ganglionic centres; second, to divulge to the ear of friendship the affections and emotions of the heart; third, to transform the deepest thoughts of intelligence into sounds which the listening spirit can remember for ages afterward; fourth, to tell the ever-attractive lessons which unfettered and progressive souls absorb from the vital system of the Infinite.

When is the tongue misemployed?

When it is made to embrace anything not welcome to its infallible standard of justice. You well know that your discrimination of *flavors* did not spring from an original intellectual perception of them; nay, the intellectual faculties acquire their education respecting foods and drinks from the testimonies and admonitions furnished by the thrice wiser tongue; which, if intelligently and conscientiously heeded, would at once set up an everlasting barrier of defence against the invasion of multitudinous medicines and epicurean habits at present so extremely orthodox and fashionable. To the human as well as animal, either in sickness or in health, one rule is for ever safe — namely: ask the organ of smell what odors will delight, and the organ of taste what flavors will please, then eat and drink (as directed in 4th vol. of the Harmonia); and the nose and mouth will notify your Reason that a swallow of fluid or a mouthful of bread after thirst is slaked or hunger is appeased, is wasteful and mischievous excess, entailing habits of intemperance and the seeds of disease.

When is the tongue an instrument of torture?

When it cries out "Crucify him! crucify him!!"—words which, while imparting no good tidings, put mighty weapons of persecution in the hands of the ignorant and prejudiced. Beware of that tongue which delighteth in the sequestered causes and private details of broken friendship; which propagates the last tale of misfortune or slander concerning individuals and families at home, or of nations' quarrels in distant lands.

When is the tongue an angel of mercy?

When, warmed by an overflowing heart of tenderness, it uttereth the words of that Friendship which could be neither purchased by the golden gifts of prosperity nor sold when misfortune sent an auctioneer to dispose of your transient possessions.

When is the tongue the noblest friend of man?

When it proclaims in thunder-tones the unreversable principles of Love and Wisdom and Liberty in behalf of every people and for all races of men; against the mischievous hatred of tyrants, against the unbridled despotism of monarchies, against the bitterness and bigotry of religionists, against every institution that works antagonistic to the largest freedom of any object bearing the image of humanity.

When is the tongue a promoter of pleasure?

When it ministers instructive anecdotes to the circle of friendship, and when, without irony and satire, it sets in harmonial motion the wheels of Wit, Humor, and convivial Mirthfulness. Yet story-telling (according to Dean Swift) is subject to two unavoidable defects; frequent repetition, and being soon exhausted—so that, he who values this gift in himself, has need of a good Memory, and should frequently shift his company.

What is the use of man's body?

The use of man's body, is: to mould and organize and develop his internal Principle—termed soul, mind, spirit—an indestructible conscious entity.

What is the use of the soul, mind, spirit?

The use of the spirit, as was said in the first chapter, is the spirit's *indefinite* problem—a mystery, which one short sentence may possibly dissipate, viz.: to give a conscious, intelligent expression to the eternal attributes of Father-God and Mother-Nature.

Is man's thinking principle, his spirit, extracted or obtained from whatsoever he breathes, eats, and drinks?

Man's spiritual body (which contains his inmost being) is elaborated and fashioned, by means of his various bodily organs, from unatomized substances extracted out of air, food, water, and the several imponderable principles. But man's inmost—his spiritual principle—is a deific essence.

QUESTIONS ON THE DESPOTISM OF OPINION.

How many forms of despotism are there?

There are three forms of despotism — two are institutional; one, is individual — namely, political despotism, ecclesiastical despotism, and the despotism of opinion.

What can be said of North America as a country?

Politically considered, and notwithstanding its justification of chattel slavery, North America, as a country, is the freest and the best. But France, England, and Germany, while laboring under numerous oppressions, enjoy more freedom of opinion. In America the despotism of opinion is mighty. It is gradually growing less powerful, methinks; still, it rules the the masses. It leads to the organization of fashion — to imitation — to a standard of judgment by which majorities govern minorities, the strong the weak, might is confounded with right, and the worst forms of tyranny and the best phases of liberty dwell side by side 'neath the shade of the nation's banner; the symptoms of future alterations.

What do you mean by an opinion?

By opinion, I do not mean anything which is demonstrable — such as the *facts* of history, the *phenomena* of science, or the *principles* of philosophy: these are susceptible of the most thorough demonstration. Opinion, on the contrary, is a vagabond, rambling about in the fields of perceptive logic — an illegitimate child of the intellect — a sort of bastard, so to say, whose parentage can never be fully traced nor legally defined. Opinion, therefore, is derived from no well-ascertained fact, from no established principle. If it were thus derived, it would no longer be opinion, but knowledge absolute, which precludes opinion.

What is the origin of an opinion?

Opinion is conceived and brought forth by such parents as *inferences, deductions, presumptions, assumptions, guesses, mistak s, misstatements, misunderstandings:* these all are eggs, each the centre of a bantling opinion; each the germ of procreative despotisms, brooded by little minds and time-serving institutions. Supernaturalism and metaphysical theories spring from conjecture—which, becoming an *opinion*, by general consent and not by understanding, attains to *authority*, and denies thenceforward the right of individual free discussion.

What have you ascertained by investigation?

By investigation I have acquired this knowledge—that all theology is a despotic theory, AN OPINION; and nothing more.

Do you make any distinction between theology and some of the doctrines of Jesus?

Yes; the doctrines of Jesus, concerning morality and spiritualism, are immutable truths. Theology, on the contrary, is not based upon Nature's facts and principles, but, as already said, upon *inferences, presumptions, assumptions*, which became despotic just like every other opinion. Knowledge has no slavery in it: opinion has no liberty. Opinion is the builder of dungeons; the inventor and proprietor of torturing racks and rods of iron; the grand Inquisitor who first kindles the martyr's fire, and then executes its terrible judgments. Such is the despotism of opinion. Absolute knowledge, being inherently positive, precludes all opinion; for ever independent of mere belief. Of course, I mean such knowledge as that which the entire soul acquires by industry through its appropriate channels of consciousness; that which, in the due process of integral growth, becometh Wisdom. And I repeat the affirmation that, church-theology is merely an *opinion;* a subjective belief; destitute of that knowledge which it arrogates to itself.

Can you give evidence to strengthen this assertion?

Yes; church-theology, for example, is believed by persons

who are in general *quite ignorant of the extents of Nature;* its laws, its functions, its relations, its harmonies, are never perceived by the believer in a dismal theology. But the sectarian mind, "never taught to stray, far as the solar walk," studies geography perhaps, and sees this globe as the *centre*, the sun and moon and stars all as so many attendent supernumeraries, and special providences as a human necessity to salvation. Our earth the centre of creation! a stationary orb, the largest, most important, about whose imperturbable majesty the entire heavens revolve! And the earth's inhabitants, the chief of all Deific concern.

Have we not outgrown this contracted idea?

Yes; thank God! the soaring soul of Science has overswept the limitations of Ignorance—the prolific source of old theology—and man's slowly but surely developing Knowledge has repressed the tides of the dead seas of error, and set bounds to the despotism of opinion.

Where did the world get the idea that this globe was the centre of the universe?

The world received it from the oriental tribes. Genesis teaches the paramount position, size, and importance of this earth; the Sun, the Moon, the myriad Stars, these are subordinate and subservient. But the "Milky Way" was long since *churned up* by Astronomy, and divided into vast constellated groups, the magnitude of some of which is sufficient to fill to overflowing our entire planetary system—out-measuring the vast orbit of Neptune—swelling over and expanding away into the immense depths of space beyond!

Can you illustrate your idea of this planetary magnitude?

Yes; "Alcyone," for illustration, is a name for one of the *brightest* stars in the Pleiades. Around this magnificent *centre*, our entire solar fraternity—the Sun, and its vast family of planets—travels swiftly, noiselessly, ceaselessly, without a moment's rest, without a moment's fatigue. And yet, like a living, breathing, harmonial Man, our planetary organization lays seemingly destitute of animation, near the centre of a wide spread bed of interlacing and inhabited stars. To the external sense he appears to be asleep, and dreaming, on the couch of

Infinitude. Notwithstanding which (apparent inertia), our solar body journeys forward at the frightful velocity of four hundred thousand miles per day; and yet, although its speed is so great, it requires eighteen millions and two hundred thousand years for our visible sun and its planetary dependencies to revolve once round "Alcyone!" This primary is nearly one hundred and eighteen millions times greater in magnitude than our sun; which again, as you well know, is many times larger than the earth, or any other related globe. Some stars are yet so distant, that thirty millions of years will sink into oblivion, and infinite scores of human beings will live and die out of matter, ere their light can reach our globe! And it will help your conception to remember that light can fly two hundred thousand miles per second. With this revelation of Nature before us, what shall we think of the oriental cosmological ideas—of the basis of the old but popular theology—Genesis, which maketh earth the *centre* of all creations, and the earth's inhabitants the source of infinite trouble to Deity!

Suppose a man should study astronomy and comprehend something of immensity, would he not, if discordant, still believe in the doctrines of theology?

Yes; theology is of necessity believed by those who are constitutionally discordant—by those who feel evils within—who infer therefrom the existence of *devils*—and possess, as they think, internal evidence of total depravity. It is a curious fact that the most *vicious persons* are the firmest believers in literal and future hell-punishments. Those who are enough unfortunate to be thieves, liars, highwaymen, pirates, slaveholders, and money-getting deacons, are fellow-believers and sometimes fellow-worshippers of the horrors and atrocious decrees of popular theology.

When does the mind lose such belief?

When the mind is well-balanced—when the person becomes measurably self-harmonial and as *much* civilized in religious matters as in current politics and in the commonplaces of life—then, popular theology *leaves* it as naturally and rapidly as the beasts of the forest flee before the peaceful march of Humanity.

Is not a dismal theology natural to certain temperaments?

Yes; Theology is naturally believed by those who have large organs of cautiousness, secretiveness, and a morbid conscientiousness. These temperaments take *judgment* into custody. It is another curious fact, that old theology (as an opinion) never gets into the *upper rooms* of the mind. It goes far underneath—lurking about in the caves and dark retreats of the cerebellum—like a polar bear sometimes, and like a viper too, that keeps sequestered because knowing its place.

Is there not much invidiousness in this assertion?

Far from it; in making this assertion, I do not forget that popular theology receives support from many talented and conscientious and benevolent men and women. But is it not worth remembering, that the most intelligent and courageous among its supporters, have been *apologizers* for the system? Have they not all failed in justifying theology to the intellectual faculties of mankind? Dr. Adam Clarke, for example, was under the necessity of writing an elaborate commentary on the Bible.

Why did Dr. Clarke write his commentary?

He wrote it simply to offer an explanatory *apology* to human nature for believing that which an intelligent and healthy Reason will eternally repudiate.

What is a commentary?

A commentary is an attempt, in many cases, to *defend* and *extenuate* a matter which is deemed either impossible, ambiguous, contradictory, or improbable. Could you look into the beginning and inceptive *causes* of the various commentaries on the Bible, I know you would be astonished to find that *each* writer worked from a disagreeable personal necessity; a method of allaying the positive protestations of the intellectual faculties and intuition. Dr. Beecher's recent scholastic work—"The Conflict of Ages"—is the most unsuccessful effort of a talented apologist; to satisfy the demands of human reason; to subdue the "conflict" between his own lower and higher faculties. The last fifty years are remarkable for apologistical sermons.

Does not the presence of evil in the world convince many of old theology?

Yes; theology, as an opinion, is entertained by scores of

honest minds, and because they can not understand the origin, the nature, and the cure of evil. (Such should read the Great Harmonia.) They consider evil to be absolute; not relative and conditional. Many believe that evil results from violating the verbal commands of God; not that evils and sins (so called) take their rise primarily from man's ignorance of his own nature, and the consequent abuse of it.

How can philosophy help the world?

The Harmonial Philosophy will do this world a monumental service by explaining the nature and demonstrating the cure of evil—a work which theology can not do. Why not? Because theology is *an opinion*—based, as already seen, upon inferences, inductions, presumptions, &c., and not upon KNOWLEDGE, which has no fellowship with opinion or despotic fanaticisms.

What other causes are there for believing theology?

Theology is believed by persons who, being victimized from childhood, now do homage at the shrine of popular and educational religion; which they would not continue to do, if they could see that *all true religion is innate;* not educational—that all true life is from within, inbred and divine; not absorbed, as a sponge drinks water.

Who profess to believe theology?

Theology is professedly believed by persons who worship at the shrine of policies, expediencies, compromise measures, shirks, &c.; by persons who believe Principle to be very good in poetry and metaphysics—congenial to fanatical reformers and revolutionists—as I shall hereafter demonstrate.

Would popular theology depart with the advent of correct knowledge?

Yes; it is impossible for an intelligent person to believe the myths of ancient Egypt.

What has been the experience of those who have sought for knowledge in the empire of Nature?

This question would require a careful compilation of the history of science, and a chapter descriptive of theological opposition to independent investigation. As this is a "delicate question," the reader will allow me to be silent for the next twenty minutes, giving time for the Weekly Pennsylvanian to answer: "We believe firmly, not only that the world is growing wiser, but better also — and nothing has conduced to this desirable state of facts more than the accuracy and solidity of modern learning. The vague mists and superstitions which clouded the intellect of past ages, have, in a great degree, been dissipated, and men begin to reason for themselves, and the people are willing to be guided by what appears in accordance with the dictates of common sense. The instructors of youth, and the promulgators of the truths of science, are no longer afraid to follow the promptings of genius, by the terrors of a brutish public opinion, which once made whole nations fools or madmen.

"When the belief was universal of the immobility of the earth, Copernicus conceived the idea that the sun was the centre of the system, and that the earth was a planet, like Mars and Venus, and revolved round the sun. And yet this founder of a new system of astronomy was excommunicated from the Vatican, in 1543, for maintaining heretical doctrines, and the papal court never annulled the sentence till 1821.

"When Galileo, his great follower in the cause of scientific truth, was thrown in the prison of the inquisition, in 1633, and was compelled to solemnly renounce on his knees, in the presence of an assembly of ignorant monks, with his hand upon the Gospel, the glorious truths he had taught, and to declare that the earth stood still, as he arose from his humiliating position, he indignantly exclaimed, stamping his foot, 'And yet it moves.' For this he was again assigned to the dungeons for an indefinite period of time, and required to repeat every week, for three years, the seven penitential psalms of David.

"But the Copernican system is now established, and has thus recommended itself to the scientific world through tribulation. That Tycho, Kepler, the Herschels, and Newton, were permitted to enunciate the result of their labors in peace, may be attributed to other causes, and in spite of the natural and universal perversity to sustain error.

"Galileo and Socrates are examples of the sacrifices men have sometimes made for the advancement of truth, under adverse circumstances, and against the preconceived ideas, preju dices, and superstitions of ignorant ages. Columbus, Fulton, and Franklin, were all opposed, each in his particular path of discovery, by the public sentiment by which they were surrounded, and nothing but their actual and unequalled triumphs saved them the reputation of being fit subjects for an insane asylum.

"How much does the world owe to Leinnitz, Leverrier, Lambert, Michael Angelo, Delambre, Descartes, and Galvani, for their painful and laborious mathematical calculations, composition of forces, and great analysis. Blot their discoveries from existence, and all becomes dark, chaotic, and given to uncertainty.

"It was fashionable twenty years ago to deny that the earth was more than six thousand years old, but the geological researches of Dr. Buckland, Professor Silliman, Dr. John Pye Smith, Mr. Lyell, President Hitchcock, and others, have proven by incontrovertible facts that it must have existed for many hundreds of thousands of years. And yet so far from these investigations leading to atheism, they lead to a true knowledge of nature. Those who contend for the limited existence stand on the very verge of denying indirectly the existence of a divine power, and uproot the whole system of natural theology. The supposition of Chateaubriand, that the earth was erected just as it is, with its millions of fossil-shells imbedded in the rocks, would overturn all the foundations of Dr. Paley's theory, and lead to the rankest skepticism. If the mountains hoary with age do not give evidence of their volcanic fires for many centuries—if the bones of fishes with their fins were not intended for motion—if the eyes of the fossil insects were not intended—then the most admirable adaptations of the animal economy do not show design or point with unerring certainty to the great Architect and Designer.

"Yet how often do the discoveries of true science pass unrecompensed, while the various systems of stultifying humbuggery meet with favor the eye and ear of the public. William Harvey, who discovered the circulation of the blood, met with detraction and persecution that destroyed his practice and reduced him to poverty, while the inventors of "cough lozenges," "flumex bitters," "liver pills," &c., roll in wealth, and dress in purple and fine linen. Before the time of Francis I., in the early part of the sixteenth century, the surgeons stanched the blood, when a limb was amputated, by the application of boiling pitch to the surface of the stump. Ambrose Bare, the principal surgeon to that king, introduced the ligature. A clamor was raised, and this experienced surgeon was hooted and howled down by the faculty of physic, who ridiculed the idea of "hanging human life upon a thread," when boiling pitch had stood the test for centuries.

"When Paracelcus, of Switzerland, introduced the employment of antimony as a medicine at the instigation of the Medical College, the French parliament voted it a crime, and passed an act making it a penal offence to administer it for any disease.

"The Jesuits introduced into Europe the Peruvian bark, and in England they at once rejected the drug as an invention of the father of lies. Frederick the Great took it in spite of the remonstrances of his physicians, and was soon restored to health.

"In 1792, Dr. Groerevett discovered the curative power of the Spanish fly in dropsy, but no sooner did his cures begin to be noised abroad than he was at once committed to Newgate by warrant of the president of the college of physicians, for prescribing cantharides internally.

"Lady Mary Montague, who had spent some time in Turkey, first introduced inoculation for the small-pox into England, as she had witnessed its happy effects during her foreign residence. She tried the experiment upon her own children, and the common people were taught to hoot at her as an unnatural mother, who had risked the lives of her own offspring. The faculty rose in arms, foretelling failure and the most disastrous consequences, and the clergy descanted from their pulpits on the impiety of thus seeking to take events out of the hands of Providence. She protested that in the four or five years after her arrival home, she seldom passed a day without repenting of her patriotic undertaking, and she vowed she never would have attempted it, had she foreseen the vexation and persecution it brought upon her.

"Almost the same fate for a time overtook Dr. Jenner, who

discovered the uses of vaccination. The Royal College of Physicians received his discovery with ridicule and contempt. Even religion and the Bible were made engines of attack against him. Erham, of Frankfort, gravely attempted by quotations from the prophetical parts of the Scriptures and the writings of the fathers of the Church, to prove that vaccination was the real Antichrist.

"Such have been a few of the results of ignorance, prejudice, and intolerance. It is to be hoped that with the common school, the academy, and college, the powers of a free press, the scientific lecture-room, the general dissemination of substantial knowledge, that such a foothold has been obtained against the flood-tides of bigotry, intolerance, and ignorance, that their dark waves will be rolling back upon themselves, no longer to disturb the placid surface of an elevating and ennobling humanity. We hope that with correct knowledge, every day becoming more and more diffused with the invention of useful labor-saving machines, the power of the loom and the anvil, the steam-engine and electric telegraph, the day will soon dawn, that it has already come, when fudge and nonsense will no longer be tolerated, but that man everywhere and on all occasions shall deal in facts, not in fancy, shall state truths and not wild vagaries hatched amid the incubations of dark ages to spread abroad and plague the world. We hope this practical, sensible era has arrived, and we believe that with such views the world will make more progress the next century than it has done in any five centuries heretofore in the struggles of an impeded civilization. Welcome an age of common sense, of correct views, of useful knowledge, the more useful because the more true."

How shall knowledge be made to take the authority of opinion in churches?

Knowledge can be made to supersede opinion, in modern churches, by calling a "convention of creeds" and publishing the results of such a convocation to the world. That is to say, let us have a senate of Christian and of anti-Christian leaders; a full representation of each system. Each creed has some truth in it, some *fragment* of a principle, which its rival has not.

Who could be excluded from such a Convention?

Hear the Echo! "Who could be excluded from such convention?" Who denied a seat in this senate? Who could be voted intruders—who, for opinion's sake prohibited?

Who could be ostracized — could Fenelon?

"Could Fenelon?"—with his sovereign conviction that holy works and charity evidence forth the soul's regeneration?

Who could be voted alien — could Luther?

"Could Luther?"—with his doctrine of justification by *faith* the inspiring element and conservative principle of character?

Who could be shut out — could St. Augustine?

"Could St. Augustine?"—notwithstanding his dismal idea of the blighted majesty of all human nature?

Who could be repudiated — could Calvin?

"Could Calvin?"—with his logical platitudes concerning foreknowledge, free will, necessity, and the unprogressive, unexpansive, fallen nature of man?

Could any one be passed over — could Channing?

"Could Channing?"—with his belief in man's boundless capabilities and endless growth?

Could a doubter be omitted — could Hume?

"Could Hume?"—with his doctrine of experience as the test of truth?

Could any be voted heretical — could Wesley?

"Could Wesley?"—with his ruling idea of a Missionary Work?

Could a friend be prohibited — could George Fox?

"Could George Fox?"—with his doctrine that the unerring spirit of God is a guest of every regenerate bosom?

Could a critic be discountenanced — could Voltaire?

"Could Voltaire?"—with his belief that what men term truth is always two thirds fable?

Could any seer be proscribed — could Swedenborg?

"Could Swedenborg?"—with his impression that the outer universe is but the drapery and imagery of a spiritual existence?

Could any liberalist be excluded — could Thomas Paine?

"Could Thomas Paine?"—with his conviction that Reason

is the only reliable Revelation, and a sufficient rule of faith and practice?

Could any person be tabooed — could John Murray?

"Could John Murray?"—with his belief in the final holiness and happiness of all mankind, and the restitution of all things?

Could any woman be repulsed — could Ann Lee?

"Could Ann Lee?"—with her doctrine of the difference between the Jewish and Gentile Christian church, of the carnality of outer marriage, and of perpetual inspiration?

Could any professedly honest person be shut out — could Joseph Smith?

"Could Joseph Smith?"—with his doctrine of a new Jerusalem, in the form of a Mormon organization?

Could any leading mind, in America or across the Atlantic, be denied a representation in this senate of creeds?

Echo still responds: "Could any be denied?" Nay; for these leaders, or their followers rather, are unable to form true estimates of each other. Each system, having obtained and bodied forth some truth, and knowing little or nothing of its neighbor, arrogates infallibility for its declarations. Opinion becomes law. Each sets desperately and spitefully upon the other. Instead of rejoicing and being happy in each other's earnestness and eloquence and efforts for man, and playing fraternally into each other's hands, the sects stoutly refuse hospitality and acquaintance, and strive to force *one creed* upon all mankind as the sum of truth in religion. They separate themselves into bigoted organizations — exhibiting folly and wickedness, passion and imbecility—and thus defeat the good which the best believers have in view.

What may be said of priests and churches?

Priests and churches, without knowing it, have deserted the path of truth. The dignity of an everlasting principle has been given to opinions; and the dismal *opinions* of theology tend to debase the mind, and plunge men into despondency.

Is priestly influence against human unity?

Yes; priests have separated themselves from others, in humbler social positions; and have made men suspicious of each other.

What is the theology of priests?

Their theology is a compound of love and hate, of heaven and hell, of rewards and punishments; and its teachers, all unconscious to themselves, breathe the spirit of hate and human differences, even while their theme is "love." Thus they divide men, and sacrifice the interests of individuals upon the blood-stained altars of sects and priesthoods. They are no friends to free thought, to free speech, to free action. They fear the human heart; they would vilify and set bounds to its God-ordained attractions. Opinion teaches the corruptions of reason; and the treacherousness of its best dictations. Opinion teaches the superiority of past traditions to present truths. And priests would have Geology retain her secrets, and Astronomy withhold her starlight, rather than see discredit thrown upon modern creeds which rest upon ancient chronicles.

Suppose we leave creeds and churches, what shall we do?

We are free to communicate with the divine revelations of our Mother-Nature. Her sweet melodious voices are ever-cheering; her revelations ever-welcome to her children. She invites them to worship in the cathedral of immensity. Her ministers are the expanded earth, the unfolded heavens, the stars above, the spheres that swell out into the depths beyond, and all the myriad hosts who live and love upon them. The unalterable universe, both positive and negative—material and spiritual, is your Sacred Book! This is the word of Father-God—containing his promises, his purposes, his principles—superior to steam-presses, to the despotism of Opinion! A proper study of its pages, so beautifully embellished by angel-hands, expands the genius of wisdom—making men active, courageous, harmonial, Beautiful. It tells man to be honest and sociable, to be reasonable and peaceable, to be just and fear not. The immutable Laws of this Book are our rules of life; and perfect obedience to them is our virtue and our religion.

What position do we now occupy, as practical denizens of the globe?

We occupy a transition place; our feet press the planks of that temporary bridge which connects the past with the future; midway between the inferior and the better era; with much of both, with neither practically. While the sun of pure wisdom, just rising over the brow of the Better Day, sheddeth its delightful rays upon the topmost minds on earth, the darkness of popular Theology—seen by them to be a despotic opinion without knowledge—appeareth all the more hideous and repugnant. The valleys of human life—the archives and alcoves of existing Doctrines—appear more and yet more uncongenial; a repugnance which increaseth sevenfold, as we continue to ascend the Alpine heights of the pure impersonal Reason. The light of the future maketh the night of the past darker; while our opponents, the comfortably-housed and the mythic-valley people, see nothing of this and have no such realizations. Gladly, we turn our steps from darkness—gladly, we look forward—away, up the hill to the City of the living God! The Past? *that* has worshipped imaginary beings; the Future? *that* will work for HUMANITY!

QUESTIONS ON THE MARTYRDOM OF JESUS.

The ponderous cavalcade of solar bodies along the milky-way is not more majestically grand than the unbroken march of human ages up the path of Time. I have been listening to the Past. It is vocal with sounds innumerable; with sounds of glad thanksgiving; and songs, also, of lamentations and spiritual distress.

The tides of life, setting their omnipotent currents through human affairs, have wafted the wrecks of different nations, different systems of government, and different religions—each bearing the mark of some chief, monarch, or martyr. Reverberating through the moss-clad dome of distant ages is heard the sad song of expiring heroes—the dying sobs of the fire-dressed martyr—triumphing over wrath and hatred and every trial, with a god-like might, seemingly defeated, but unfailingly victorious. Amid the gathering clouds of smoke, and through the folds of tempestial fire, the martyr sees angel faces full of joy!

What are the characteristics of a true martyr?

A true martyr is one who bravely meets terrors and tortures, imposed by many and strong enemies, rather than relinquish or disavow a cherished conviction; one who, with a moral enthusiasm transcending the instinct of self-preservation and every selfish motive, fearlessly embraces *death* in its most terrific form, in order to bear faithful witness to the sovereignty of some divine principle.

Where shall we look for the world's true martyrs?

Open the history of Asia, the history of Europe, the history of America; and behold the martyrdom of the great and good. 'Neath earth's flowery bosom lie the smouldering ruins of nameless men and women — who have made personal resistance to crime and to tyrants —

> "Where do they sleep? the fearless and the true,
> Whose holy deeds around their pathway threw
> A glorious light —
> A light which, streaming o'er the mists of time,
> Illumines every age and every clime
> With radiance bright."

Is it not natural to revere the birthplace of Jesus?

The Christian's sensitive reverence for Palestine, the native land of his Savior, is both natural and beautiful. The elements and aspirations of patriotism, of poetry, of pathos, of prayer, of perfection — yea, all the tender sentiments of filial love, all the sacred prejudices and imaginations concerning religion, all the painful struggles of time and the awful mysteries of eternity — come forth at the magic touch of this strange, eventful history. The lone star of Bethlehem, to the poetic believer, hath the effulgence of a thousand suns. The flowings of the sacred waters, over the bright sands and along the purple shores of the Holy Land, seem like the golden sounds which fed the silent air of Eden. Gently descend the dews of Herman. The widow's overladen heart findeth rest beneath the welcoming shade of the Cedars of Lebanon. The winds of the sea of Galilee steal with dreamlike stillness over the fertile plains of Judea. To the banks of the baptismal river the Christian goes for contemplation. It sings a song to him whose "raiment was of camel's hair." And it breathes blessings upon him who "came from Galilee to be baptized." Its music leaves her soul upon his heart. "He casts a wishful eye to Canaan's fair and happy land" — and yearningly, looks forward with faith and hope to the place "where the wicked cease from troubling." No! I do not wonder that Palestine is a "Holy Land" to him who entirely believes, that one of its rural barns was the palace which shut from vulgar eyes the birth of a heaven-descended Prince — that one of its uncarved and uncushioned mangers cradled the Eternal Savior of the World — whose feet had pressed the soil; whose sympathetic tears had watered it; whose breath, freighted with words of comfort for the friendless sons of men, had mingled with the air; and whose hand had written in the sand, "Let the sinless man cast the first stone."

What does history relate on this subject?

Sacred history relates that, in twilight's pensive hour, a young man sought the wilderness. Retiring winds waved the dreary depths, and music made of melancholy sort. He had travelled in Egypt; lived there till the death of Herod. Golden domes of pride, sacred temples of error, and towers of war, he had seen; had met and mingled with the world. But the spirit of God moved within. And the angels, lifting their voices o'er the wild uproar of the wilderness, bade him "Onward." With pathos true and touching, the voices of Mother-Nature spake to his weary soul. Anon, the heavens opened: and he "saw a spirit from Father-God descending like a dove." Then a voice said: "This is my beloved Son, in whom I am well pleased."

What may be said of the Jews in this connection?

The Jews were the most imbecile worshippers of Force, and knew not the Father. They were worshipping the imaginary God of the patriarchs and prophets; not the unfailing Source of the spirits of all men. They studied a creed; not the volume of creation. The Jews were the best and the worst of men: virtuous and vicious, witty, serious, and sometimes gay; learned in many arts, generous and brave at times; invariably hypocritical and avaricious, equally infidelic and faithful, meterialistic and spiritual.

"The Jews must be taught the way, the truth, and the life," said the young man, . . . and, after forty days of interior preparation, he went forth to teach.

According to Bible history, who heard him gladly?

The poor heard him gladly; mainly, because he was born of the humblest among them; and advocated their cause. He opened his mouth and taught the multitude; and he healed many that were sick. He did this without reading from the then popular bible, or using remedies from the then orthodox drug-store.

What followed this repudiation of the then popular authorities?

The physicians and lawyers and clergymen of the times reasoned against his claims; they doubted his power of discerning spirits; and openly ridiculed his psycho-magnetic miracles. Some of his own converts traduced and deserted him. And they had him arrested on a charge of heresy to the Jewish church, and conspiracy against the Roman government. They tried him without justice; and crucified him without mercy. What a great martyrdom! What a faithful witness did he bear to the Father-God who inspired him; a martyr to his spiritual principles!

According to recent discoveries in psychical science, how would you explain the birth of Jesus?

Matter is the servant of mind. Nothing is more obvious than the sympathetic alliance of these two eternal principles. Mind is the moving Principle: matter is the Principle which is moved. And it is well established that the productive mind influences and moulds the body and soul before as well as after birth. History is brimful of examples, and settles the doctrine as true, that the unborn child is psychologized by the maternal spirit. (See 3d vol. of Great Harmonia.)

Can you not give examples of maternal psychology?

Yes; there are many examples. Five months before the birth of Caligula, the Roman emperor, his mother *dreamed* that a supernatural being brought from the sky and gave her an eagle, which changed slowly into a venomous serpent, and was stoned to death by the multitude. The angel said: "The eagle is power; the serpent is tyranny; the last is assassination." Justified by her imagination only, she insisted that the history of her unborn child had been symboled forth. This terrible impression acted like a charm upon the coming spirit; and, lo, the life and death of Caligula was an exact fulfilment of his mother's dream.

What happened to the mother of Nero?

In a dream the mother of Nero saw a dove descend, holding in its mouth a scorpion which was dropped upon her bosom, and presently stung itself to death. A few weeks prior to the birth of her son, this dream was repeated. She said it denoted *peace*, first; next, *persecution;* the last, *suicide.* And the history of Nero was an exact correspondence.

Had the mother of Moses such experience?

Yes; while in the house of Levi, a young woman had an impressive *dream* in which she beheld a beautiful damsel, leaning over the river's brink, with her sweet face beaming compassionately upon the form of an innocent child. Presently this child became a great man; and his might was felt in all the earth. An angel now descended from a high mountain, and said: "Behold! so shall it be with thy son." . . . . . Not long after this dream, the woman became the bride of a distant kinsman. And twice before the birth of her first child, the same dream was impressed upon her; and the same angel appeared, with the same message. Of course the psychological effect was complete. Her son's name was "Moses."

Can you mention an example less remote?

Yes; a woman of considerable physical courage mounted a horse, rode side by side with her soldier-husband, and witnessed the drilling of the troops for battle. The exciting music and scene together inspired her with a deep thirst to behold a war and a conquest. This event transpired a few months before the birth of her child, whose name was—"Napoleon!"

Relate the history of psychological effect wrought upon the spirit of Dante's Mother?

During the important period immediately preceding the birth of Dante, his young mother saw a vision of startling grandeur and great depth of significance. She beheld a populated globe, of symmetrical proportions, rise gradually out of the sea, and float midheavens. It was decorated with every conceivable element of natural and artificial beauty. Upon a high and grand mountain, which melted away into the distant horizon and sloped gracefully into lands and lakes that spread out to the left, stood a man with a brilliant countenance, whom she knew to be her son. Pointing with his upraised hand, he bade her look down to the right of the mountain. She beheld a precipice of abrupt descent; like the wall of an immeasurable gulf, with depth unknown. Whereupon she thought she fainted with excess of fright. But her son was serene as a morning star; and, looking again, she saw no evil. After this beautiful and thrilling vision, Dante's mother had only in view the greatness of her unborn child—whose genius as a scholar and poet, as the creator of a world of fancies, is known throughout all the lands of civilization.

Are there other illustrations of the marvellous effects of mind upon the unborn child?

In further illustration, I might refer to hundreds of similar cases among poets, painters, musicians, mathematicians, and religious chieftains. One more instance, however, will suffice: to demonstrate the mysterious influence of mind upon matter; and more particularly, to prove the predisposing effect which a mother's spiritual convictions exert upon her coming offspring. The wife of a very poor, but respectable, mechanic *dreamed* several times, before the birth of her child, that an angel came to her and said: "Hail! thou art highly favored—the Lord is with thee." The angel looked lovingly down upon her; and she, not comprehending the intent of his message, was troubled. But the spiritual visiter soon allayed her anxiety, by saying: "Fear not—thou shalt bring forth a son, and thou shalt call his name *Jesus* . . . . he shall be called the son of the Highest . . . . he shall reign over the house of David for ever . . . . and of his kingdom there shall be no end." In due course of time this woman's impressible imagination was operating, with full belief, expecting the literal fulfilment of her vision. The result was accurately daguerreotyped upon the spirit of her unborn babe. And this person lived and died on the scene of history, as if his whole soul—impelled by some supernatural predisposition—was struggling to fill the sublime and immense measure of his mother's dream!

What is there so wonderful in a name?

"Jesus" is the Greek for the Hebrew word "Joshua;" and the term "Savior" is the English rendering. The word "Christ" was annexed to distinguish him from many others bearing the first name. "Messiah" is the Hebrew for the Greek word "Christ;" and the term "Anointed" is the English translation.

The Jews called every political or religious Chieftain *the Lord's anointed*—because their doctrine was theocratic—thus, Saul and David and Solomon were considered the especial Agents of God; and Isaiah calls CYRUS "the Lord's anointed" which is the same as the word Christ, or Messiah. "Christ" is a term which literally signifies a divinely-commissioned Agent or diplomatized Physician. It would be perfectly correct, therefore, to say—"Joshua, the physician," to designate him among the inhabitants of Palestine; or, still more literal, "Doctor Joshua, the martyr of Calvary"—thus giving to this spiritual Essenian a just and sufficiently conspicuous position among the world's great martyrdoms.

What can we be certain of in his early history?

Aside from the penetrations of clairvoyance, and without the testimony of spirits in daily correspondence with men, there is nothing known of Joshua's childhood and youth.

What did the early philosophers say?

Very little; nothing reliable. Celsus, an Epicurean philosopher of the second century, testifies that Jesus (or Joshua) spent several of his childish and youthful years in one of the most densely-populated spots of Egypt; that while there, he acquired considerable intelligence—and learned the art of healing by mysterious words and manipulation; and that, after returning to Palestine, he assumed a special mission, and professed to hold an incomprehensible correspondence with the Father of spirits. But Origen, a primitive Christian father, regarded Celsus as a heretic, and answered him accordingly.

What may be said concerning his reputation?

The wilderness of Judea echoed to the herald-notes of good honest John. He sowed the seed in Palestine; but expected to reap on the other side of Jordan. Joshua seemed to have had no understanding that he was the person referred to—and so, being of a religious cast of character, went like any other converted spirit "unto John to be baptized." But John "forbade him," and said—"I have need to be baptized of thee." Here, doubtless, Joshua *felt the hidden voice of his mother's dream;* and, with a beautiful grace which became his earnest soul, he baptized the prophet. And forthwith his friends had, as they supposed, reason to expect great words and greater deeds. His fame "went throughout all Syria;" because he had cured many sick.

Shall we say that this reputation became a misfortune?

We love to have miracles wrought *for the single glorious purpose of benefiting suffering humanity.* And we love to contemplate Joshua in this unselfish work; a motive which alone actuated his first efforts. After a while, however, we behold him working, so to speak, for his reputation. "That ye may know," he says (Matt. ix. 6), "that the son of man hath power on earth to forgive sins"—then he healed the sick of the palsy! His miracles, instead of serving the good of the suffering merely, were appealed to by him and others as *proof positive* of his divine commission. (See John x. 37; xi. 15; xv. 2, &c.)

Jesus had extraordinary power; was that power limited?

"Command these stones to become bread," said the spiritual skeptics. Did he give them a sign? The populace did not believe in physical manifestations. They required evidence. "If thou be king of the Jews, save thyself." He was nailed to the cross, and had the *reputation* of being both a medium and a god. But could he draw a nail? Could he descend from the cross by any supernatural means? If so, why not? All that the people asked for was—"evidence." Strange history! a table never moved, a chair never trembled, water never became wine, when the skeptics asked for a manifestation. No! but the wonders were wrought when the *Professor Faradays*, and the *President Mahans*, and the *savans*, of those days—were not prepared to detect the methods of deception. Joshua was said to be almighty. *Yet the success of his might was conditional.* "He did not many wonderful works, *because of their unbelief.*" We marvel that man could limit thus the ways of God. Upon rational laws, however, all is quickly explained.

Is truth aided when we confound persons with principles?

Nothing is more unfortunate. The universal deification of local *persons*, and the consequent co-extensive obscuration of general Principles, is a familiar phenomenon in the religious world. Perhaps it should be described and deplored as a reptilian error, gnawing perpetually at the heart of man's native religion—as an invidious serpent crawling about in the garden of his soul, ever tempting the higher sentiments to substitute persons for principles—inducing the spirit to worship empty creeds and godless ceremonies, as if these were the *summum bonum* of all saving righteousness.

Should we hold Jesus responsible for the short-comings and mistakes of his professed followers?

No true harmonial philosopher, no rational modern spiritualist, will ever hold Jesus responsible for the innumerable absurdities of many who claim him as "Master." The holy principles of that spiritual religion which was *patented* by the bench of Bishops under Constantine and *labelled* "Christian" by later and lesser authorities, would be transcendentally effulgent and magnetically attractive, could it be but safely exhumed from the popular cemetery of ghostly creeds. Well-meaning clergymen there are in abundance who walk through the streets of their profession, with step attuned to mournful measure, dressed in garments of grief, a cloud enveloping each face, as if unexpectedly bereft of some world-wide benefactor. Alas! it is too true. They have destroyed their best friend. It is the departure of Nature's own religion. *The Christ-principle of universal Love** has been sepulchred beneath a solemn outward hero-worship of the Martyr of Calvary.

"All hail the power of *Jesus' name,*
Let angels prostrate fall;
Bring forth the royal diadem,
And crown *him* lord of all!"

Time hath been when my spirit marvelled at the extravagance of this "obituary notice," at this ghostly procession of priest and parish—but I was but a child then, and saw delight, as many still do, in things of show and circumstance. Now I half sympathize with these mourners, and I half call them to repentance. The system and forms of religion I term supernaturalism. On the *first* day of each week, according to the

* The reader is referred to more ample explanations, of Jesus and the Christ-principle, in subsequent pages.

most approved almanac, our evangelical clergy visit the *cemetery* of supernaturalism—the system and ceremonies of religion! This "churchyard" hath a sorrowful history. The fearful tempests of eighteen centuries have passed over it. Creedal strifes and sectarian storms, that have rolled down these grim and gory ages with the terrible strength of a thousand cataracts, have swept day and night through the sepulchral caverns of this deadly place; and the vampyrean voices of *terrors* and *tortures* and *miseries* dark that have cursed and crushed humanity—all mingle their sobs with the hideous bellowing of Romish *Bulls*, with the deep hollow barking of protestant *Dogmas*, with the sickly mewing of the Westminster Shorter *Catechism*. Every sabbath the clergy visit this cemetery, and, aided by such as feel disposed, mourn o'er the moss-covered grave of Nature's own religion.

What is the ceremony which is attached to this burial?

The burial ceremony, which is modified more or less by each sect, consists—first, in singing "Hark from the tombs"—second, an invocation to an unknown god—third, reading through and remarking upon "the Northwest passage" of some handsomely-bound book—fourth, preaching a funeral discourse with the ghost of an old idea for a text—fifth, another song of sadness and supplication—sixth, a benediction, with a promise to meet next Sunday and rehearse the drama of burying "Christ in creeds," or absolute religion in its fashionable surroundings. Practical and undefiled religion once consisted in a well-ordered life of universal good will—but consists now in believing the creed, in adhering to the form, in being popular, and rejecting the doctrine of progressive development.

What is the consequence of the deification of persons?

All inequality is productive of discord: all over-statement is injustice; and the deification of persons is a "spot on the sun" of righteousness. Every exaggeration of supposed gods, every over-statement of the wisdom of spirits, is followed by a corresponding diminution of mankind.

Can you explain your idea more at length?

If you take from man's character to enrich the character of the gods (of spirits or angels), the penalty is heaviest with man: for man, not gods, needs elevation. You dress your gods and saints in richest robes; while on your own person hang innumerable rags and tatters! If I were to tell you the exact reason why we see so few noble men and noble women among Christians—so little individual integrity and self-sustained intelligence—I should say, in the main, that the people have allowed themselves to be led captive by unspiritual teachers: have, in short, put their souls upon a gilded waiter, and, with bended knee and unreasoning reverence, presented them to the gods of tradition and the times. In truth, the Christian world has given so much intellectual wealth toward maintaining in poetic elegance the celestial aristocracy—toward praising and extolling the virtues and qualifications of the *godheads*—that, now, the people have not enough veneration for *human heads* remaining to commence even a respectable *retail* business in the line of practical individual Religion!

How shall we apply this in justice to martyrs?

By magnifying the trials and sufferings of Joshua—who wrought but thirty-six months for humanity—we take away our sympathy from those who need (if they do not deserve) it more a thousand-fold.

Besides Joshua, are there not other martyrs?

The body of Joshua could not suffer more than those by his side; and his *soul*, being lifted by the consciousness of self-sacrifice to a principle, must have suffered less. There is such joy in right-doing! Shall we not think of Stephen, Peter, Paul; of the martyrs of Italy, Spain, Portugal; of the victims to the French revolution. The manly martyrs to science—Galileo, Tycho Brahe, Copernicus, Kepler—of the inventor, rapt in the idea of "Eureka," insensible to poverty and disease which set upon him like wolves upon their prey—shall we not think of these with justice?

Are there different phases of martyrdom?

Yes; there are others still—the artist, the musician, the needlewoman, the orphan, the deformed, the insane! What living martyrs, these! Open the history of individuals, and behold the martyrs to envy, to jealousy, to misunderstanding, to a bad temper, to a bad marriage, to wrongs unwritten, to evils not yet revealed! This spiritual martyrdom is not comparable with physical crucifixion. Many there are who carry about with them *an inveterate foe* to private peace and to public usefulness—some hateful habit or poisonous propensity—pursuing their conscience day and night: a perpetual martyrdom from which they may not escape. *Such nail themselves to the cross*, give up the ghost many times a year, and sweat great drops of agony when alone! These are self-crucified—upon whom good angels look, with tearful eyes and saving sympathies!

What is martyrdom usually a result of?

Martyrdom is the result of an individual *protest* against crime—of personal *rebuke* to ages of wrongs and mistakes; the forcible crucifixion of one imbued with the conviction that "resistance to Tyrants is obedience to God." Viewed in the light of an individual protest, to a religion of forms and a government of policies, the crucifixion of the Son of Joseph and Mary is a glorious example of spiritual supremacy. Despotic opinion drives in the earth a stake of iron, Ignorance chains a reformer to it, Prejudice brings the fagots, Fanaticism kindles the flame, the State smiles approvingly, the Church makes a prayer, and the shell of an immortal being is burned to ashes! Poor disciples of Ignorance! little do they think that the martyr's pile is "a chariot of fire" on which his soul rides into the kingdom of heaven! The Reformer's grosser form, his spirit's coverings, may be dissolved in the flame; but the Thought—the idea, the principle, for which he died—*that* lives after him. Nature hath ordained that children shall reap the harvest of error-seeds sown by their forefathers; and learn thus, perforce of a consequent necessity, to *till* and *plant* and *eat* with truth.

Can you illustrate this law of justice in Nature?

Yes; I can let you into the idea by means of a parable. A mythical tradition relates that the earth was once inhabited only by twelve valiant and ambitious knights; at a period when there was neither sun nor moon, and the world was swimming in an ether of unbroken blackness. One among the twelve, more beautiful and gentle than the rest, became the victim of their envy and ambition. Under pretext to destroy him, each challenged the other to combat: making the conditions of defeat, certain and immediate death by burning. Accordingly a large fire was kindled, and the warriors proceeded to fierce contentions—when, by the concerted force of the others, the most beautiful and envied knight was made to yield, and, as in the case of Joseph, was sacrificed by his jealous brethren. He was thrown into the flames which quickly consumed his body, and it disappeared in the burning pile; but, lo! as his life was extinguished on earth, in the same rapidly progressive manner, there came out in the firmament a *Golden Sun*—giving forth heat and light, illuminating the broad surface of nature, awakening birds of song, and unfolding flowers in strong places! With a wonder surpassing speech, the envious knights recognised in the face of the glorious sun the spirit of their beautiful and innocent brother. Beholding his triumphant resurrection, they were mortified at their own defeat. Ambitious of a similar promotion, one of their number leaped into the fire, and experienced the tortures of burning; but as his head disappeared in the flames, the remaining ten beheld the appearance of a pale and sickly *moon* whose comparative insignificance deterred them from further search after glory in that direction.

What truth does this fable illustrate?

This fable typifies a sublime truth; it bodies forth the destiny of two classes. He who aspires to the martyr's crown of thorns, to the end that he may be famous and popular in history, becomes but a pale *satellite* in the firmament of Justice; while, on the contrary, he who, forgetful of self, dies by the hand of violence to vindicate what he considered to be a great Principle, comes out like a golden Orb in the starry dome which overarches the temple of Humanity.

Is there a principle of distributive justice in the affairs of the world?

There is an irresistible Gulf-Stream of distributive justice, with ebbless tide, palpitating with deific energy, *setting straight through the Ocean of human life*, which compels a benefited posterity to crown with glory the Man who suffered martyrdom by mistaken ancestors. Children bless what fathers curse. And the martyr awakes, Phœnix-like, from his ashes, and soars o'er the fields of former persecution, unmolested evermore and cheered with songs of praise.

> "Thus the world goes round and round,
> And the genial seasons run—
> And ever the truth comes uppermost,
> And ever is justice done!"

What are your impressions concerning the infallibility and standardship of the Old and New Testaments?

It should go abroad, that this (the Harmonial) platform, so long as I have anything to do with it, is free, in the largest possible acceptation of the word, to every person of goodness of motive, himself being the judge, to controvert or correct any position which may be taken. It is to be understood, therefore, that I am always in a condition of mind to be taught. I welcome all persons who differ from me in regard to the Scriptures. Let us all seek the path of rectitude and righteousness.

Are all readers prepared to look at this question dispassionately?

No; it seems to me that many are not simple-minded enough to get at the plain unvarnished truth. Many are too much afraid of the speech of the world; not enough in possession of their own faculties and individuality; all the time fearing that they shall utter some sentiment which will be heralded throughout the world as too radical, and heretical absolutely, to the recognised doctrines of the Christian system. Of this class I know there are many. I know also that there are a few, a blessed group, who, standing beautifully above such fear, have attained unto considerable truth in the way of independent investigation; not only by interrogating what are called the manifestations of spirituality, but, also, by a free and candid examination of the cardinal doctrines which underlie the Churches of the Nineteenth Century. It will be found that those who have investigated the semi-popular spiritual phenomena, who have interpreted for the soul's benefit the principles of Christianity, and arisen above the standards recognised as orthodox by the world, are persons whose marks and works will be looked upon by the people of the future ages, *not as authorities*, but as guideboards to still greater and higher revelation.

What do ministers say concerning the Scriptures?

We are told by honorable gentlemen who keep the pulpits, that the Bible is the inspired truth; the word of God. Now, it would be entirely *just* to ask: how is it possible for ministers to make this assertion intelligently, unless they have received and comprehended a superior revelation?

How is it possible for any natural-minded man, one who has merely gone through the colleges and been otherwise artificially prepared for the ministry, to have sufficient illumination wherewith to pronounce the Bible to be surely and truly the word of God?

It is impossible. To accept that as truth which *is not within the comprehension of the intellect*, is a position similar to that taken by every leader and devotee in heathenism. One man, for example, believes in Juggernaut because it was believed in by his forefathers; not because of any understanding concerning it. Another believes that all religious truth has descended from on high, through the Shaster of Hindoostan. Why? Because *it is said so* by the masters and worshippers of that great production. So it is in our own vast country. Plenty of persons there are, even my next-door neighbors, who believe the Bible to be "the word of God." Do they believe because of intellectual apprehension of any principle contained in it?—because of any wise comprehension of the scope and drift of the whole? No. Why, then, do they believe? I answer, in consequence of the teachings of their fathers and forefathers—of those about them who occupy high places, clothed with a little brief authority—whom, even from the earliest youth, they were taught to reverence as the true teachers of this book and its truths. How can we pronounce that to be supernatural, unless we have a revelation *superior to it*, by which to comprehend and decide the question? To affirm that the Bible is truly and totally the communication of God, through different men to the world's inhabitants, without any supernatural revelation (which modern ministers do not profess to have) is, to say the least, an appropriation of authority based upon opinion, which more simple-mindedness would banish from the intellectual and wisdom faculties.

Does the general mind easily recognise, through facts, the existence of a principle?

Nothing is clearer to me than that the human mind, when in its highest condition, naturally recognises principles; and recognises, also, that those principles tend to external embodiment. For instance, there is a principle of architecture in the human mind. What then? In the course of human development, houses are built, ships are constructed, and different forms and structural beauties come forth on both land and sea; they come as the *external manifestations* of a principle in the soul of man. So, also, in the soul, there is a principle of Love. This principle is an abstract, a vital, essence; but comes directly outward into manifestations. It begets the blessed relations of brother and sister, the relations existing between child and parent, between husband and wife, relations which go on backward, and forward, interlocking and interlacing throughout, binding the world together. Then homes are sought and found. All the delightful experiences of home, and all the bewitchments and inversionisms of society, are the external manifestations of this soul-principle called Love; so, also, is every other relation and event and condition the result of some principle in the constitution of man, flowing into outward embodiment and expression. As soon as men feel an affection for something, they get the intellectual impulse to carry out and accomplish. The emotion to construct a house or steamship, is followed, in due time, by the executive power by which to elaborate that emotion. In a word, there is an attribute of wisdom in the mind — a power to express outward order, form, and proportion — by which man intuitively sees eternal principles.

Does this principle of wisdom come also into open manifestation?

Yes; and with it cometh another manifestation — *the worship of the manifestation* — exposing the soul's utter forgetfulness of their source. Many persons there are, who, having come out from Catholicism, look back into the Romish Church and wonder how intelligent minds can still worship at the shrine of Idols and graven Images. Now, I tell you that an intelli gent Catholic looks directly through the image of Virgin Mary to *the principle* which she is supposed to represent. But another, less intelligent and more material, thinks he must worship the object. So, there are Christians in this country occupying the same position in reference to this question of the Bible.

What do you mean by this assertion?

I mean that they forget the divine principle in man which seeks to express itself in books, in ideas, in shadows, types, and symbols — confounding, thus, the principle with the embodiment, the spirit with the letter. They take the embodiment as the essential, forget the principle, and bestow at last unlimited reverence and affection upon the book itself. An intelligent Catholic thinks he sees the principle of divine illumination coming down from heaven, a blessing which was vouchsafed originally to the wife of Joseph; yet he does not worship the image of Mary as the ultimate of a religious obligation. It is only the uneducated Catholic who does that. Even so the educated Christian is not absorbed in his reverence for *the book*, for the perishable pasteboard and the printed letter which killeth; but he sees through and beyond it all, *sees a divine principle*, which is no more dependent upon the book for expression than the Virgin Mary's image is necessary for the existence of the state of virginity which it represents. When I meet an *intelligent* and spiritual Christian, Catholic or Protestant, I find a man, a brother; at once ready to clasp hands, and to converse, without trembling, concerning the question of the Bible. But when I meet a person worshipping the book, *forgetful of the principle*, then do I find one who looks upon me and those who think as I do, as hopelessly infidel. He pities me in my skepticism; and I pity him in his. The difference between us is this — he worships the book without the spirit; while I reverence the spirit, without the book. We should remember that all manifestations of principles are necessarily more or less imperfect. It can not be expected that we should get, through all the ages of antiquity, a perfect transcript of what Jesus, John, and Paul, thought and accomplished. No one can either believe or expect it, who has any reliable knowledge of human actions or human history.

Are there many persons capable of separating a principle from its manifestations?

There are very few persons, it seems to me, who have the power, the self-subordinating abstractedness, to look through forms to principles. Most persons lose all idea of *principle*, when they begin to venerate the manifestation. Christians, for example, are sensitive when we refer to the man Jesus; as if the existence of the man was *necessary* to the existence of a Christ-principle; as if Jesus, the blessed brother, was *one and the same* with a saving principle! We will say that principles are eternal, and if eternal, they are universal; but every one knows that Jesus was a man of Nazareth—not ubiquitous, in all the worlds like a principle—not even in all the lands of this world. He was a local man; with local characteristics. A principle of truth, on the contrary, can be confined to no centre; to no one land or nation; to no one sea, though it should flow in Galilee. It is boundless as infinitude; without variableness or turning shadow. A man, on the other hand, has his peculiarities, his idiosyncracies, which necessarily become interfused more or less, and confounded eventually with *the principle* which his character and acts are said to represent. No enlightened one will deny, I think, that Christ was the best representative of a Love-principle.

But is a representative essential to *the existence* of the principle represented?

No; the principle existed before as well as since. The "Christ-principle" I call it, simply to be familiar and accommodating. Jesus was a local man; the "Christ?" that means a principle. *Jesus*, as you remember, is a Greek word for the Hebrew *Joshua;* but "*Christ?*" that signifies *Savior*, or a physician: that principle which elevates, bathes, beautifies, permeates, spiritualizes, the soul of man—bringing it into harmony with angel, with seraph, with the heart of All Things. The Christ-principle, then, is universal. It shone through several natures before Jesus, shone through him when he existed, and still shines through every good word and work. Jesus was prepared, by organic arrangements and intuitional characteristics, to shadow forth and exhibit the nature of Love.

Can you impart your impressions concerning Jesus through language?

Nothing exalts the mind quicker than a perception of its own possibilities, even though foreshadowed by the existence of some other mind. Let us, then, contemplate Jesus as a man. His general organization was indeed remarkable, inasmuch as he possessed combined the perfection of physical beauty, mental powers, and refined accomplishments. He was generally beloved during his youth, for his great powers of discernment, his thirst after knowledge, and his disposition to inquire into the causes of mental phenomena, of the conditions of society, and of the visible manifestations of Nature. He was also much beloved for his pure natural sympathy for all who were suffering afflictions either of a physical or mental character. His benevolence of love toward all without distinction; his constant yearning for the companionship of those who were considered good and righteous; his marked respect and affections for those who were much older than himself; his constant visits to those who required relief from their afflictions; and his kind words of consolation to those who were depressed either by disease or unhappy social circumstances—all contributed to render him an object of general love and attachment. These were the peculiarities which distinguished him from all other persons then living.*

How, then, do you behold Jesus on the scene of history?

I behold Jesus as a great and good Reformer; as connected with no marvellous or mysterious aristocracy, but as being born of lowly parents, and fostered in the bosom of their domestic habitation; as possessing intelligence to a surpassing degree; as manifesting unbounded love, benevolence, and sympathy; as healing the sick, restoring the blind, curing the lame, and visiting the disconsolate in their afflictions; as preaching love, morality, peace on earth and good will to men; as instructing the multitudes in the paths of pleasantness and peace; and as loving all and disliking none. I behold him as being condemned, nailed to the cross, and dying a

* See Nature's Divine Revelations, p. 561.

martyr to the cause of love, wisdom, and virtue![*] Such is one of the parts in the great monument which an ignorant and misdirected world have erected to their own shame and folly!

Do our modern Churches worship *the manifestation* of a principle and not the principle itself?

There are cultivated members, I know, who consider that the spirit giveth life, that the letter killeth; but they are too quickly counted. With these minds I have no difference, on this question. But those who absorb the symbol and lose themselves in the letter, in the manifestation—forgetting that principle which giveth life and light to the symbol, letter, or manifestation—such, create a difference which will continue through all this world. Such worship the Virgin and forget the principle she represents; worship the Bible, and forget its value as a history. There is a principle of wisdom in man, which, when cultivated separate from books and arbitrary standards, would be a sufficient source of salvation. It is not necessary to read the Bible, nor to worship it, or to know where it was printed, in order to be saved. Salvation consists in part of self-regeneration—in absorbing into one's nature, and exhibiting from it "The Christ Principle," the principle of Love—shoreless, boundless, having neither depths nor heights, yet always within the sensibilities and comprehension of a true human spirit.

What is the most reliable definition of popular Christianity?

It should be borne in mind that Christianity, as understood by the Church, is a system of symbolisms, of ordinances, of *subjection* to higher authority. Frequently it hath been said, "Christianity has not been lived out"—that all we want is an opportunity, by social organization and other instrumentalities, to live out the great ideas taught by Jesus. The doctrines taught by the Church in reference to him, have been lived out. Men are living, so to speak, upon the husks of the fossiliferous past; yet many believe that the Church is giving them water, food, and raiment. Men engage themselves with the forms and symbols of religion, and force themselves into subjection

[*] See Nat. Div. Rev. and the second vol. of Great Harmonia.

to the supposed holy ordinances of the past, seek to be in harmony with the Churches, and lose thereby the Christ-principle which Jesus tried to exhibit, namely: the spirit of love—universal and unextinguishable philanthropy. That, I repeat, is the Christ principle.* But Jesus was a man of Nazareth. Some good did come out of Nazareth; yea, out of the man who was born there. But who will worship the local man? In the record of him—there are manifestations of a heavenly principle. When we behold a demonstration of the principle of Love, then do we perceive that which partakes of the Divine,—an exhibition of the principle of intelligent forgiveness—and we should bow before it, worshipping it as quick and profoundly in our next neighbor as in *the record* of the man of Nazareth. In proportion as men become absorbed in the symbol or the letter, they become materialistic, and forget or fail to recognise the spiritual side of the principle. It has been reported recently of a little street-girl in New York, that, on being unexpectedly benefited by a woman to her unknown, she asked "if she (the good woman) was not God's wife!" This was a manifestation of "Christ" to the little girl.

Can any man believe and be saved through the "Christ," and yet separate his thoughts from Jesus?

Yes; every man can and should do so. *Jesus taught the principle of love.* His words and works give out the light and beauty which his soul had received upon that principle. Men both see and feel this principle, in all its heavenly bearings, when in their highest states. This is the principle by which men shall be saved from hatreds, imperfections, perversions, and inversions, throughout the world. The way to be saved, then, is to act wisely upon "The Christ-principle"—not to be a follower of Jesus. The paramount question is *not* what he did, nor what he thought. He had to live, do, and die, for himself. He may have had affections, peculiar to his nature, which you can never realize. In the midst of all, however, he manifested a loving forgiveness, a womanly gentleness, a hospitality of soul, which, whenever demonstrated by

* See a work by the Author, entitled, "The Approaching Crisis."

any human being, is the most beautiful indication of the presence of God.

What do you see in Christianity so very objectionable?

Every calm reader will see at once that I object, first, to *the materialism* of the Churches; and, second, to the worship of *the Book* as an authority above man's pure Reason. I am an entire believer in *the principle*, which lies in the foundation of Christianity, not the follower of any one man who is claimed as the immediate incarnation and expounder of it. I have reverence sufficient to worship that principle of wisdom and happiness which cometh directly and at all times from the Infinite God. When I behold this principle nestling in all human hearts, waiting an opportunity for expression, then do I see evidence that the Christ-principle is universal; that it can be appropriated by all nature, and exhibited just so far as our social circumstances and organic dispositions will permit and suggest. Therefore, I can not blame the man who fails to exhibit Christ; because, if I seek, I find so very much in or about him which will explain adequately the absence of such manifestation.

Where did the doctrine of denunciation, of blame and praise, originate?

The scolding propensity is of heathen origin—is of ignorance born. The forgiving principle is Christian. Men admire Jesus when he acted upon the Love-principle. They admire him yet more, when, nailed to the cross and interiorly expanded in this principle, he prayed—"Father, forgive mine enemies—these Jews—they know not what they do." Men reverence that exhibition; and many worship the man. I wonder not that almost every artist, with power to bring his thoughts out upon canvass, goes to work to exhibit that sublime spectacle. But when men read how Jesus went to lash the money-changers, a shudder comes over them; and he does not now stand within the circle of their reverence. Here comes his peculiar individual character; with no exhibition of a Christ-principle. The love-principle, no person, except him, had the organic power or social ability to express. When he takes upon himself the Mosaic Characteristic, to whip and scold men into the traces of belief and duty, he seems to be no longer the inspired son of God. He seems now as one among other men, excited as others are by opposition. You intellectually see, then, that it is *the Christ-principle* which is adequate to save us, and not the man Jesus of Nazareth. Man may pray to and through the Lord Jesus, but unless he put on practice the Christ-principle, he can not be saved.

This word "saved" is a common term in theology, signifying an eternal rescue; what do you mean by this word?

By the word "saved," I do not mean from a place of endless suffering, but from immediate discords, immediate anxieties and troubles in this world, saved from discords, and mental anxieties for many indefinite periods in the world to come—saved, not from eternal perdition, but from derangements of soul and society. Put on the Christ-principle, through wisdom—put on that which Jesus put on—and then, behold "God manifest in the flesh!"

What relation is theologically assumed to subsist between the early Jews and the scheme of salvation?

It is assumed in theology that the Jews were the chosen and favorite people of God; that he selected, them, out of all nations of the earth, in order to manifest his interest; to bring about the workings of the scheme of salvation. Every one who has read their history, knows that the Jews were—morally, in tellectually, socially, physically—no better than wandering tribes and several nations about them.

What testimony can you adduce to support this assertion?

The testimony of Isaiah, in reference to that people, is very much in point. He affirms them to be—"A sinful nation, a people laden with iniquity, a seed of evil-doers, children that are corrupters." In another place, he says: "Thy princes are rebellious and the companions of thieves. Every one loveth gifts and followeth after rewards. They judge not the fatherless, neither does the cause of the widow come unto them." Such is Isaiah's testimony in reference to that people, the ancient Jews; an enslaved race which the Church believes to have been especially raised up by Deity; that he might openly manifest his preference, and prepare the way for a tragical system of salvation! He has given us yet another testimony concerning them—"For every one is a hypocrite and evil-doer; and every mouth speaketh folly." It would be difficult to find in any class of people more corruption. Isaiah further says—"They have erred; through wine, through strong drink; they are out of the way. *The priest and prophet have erred through strong drink. They are swallowed up of wine. They err in their vision; they stumble in their judgment; all their tables are full of vomit and filthiness, so that there is no place clean.*" Such, I repeat, is Isaiah's testimony in regard to the people which (as the Churches believe) God raised up for his special purposes; a peculiar tribe of semi-religious individuals, not so good as many contemporary races.

Were the Jews more susceptible of spiritual influx than other oriental tribes?

Whatever may have been the opinions of the early Christians (who were mainly converts from the Jews), in regard to this nation, I have at present no positive perception; and yet, I get an impression that they were more susceptible to spiritual intercourse than many about them, except the devoted seers and poets of Asia. They had all kinds and degrees of impressions, except the impressions of pure wisdom. Every one which came bolting into the soul, so to speak, the recipient called a "thus saith the Lord;" and if the prophet made a mistake, he said—"It is not I but the Lord that deceiveth." No prophet or medium could admit that he had made a mistake. It was said—"The Lord said unto Moses or Aaron." Intelligent men would say, to-day, that some agents or spirits have erred. Men can speak now from the era of more light. The Jews seemed to be a race of mediums, fortune-tellers, soothsayers, &c.; especially certain persons among them, as Moses and his most active agents. How strong and deep was his impression to leave Egyptian bondage; to go forth; to bring out the people; to start a new system of government; and to establish, out of the best of the old, a new religion.

Was not this marvellous proceeding of Moses the execution of a providential arrangement?

No; there was nothing supernatural in his proceedings. Moses was educated at the very centre of education; at Pharaoh's house; had the advantage of all the lore of Egypt; was a recipient of the civilization which clustered about the discipline of a powerful king. It was not wonderful, therefore, that he was intellectually enabled and morally qualified to form a system of religion called "The Ten Commandments," and a theocratic government full of barbarism and tyranny. It is not at all wonderful, that, being a medium as hundreds now are, a voice came to him out of the clouds—"Thus saith the Lord; Go forth, and do this and that." It is precisely in accord with our experience; only we have more than he had; and with a rational philosophy to explain, we say that the Lord is not addressing us; but, on the contrary and more beautiful, that it is some friend, some spirit, some angel. Moses, however, gave out his impressions as *absolute authority;* not to be questioned. But men have learned better; progression has been made even in Religion. We do not now give out such communications as authority; but as that which should be questioned—believing that portions of every communication are always good—as aids and stepping-stones to better things.

But were the Jews not more acceptable to Jesus than other people?

In the New Testament I find a continuation of the same unfortunate testimony concerning the Jews. Isaiah's testimony was entirely corroborated and confirmed by Jesus; in words with which most Bible-readers are familiar. They are to be found in Matthew's report: "Woe unto you scribes, Pharisees, hypocrites"—that is, editors, conservatives, all mere professionists—"for ye shut up the kingdom of heaven against men. Ye neither go in yourselves, neither suffer ye them that are entering to go in. Woe unto you scribes, Pharisees, hypocrites,"—editors, conservatives, speculatists, professional men—"for ye devour widows' houses"—now think of South and Wall streets, New York—"and for pretence make long prayers"—Trinity church directly in front of Wall street—"therefore ye shall receive the greater condemnation." The word "condemnation" is very positive and appropriate here; but would not be proper out of this connection; it would elsewhere sound like an oath; but here it looks like a cannon-ball loaded with earnest and deserved rebuke. This bombardment of the Jewish character is intensely wholesome! "Woe unto you scribes,

Pharisees, and hypocrites, for ye compass sea and land to make one proselyte"—think of the missionary enterprise in South America and elsewhere—"and when he is made, ye make him ten-fold more the child of h–ll (prejudice, and superstition) than yourselves." ☞ The word "Hell" in a correct version (?) might be rendered "discord." Again Jesus says: "Woe unto ye scribes, Pharisees, and hypocrites, for ye pay tithes of anise, of cummin, and have omitted the weightier matters of the law—judgment, mercy, faith. These ought you to have done and not leave the other undone. Ye blind guides, which strain at a gnat and swallow a camel." That is to say—Woe unto you editors, speculatists, conservatives, politicians, hypocrites, capitalists, for ye prepare your ministers for the work of being artistically eloquent and entertaining—teach them to turn long and beautiful periods—but within, ye and they are full of expedients, enslavements, big salaries, and excesses of living. (This reading is in anticipation of the Bible revised and improved.) Thou blind Pharisee, ye who know nothing of spiritual worlds, cleanse first that which is in thy cup and platter, so that the outside of them may be also clean; woe unto you scribes, Pharisees, and hypocrites, for ye are like unto whited sepulchres, which *appear* beautiful, but are in reality full of dead men's bones—fossils of ancient myths and decayed theologies.

To whom did Jesus apply the language quoted from Matthew's report?

This is the description which Jesus of Nazareth transmits to this day, of the people against whom Isaiah also testified; and yet, the Jews are believed in all Christendom to have been the chosen people of God! He delineates and denounces them as scribes, Pharisees, and hypocrites, full of all uncleanness, of discord, of selfishness, of ambiguities, and inversions of character. It is not only believed by Christendom that the Jews were the "chosen people of God," but this belief is essentially important to the Christian system; because, Jesus himself gave his whole work to that people. This sectarian attachment shows the idiosyncracy and ante-natal tendencies of the man. He was not universal, like a principle; neither was he cosmopolitan. Jesus implies that his mission was local; he did not deny being a king of the Jews; his doctrine was not to the Samaritans, nor to the Gentiles, but to the Jews particularly. He preached to them, and did many works for them; gave them laws, and a blessed new commandment; considered that he was in a line of successive supernaturalisms, beginning with Adam and passing through Moses; that he was legitimately in the line descending from the house of David; the rightful heir to the throne of Judea; and lastly, according to the plan, was destroyed by the very people whom he came to save and exalt. Every impartial person — every reader of the opinions he entertained — will acknowledge that he was not a world-wide and cosmopolitan reformer.

Suppose we admit your ideas on this subject, what is the most needful want of the mind?

The mind needs to grasp the idea of a universal principle. The expansion of a local person into a principle is impossible. No one can be a follower of Jesus, and, at the same time, be a world-wide reformer. Jesus made — as every other individual must — comparisons and distinctions. He saw on one side a Gentile world; on the other, a world of Jews. He acted as a Messiah to that people. He was psychologized, in part, by the corresponding conviction of those who surrounded him. To them he had to teach; to deliver the word of salvation. He believed in the existence of human sheep and goats; of persons good in heart, and in hearts of evil. His, was not a universal system of perfect reform; yet his every word looked eventually that way.

What is the central doctrine of popular Christianity?

The doctrine taught to the world is, *subjection to higher authority.* This is Christianity, as understood at the present time. It is the doctrine of submission. Obey your existing rulers; be the friends of popular law and order; servants, obey your masters. Those who say Christianity has not been lived out, in this sense, have not yet ascertained the history of that system which they profess to believe. It can be shown that Christianity — *as a system of subjection to higher authority* — has been practically tried and lived out. Christianity is fixed in human history. Therefore it can not be said that this century is living under it truly. Most receivers are living upon the *forms* and *symbols* and *husks* of that which has gone into history. No one enlightened mind will live upon the symbols, the letters, and authorities of the book. Men have souls of their own; they may receive illuminations of the present and the future.

Are there many persons prepared for your impressions regarding Christianity?

There are not many persons prepared to hear, in the midst of all their conscious imperfections, that they *have lived out* the doctrines of Christianity; even when taken in the sense of subjection to external authority. But it has been lived out in the Catholic Church. The Catholic Church was the first well-authenticated system; of the slavish subjection of the lower to the higher. It requires the obedience of the body of the Church to its heads or potentates; and lastly, the obedience of the potentates to the special commands of Joshua. Paul, the best Jewish expounder of the Christian system—much better than any popular commentator—teaches, that the husband should be *subjected* to the Church; that the wife should obey the husband. As the Church should be *subject* to Christ; even so should woman be *subject* to her husband. Agree quickly with thine adversary, lest he cast thee into prison. Subjection is Christianity, in its primitive sense; and, in this sense, Christianity has been lived out. It has done, in this respect, all it can do. George Fox's school have carried out the doctrine of *obedience* of the lower to the higher; of the body to the soul; and the soul to the still more inward spirit. The Quakers have advocated and practised the idea of *non-resistance.* They would be overcome by evil rather than use carnal instruments in opposition to it. The Quaker system, in one sense, is the best exposition of Christianity. It is an illustration that *subjection* is a Christian doctrine. They endure all manner of unrighteousness rather than resist with the same weapons. They will not do evil that good may come.

What are the general facts regarding subjection in Christian countries?

Through all Christian countries there are multitudes of people subjected to authority. There are those, here, who think that the Book is the word of God; a final authority, in faith and practice. You may speak of the doctrine of "good will to men" to the end of days, but you will not satisfy the Church. The Church says, "Tell me that the Bible is the word of God, and I will call you a Christian." But this would not be in accordance with a law of progress.

Does any one believe that the Book is essential to Salvation?

Yes; there are many externalists and authoritarians who think so, and yet such know that there was no Bible for Matthew. Paul had to write his own letters—his own bible—from his own inspirations. He wrote to the Thessalonians, to the Galatians, to the Romans; and why can not you also write?—"write" in your lives, in your deeds, of friendship, and affection? What more beautiful letters than such? Write out of the bible of your own soul, where liveth for ever the Christ-principle! Come to this spiritual platform, and see how the subjection of the lower to the higher, of the weak to the strong—which is in the main a Christian doctrine—will be supported by natural and healthy influxes, emanating from the Love or Christ-principle, saving you from hatred and malice and revenge. Worship that principle; not a man. Defend not the book, but the doctrine of love to man and love to God: this is the sum and substance of all Religion.

Suppose we should resolve from this hour to set ourselves against authority, and live the true life, what regard shall we bestow upon the New Testament writers?

It matters not what Matthew, Mark, John, or Jesus said, thought, or did. The question is, dŏ you, in your life and soul, advocate the principle of Universal Love. The whole question turns upon this point—whether you will worship *Principles* instead of persons—whether you will take *the spirit* in preference to the letter—whether you will take the idea rather than the symbol. When you read the book properly it ceases to be an authority. The good principles of the book should be regarded as aids, as helps, as stepping-stones, to higher and better revelations.

By what authority can the Bible be decided as the word of God?

No person, as I said, is capable of pronouncing the Bible the word of God, unless he is sufficiently inspired by a higher rev-relation. If any man pronounces it to be the word of God, without such higher revelation, his *say-so* is worth as much as a similar affirmation by the worshipper of Juggernaut. He affirms, not by intelligence, but by the faith; inherited from his forefathers, endorsed by antiquity. Our worship of the past is in proportion to our ignorance of it. More reverence for PRINCIPLES will lessen confidence in personal embodiments.

But is there not something natural in the association of a person with a principle he may have represented?

Yes; he who loves the Christ-principle will also love persons in proportion as they manifest it. Jesus was, to a beautiful extent, the "Son of God." Why? Because he made the best practical exposition of the Principle. If, however, we should learn that the doctrine of *subjection* (which he taught) can be improved by a principle of wisdom—which will bring order and form in society—then we would say, that, although he advanced the temple which was based upon the proceedings of Moses, yet future generations must put on the turret and build the dome. This spiritual temple was began in Egypt; the building continued through all the prophets and seers of intermediate ages; but—how many spacious chambers and galleries of immortal beauty were added by the Man of Nazareth!

Do you mean to teach that spirits are helping man to build this temple?

Yes; it is yet going through the process of erection; every man here, and every angel yonder, is a builder. When men come into the higher rooms, then they draw close to the region where communications are both easy and natural. Spiritual men are no longer believers. By actual experience, spirits communicate with the sons of men. Every one, disposed to be in harmony with these principles, is a builder of the temple of progressive redemption. We have but little to do with the past; only so far as it sheddeth instruction. The past is fixed eternally; no man can alter it. No praying, no preaching, no spiritual device, can possibly erase an action or efface the history of an institution. The great point is, to live from this hour in reference to the symmetrical erection of the Spiritual Temple. Men will be beautiful and happy in proportion as they regulate their existence by the Twelve Commandments.

QUESTIONS ON

THE MYTHS OF MODERN THEOLOGY

MY thoughts were meditating upon the unutterable splendor and unchangeable order of the Universe. I was thinking how ten thousand times ten thousand orbs were shining in the still depths of immensity — each in its own beautiful sphere — each performing its duties in the great fraternity of worlds — each full of eternal, inherent, immutable essences, and replete with properties and principles which, while they secure obedience, also themselves obey; and then I contemplated the Heart of hearts, the Divine Cause, the Fountain Source of all these ponderous, manifold, and beautiful existences; how the Eternal Cause "acts to one end, but acts by various Laws" — unchangeable; the same yesterday, to-day, and for ever — a Being who lives and acts as far from the finite as I live and act from the Infinite; constitutionally and essentially without variableness, neither shadow of turning — perfect, without any of the weakness common to human nature, and not to be compared with man in any particular; impartial, an eternal effulgent Sun shining upon the just and unjust, without preferences; altogether lovely and attractive; whose thoughts are not as our thoughts, and whose ways are not as our ways; the altogether Good, the altogether Great, the Everlasting, the Infinite.

Do the world's theological teachings ever come before you, when thus meditating?

Yes; my meditations were as the foregoing, when my eye caught the following passage on a page of the New York Observer (for July 28, 1853), which painfully contrasted with my blissful thoughts:—

"THE PATIENCE OF GOD.—There is no subject more wondrous than this 'the patience of God.' Think of the lapse of ages during which that patience has lasted—six thousand years! Think of the multitudes who have been the subjects of it. Millions on millions, in successive climes and centuries! Think of the sins which have all that time been trying and wearying that patience—their number, their heinousness, their aggravation! The world's history is a consecutive history of iniquity, a lengthened provocation of the Almighty's forbearance!"

Will mankind ever discard such mythology as this paragraph presents?

Certainly; behold what a soul-degrading conception of our Father-God! The good man and the great-minded can revere only a Being *whose character is fixed in all the perfections of the celestial life*, affectionate and beautiful always; no changeableness—beyond the capability of alteration or extinction—a Source of Love and Wisdom perpetual.

The New York Observer is unceasing in its efforts to spread old notions among the people. "The patience of God!" It sounds like a voice from the tombs of oriental mythology. The Egyptian gods, many and beautiful, had human frailties. Grecian gods would occasionally get into a furious passion and "lose all patience" with the absurdities of mundane transactions. The capricious and nervous gods of the Aztecs, with sleepless eyes and fleetest locomotion, would perform wondrous things within volcanoes and under burning mountains. The Persian angels of depravity were permitted to frighten people by means of "thunder and lightning," and thus secure their attachment and loyalty to Allah and Ormudz. But to teach, in the middle of this century, such weaknesses as characteristic of our own ever-just and ever-loving Father-God, is at once an insult to the reason and intuition of every living man, and a hinderance to the cause of theological discovery and improvement.

Moved, perhaps, by a desire to impart more theological information, the Observer states, in the same irreverent and blasphemous paragraph, that "of all the examples of the Almighty Power, there is none more wondrous or amazing than *God's power over himself.*"

Intelligent reader: think of this dispassionately. Here, the Observer is commending the Living God as *an exemplification of self-control;* he don't get angry in a hurry; suffers exceedingly with the short-comings of puny man; is almost aggravated to destructive passion with sins of human beings (sins which can only injure the sinner), and yet, like a self-regulated philosopher, the Almighty controls his temper and is yet longer gentle with venerable offenders!

What a miserable myth is this! That doctrine which is father to it, must be "totally depraved," corrupt in its very core. It will do, perhaps, for uncivilized and undeveloped minds; but from all such degraded and degrading conceptions of the great "I AM," let the good spirit of Father-God deliver us! Theological myths are possibly pleasurable to the Observer people—that is, if one is to judge a tree by its fruit, or a religious publication by the odor and tone of its articles; nevertheless, let us work diligently for the ultimate destruction of all such trees, and of all such mythological teachings, and do all we possibly can toward making the wilderness of modern theology to blossom as the Rose.

Suppose we conclude to issue a paper precisely unlike the New York Observer, how should we announce our intentions?

If you desire to issue a Harmonial paper, with its columns wide open to a candid discussion of the colossal ideas of universal Reform, you should unroll your banner on the bosom of the free air, with this device: "*Freedom of Speech, and Liberty of the Press!*"

What does the New York Observer teach in regard to the religious education of children?

"Children should be early taught," says the Observer, "that the Bible is the great authority; and that when it speaks upon any point the question is settled for ever. They should be taught to go directly to the Scriptures to find what is good and what is bad, what is true and what is false. Thus, with the blessing of God, *they will acquire the habit of constantly subordinating their own notions and inclinations* to the plain declarations of Scripture. It is a good sign to hear a child often use the expression, '*The Bible says so.*'"*

The Observer's efforts to manufacture crudities, to multiply sectarians, are unmeasured and unceasing. Children are urged to regard the Bible as the great authority. If the young mind repels the unnatural thought, then they should be "early taught" to adopt *the authority* at all events, no matter how severe the trial may be. Authority, as already shown, is the language of despotism; it attempts to form the convictions of the mind. Authority has built the gibbet and the cross: all that blackens the pages of history, was originated by the bigotry, the sectarianism, and the superstition, whose only parent was *arbitrary authority* — OPINION. And children should be "early taught that the Bible is the great authority."

What shall be done with a system of religion which promulgates doctrines so despotic?

What shall be done? The declarations of Science must be denounced; Reason must be silenced; Experience, upon its bended knees, must confess to lies; Truth must conform; Virtue, be vilified; Justice, denied; and the whole nature of Man must bow in resistless obedience to the dicta of arbitrary authority — yea, all this must be done, in order to be a consistent receiver of theological monstrosities.

The authority of mere Opinion must be imposed upon the plastic mind of youth; pressed, regardless of all healthy resistance, into its very substance! The youth grows to manhood with the shackles upon him. His mind is in bondage to authority; he can not think. He worships, not the Truth, but *the authority;* he is therefore a bigot and a slave! According to the New York Observer, the *book* is the final authority. The Bible may be (as it is) a combination of good things and bad things — it may present truth on one side and error on the other — but, no matter! its authority must never be questioned. Poisonous and unnatural as the doctrine of authority is, it is not more perni-

* See the Observer of July 7th, 1853.

cious than this: "that when it (the Bible) speaks upon any point the question is *settled for ever*."

Would the Observer have this opinion "early taught" to the young mind as religion?

Yes; and yet every enlightened person knows that the Bible is wrong in scores of things. Its geology is wrong, its chronology is wrong, its astronomy is wrong; it is wrong in many prophecies; and there are doctrines, precepts, and practices, unfit for the child to learn or the man to follow. In one place we are informed that "God is no respecter of persons," while, in another place (Exodus xxxii. 37), we read this most horrible contradiction: "Thus saith the Lord God of Israel, Put on every man his sword by his side, and go in and out from gate to gate throughout the camp, *and slay every man his brother, and every man his companion, and every man his neighbor*." In one part of the Bible (Matthew vii. 12), we read this most perfect of all laws: "Whatsoever ye would that men should do to you, do ye even so to them"—but in another place (Deut. xiv. 21) we read this most unwholesome of all commandments: "Ye shall not eat of anything that dieth of itself; *thou shalt give it unto the stranger that is in thy gates, that he may eat it*, or thou mayest sell it unto an alien."

The Observer esteems it a "good sign to hear a child often use the expression—*The Bible says so*." How replete with absurdity is such a thought—that Children, without experience and unable to form an intelligent idea of any great question, should quote the Bible as the *totality* of truth!

Do you mean to teach that men are freely to examine, and sit in judgment on the Bible?

Certainly; when the Bible speaks upon any point, *that point* should be examined as freely as I now criticise the New York Observer. The Bible says a vast number of things which are wrong, and unworthy of a place in a book which claims to be the Word of God. On its pages are to be found good precepts and evil ones; truth and error; wisdom and ignorance; and the child that "early" learns to receive everything the Bible says, as *absolute truth*, has a painful and difficult lesson to unlearn in after years. The Bible itself teaches us to "prove all things, and hold fast that which is good." A book is certainly included in the category of "things." So the Bible testifies against the New York Observer, and not less against its own contents. Sectarians are already too numerous for the world's good; and there is scarcely a religious journal in existence cal culated to increase the number more rapidly than the Observer; I hope, therefore, that some moral revolution will effectually reform it.

Originally, these criticisms appeared in the New York Reformer; over the author's *nom de plume* "Silonius." Next, that paper contained a rejoinder, signed "Senex"—given below; as a fair exposition of feelings of hostility experienced by those whose honest convictions are freely declared to be unsound and absurd.

A WORD TO "SILONIUS" BY "SENEX."

"*To the Editor of the Reformer:*

"'*The Bible says so.*' Yes; 'the Bible says so.' This was the teaching of our early days, when we listened to the solemn admonition of a dearly loved, but now sainted mother, in the calm quiet of a New-England Sabbath eve. 'The Bible says so' has been our guiding star through many a dark and cheerless night of sorrow. 'The Bible says so' has rung in our ears, when with attentive spirit we have listened to its teachings. 'The fool hath said in his heart, there is no God.' 'Thy word is a lamp to my path.' 'Hold thou me up, and I shall be safe.' 'God is no respecter of persons, for whosoever worketh righteousness shall be accepted of him.' 'The way of the transgressor is hard.' 'Children, obey your parents in the Lord, for this is well pleasing in his sight.'

"Are the doctrines of the modern school of Progressives any more favorable to morals, virtue, or honesty, than this old-fashioned New-England teaching, 'the Bible says so'? Are the men and women who have fellowship in public assemblies—the Rev. Browns, the Abby Kellys, the Bloomers, the *She-isms* of all grades, the *He-isms* of all stripes—any more industrious, or intelligent, or useful, than those taught in all the strictness of a New-England household, with the watch and 'the Bible says so'? Are the 'higher law' doctrines of the present day, any better than the *highest* doctrine of the New-England Church—'the Bible says so'? In a word, does it make a man the worse citizen, or a woman the less useful, or a boy the more idle and vicious, to have been taught this *doctrine* —'the Bible says so'?

"Well will it be for our country when such men as 'Silonius,' with all the host of Bible-scoffers, Sabbath-breakers, and law-destroyers, shall find the 'Harmonia' they are so anxiously looking for and expecting, and, gathered in one grand phalanx, shall confine their teachings to themselves and the children of their own begetting, and no influence of the kind now exerted shall poison the rational teachings founded upon the Bible and its 'says so.'

"Yours, "SENEX."

A KIND WORD TO "SENEX" BY "SILONIUS."

To the Editor of the New York Reformer:

DEAR SIR—As Editor, a position both conspicuous and exceedingly responsible, you will doubtless be assailed—more or less each week—with communications leading to popular Conservatism, or else to principles of Progression. So far as such communications serve the ends of human enlightenment and reformation, you have resolved, I hope, without fear or favor, to admit them. On this impartial principle, you admitted my strictures on the New York Observer; and, subsequently, the brief criticism of "Senex;" to whom I now have a few kind words to communicate.

Senex misunderstands me: I do not undertake to denounce or repudiate the moral teachings of the Christian's Bible; nor would I utter a word to detract a particle from the poetry and beauty of those ideas which have been, to his mind, "a guiding star through many a dark and cheerless night;" but against the erection of the "say so" of any man or Book, as an arbitrary standard—superior to the "vital spark of heavenly flame" that glows within on the altar of Reason—this, in accordance with my living conscience, I will write and speak against with all my heart, mind, and strength. Senex asks.—

Are the doctrines of the Progressives any more favorable to morals, virtue, and honesty, than this old-fashioned New-England teaching—'the Bible says so'?

Yes; dear Senex, a thousand times more favorable! New-England theology has tried hard, with its solemn teachings and ceremonies, to bring peace on earth and good will among men; but it does not succeed. It labors every Sunday; and thus keeps old ideas and superannuated theories popular. It is well calculated to make bigots of young minds; and conservatives of older ones. Morals, virtue, and honesty, of *an ordinary* kind, are abundant in New England; the cash-book and ledger furnish the code of commercial morals; but the universal principles of reform and Brotherhood—which Jesus taught—are well nigh buried; lost beneath the superabundance of forms and rituals. If Jesus had confined his intuitions and mental attributes to the "say so" of the Pharisees and Sadducees—to the arbitrary teachings of the Talmud or revered gospels of ancient tribes—do you suppose he would have introduced a purer and more spiritual form of religion? Modern Progressives have in him a glorious example of independence to follow; and as to "morals, virtue, and honesty," why, good Senex, fear not—"the Lord God *omnipotent* reigneth;" therefore, all are and must be safe eternally!

Do you believe in the perfect independence and individuality of the human mind?

Yes; all external and objective authority is prejudicial to the symmetrical development of our interior nature. Thousands of persons, like yourself, dear Senex, have borrowed and begged, and procured a species of negative, transient *comfort* from the "say so" of some revered authors. But does such consolation "in a dark and cheerless night" add anything to your manhood? Does it start you intelligently to action; for the harmonization of your brother man? Suppose you see some new scheme for improving the structure and commercial antagonisms of human society, dare you leave your old-fashioned New England "say so," and tread the new path?

"The man is thought a knave or fool,
  Or bigot, plotting crime,
Who, for the advancement of his kind,
  Is wiser than his time.

For him the hemlock shall distil;
  For him the axe be bared;
For him the gibbet shall be built;
  For him the stake prepared;
Him shall the scorn and wrath of men
  Pursue with deadly aim;
And malice, envy, spite, and lies,
  Shall desecrate his name.
But truth shall conquer at the last—
  For round and round we run,
And ever the right comes uppermost,
  And ever is justice done."

Senex asks: "Are the 'higher law' doctrines of the present day any better than the highest doctrine of the New England Church?

Yes; the higher law of Nature is *higher* than the theology of any church; than the authority of any book. But the higher law of Nature is no higher than *some* of the teachings of Jesus.

Why do Nature and Jesus agree in this law?

Because Jesus found his authority within. He taught *this* principle and *that* precept upon the authority of his spiritually-illuminated intuitions; never relied upon any "say so" or external authority; he appealed to Father-God and to Mother-Nature. And I am compelled to be *as true* to the light within me; as free, from outward standards of judgment.

Senex speaks of the "host of Bible-scoffers, Sabbath-breakers, and law-destroyers" as being worthy only of a place by themselves; and he boldly intimates that they should be peremptorily rejected by the world as so many enemies to its righteousness! But, seriously, would it not be well for truth's sake to remember that *these very anathematized individuals* are the Temperance men, the Anti-Slavery men, the Peace men, the Anti-Superstition, the Anti-Bigotry men, of this wonderful age? They head every grand reform. They lead in all the soul-developing and nation-revolutionizing principles and thoughts of this century. These men and these women are earnest. They believe in the eternal Father-God; and they work because they believe—because they know. They ignore the Church for its barrenness and bigotry. These are the spirits who lead in the bravest and self-denying enterprises of the day. As a public teacher recently declared—"the skepticism of these minds is not flippant. It is not a peculiarity alone of radicals and fanatics; many of them are men of calm and even balance of mind, and belong to no class of ultraists. *It is not worldly and selfish.* It is calm, abiding earnest."

Strange, is it not, friend Senex, that all the great social and spiritual and theological Reforms of this day should be commenced and prosecuted by the so-called "Infidels?" It was this magnanimous independence, this conscientious breaking away from established forms and the "say sos" of prevailing authorities, which originally offended the pious Jews when Jesus went forth to preach fresher forms of spirituality and reformation. This infidelity caused the noble Nazarene to be anathematized, and then crucified.

Most people, with a goodly share of intelligence, believe a mass of insurmountable inconsistencies, in an orthodox creed, which they would reject as error, could they be induced to compare them, one with another. Fearing lest this comparison will be too long procrastinated, I will myself proceed to give the reader twenty-eight affirmations of a bible-believer, and show, by means of a parallelism, that fourteen points of faith (one half) are exactly antipodistical to the other half, but which, by a church-receiver, is imagined to be every way compatible and harmonious.

What is the first affirmation and contradiction?

I believe that God is unchangeable; the same yesterday, to-day, and for ever; without variableness neither shadow of turning.

I believe that God repented himself that he had made man; it repented him at his heart; and he cursed the ground for man's sake.

What is the second?

I believe that the first pair were pure, and without inclination either to good or evil.

I believe that Eve committed the first sin through an exercise of her own free will, or individual sovereignty.

What is the third?

I believe that God is superior to both time and space;

I believe that man himself can *determine* in this world, by

that he is omniscient as well as omnipotent; that he saw the *end* from the beginning; and that he fore-ordains and pre-arranges all events in the progression of time.

the life he leads and the character he forms, whether he will enjoy everlasting bliss or suffer eternal misery.

What is the fourth?

I believe in the divine origin and sanctity and universal obligatoriness of that commandment—"Thou shalt not kill."

I believe that Moses and Joshua received divine commissions to *kill thousands of human beings* for the glory of God and the advancement of his righteous kingdom.

What is the fifth?

I believe in the divine authenticity and universal applicability of that commandment—"Thou shalt not commit adultery."

I believe that Moses and Joshua received orders from the throne of Grace to war with the Midianites, and, after putting to death all the male and female parents and male children, that he then gave the unmarried and virgin females for the use of the men composing the army.

What is the sixth?

I believe that God is superior to all human weaknesses; that he is never arbitrary in his governments, providences, or punishments.

I believe that God is "a jealous God"—visiting the iniquities of the fathers upon the children to the third and fourth generations; that he will have mercy on whom he will have mercy, and whom he will he hardeneth.

What is the seventh?

I believe that God is ever regardful of the happiness and welfare of his creatures; and full of compassion and of great

I believe that God sent plagues and suffering among the Israelites; kept them wandering to and fro in the wil-

mercy; that his anger endureth but for a moment.

derness *for forty years;* because he was, during all that period, angry with that people.

What is the eighth?

I believe that God is no respecter of persons; that his sun shines upon the just and the unjust.

I believe that God made a special selection of certain personages — the prophets, writers, and apostles — to act as his attorneys among the earth's inhabitants.

What is the ninth?

I believe that the Old Testament is mainly set aside and superseded by the New Testament (or dispensation) which began with the life and preaching of Jesus; that the latter has repealed the laws of Moses to some extent, and introduced better and diviner rules of faith and practice.

I believe that the Bible is harmonious in all its parts; law with law, prophecy with fulfilment, precept with practice, cause with effect; that, the rejection of one part is tantamount to a repudiation of the whole.

What is the tenth?

I believe that the law of "an eye for an eye and a tooth for a tooth" can never be harmonized with "return not evil for evil, but overcome evil with good," because the two laws belong to different eras of the divine administration.

I believe that the true follower of Jesus must "resist not evil," must love his enemies with a brother's faithful love; nevertheless, I believe that it is always Scriptural to "resist the devil" so that he shall flee away.

What is the eleventh?

I believe in the commandment which says, "Bless them that curse you, do good to them that hate you, and pray for them which despitefully use and persecute you; that you may be

I believe that those who did not love the Lord, but who cursed and despitefully used him, or disregarded his laws, shall, at the close of the *judgment day*, "go away

the children of your Father which is in heaven"—for by so doing, we but imitate the great and good God.

into everlasting punishment," be cast into outer darkness where shall be weeping and gnashing of teeth, for so does the good God punish the wicked and the guilty.

What is the twelfth?

I believe that with God all things are possible; that he is omnipotent, and nothing can stay his hand.

I believe that it is *impossible* for God to tell a lie; or do aught contrary to the perfections of his attributes.

What is the thirteenth?

I believe that God is a spirit—boundless as infinitude; "living through all life, extending through all extent;" illimitable and everywhere pres-

I believe that there is a hell where the spirit of wickedness, alone in his glory, prevails and rules supreme; that, therefore, there is a portion of infinitude where the spirit of an *omnipresent* God lives not, because it can not enter.

What is the fourteenth?

I believe that the Lord God saw everything that he had made, and pronounced it *good.*

I believe that the serpent was the most wicked and mischievous of all the beasts of the fields which the Lord God had made.

Do you mean to affirm that contradictions and irreconcilable inconsistencies, like the above, constitute the popular orthodox creed?

Yes; and several pages might be added of similar incongruities and monstrosities; taught from the fashionable pulpit; taught in the most flourishing Sunday-Schools; taught as consistent and soul-saving wisdom. When such elements of faith enter the human mind, there is not much room left to noble thoughts and great principles. That clergyman is estimated as most accomplished, and that layman the most successful for the American Tract Society, who is so skilful in handling Scriptural texts that no contradictions shall come to the surface, and be detected by the common, unskilful thinker. Overflowing with grammatical verbiage, these tract and sermon writers almost always succeed in concealing the intrinsic absurdities which lurk in their orthodox creed. To the ordinary reader of tracts and religious periodicals, the opinions of a Doctor of Divinity are seldom questioned. And I would respectfully ask:

What absurdity have the so-styled wise men of the Church not sanctioned?

Not to mention the multitudinous instances of opposition to the several civilizing sciences, of which they are guilty, we will present no stronger proof of their propensity toward absurdities than that they, as a body, endorse the above peculiarities of an orthodox creed.

When will mankind learn to explain and be enabled to practise the Philosophy of Truth?

The time hath already come to the individual who, without boastfulness, permits his intellectual faculties to perform their office. To him the laws of the Universe are unchangeable; harmony reigns triumphant everywhere. Persuaded by the never-changing testimonies of Creation that there is a Great First Cause—a divine principle of Love and Wisdom—how can the human mind be so sadly blinded and misguided as ever to adopt the popular pagan theories of heaven or hell! We make (or have made by the confluence of external circumstances for us) our heaven and our hell as we journey forward; they come not as arbitrary rewards and punishments, but as inevitable *sequences* to right and wrong doing. Why not, then, be philosophical henceforth; and resolve to act as intuitive Reason alone may sanction.

It is stated in "Nature's Divine Revelations" (page 547) that the Bible was compiled at the Nicene Council; does history give us any proof of this assertion?

Just at this time there is no external question more important. And there is, perhaps, nowhere to be found a more concise, consecutive, and conclusive answer than the following, which I submit to the world with undisguised pleasure and grateful confidence:*—

* The reader is supposed to infer from the above language, that the author's companion, Mary F. Davis, is the writer of this valuable answer to the Nicene Council question.

The proceedings at the Council of Nice are, like all events in the ancient history of the Church, veiled in obscurity. Indeed, a strong desire seemed to possess Eusebius and others who were present to conceal its details from the world, or at least to clothe the whole affair with the garb of mystery. Thus Pappus tells us that the Bishops, having "promiscuously put all the Books that were referred to the Council for determination, under the communion-table in a church, they besought the Lord that the inspired writings might get upon the table, while the spurious ones remained underneath, and that it happened accordingly."

This recital is quite in accordance with the usual practices of the Church Fathers, who are referred to with so much reverence by the modern priesthood, but who, if we credit the concessions of Dr. Mosheim, were artful, wrangling, and grossly dishonest men. He declares, in vol. i., p. 198, that "It was an almost universally adopted maxim, that it was *an act of virtue to deceive and lie*, when by such means the interests of the Church might be promoted." As regards the fifth century, he says: "The simplicity and ignorance of the generality in those times furnished the most favorable occasion *for the exercise of frauds;* and the impudence of impostors in contriving false miracles, was artfully proportioned to the credulity of the vulgar; while the sagacious and wise, who perceived these cheats, were awed into silence by the dangers which threatened their lives and fortunes, if they should expose the artifice."

In a translation of Michaelis, the pious and learned Professor of Göttingen, by Bishop Marsh, we find the following startling assertion: "It is a certain fact that several readings, in our common text, are nothing more than *alterations made by Origen*, whose authority was so great in the Christian Church, that emendations which he proposed, though, as he himself acknowledged, *supported by the evidence of no manuscript*, were very generally received." Origen was undoubtedly of the greatest importance in giving form and permanency to the institutions of priestcraft, as he was a man of extensive learning, and was very industrious as a writer and compiler. He is said to be the first author who arranged a distinct catalogue of the books of the New Testament, which catalogue embraces the same as are now admitted into the so-called Sacred Canon, excepting James and Jude, and these he owned in other parts of his writings. This compilation, which was made about 210 A. C., served doubtless as a precedent in all subsequent councils; and there is every reason to believe that, to the ingenious interpolations and omissions of this ancient savant, the New Testament owes whatever it possesses of grace, harmony, and historical congruity. Taylor, however, acquaints us with the fact, that this same Origen afterward relapsed into Paganism, and publicly denied Christ.

Bishop Faustus, an eminent Christian writer of the fourth century, declares that "It is certain the New Testament was not written by Christ himself, nor by his apostles, but a long while after them, by some unknown persons, who, lest they should not be credited when they wrote of affairs they were little acquainted with, affixed to their works the names of apostles, or of such as were supposed to have been their companions, asserting that what they had written themselves was written *according* to those persons to whom they ascribed it."

Scaliger asserts that "The fathers put into their Scriptures whatever they thought would serve their purpose;" and Mosheim, the great Church historian of modern times, tells us, in vol. i., p. 109, that the "opinions, or rather the conjectures of the learned, concerning the time when the books of the New Testament were collected into one volume, as also the authors of that collection, are extremely different. This important question is attended with great and almost insuperable difficulties to us in these later times.'

In regard to the books of the Old Testament there seems to have been equally as much dispute during the first few centuries; and many Chronicles, Psalms, Prophecies, etc., were alternately accepted and rejected by the different councils, amid fierce and fiery altercations.

But while so much doubt attends our investigations in the misty labyrinths of ecclesiasticism, many things seem to point out the Nicene Council as the one whose decisions were most authoritative respecting "the inspired book." The catalogue of Eusebius, who was the most influential and learned among the attendant bishops, was exactly the same with the modern one; as was also that of Athanasius, who was his contemporary. This council is alluded to by both ancient and modern Church historians, as "one of the most famous and interesting events presented to us in ecclesiastical history," and a universal regret is expressed that its acts were not committed to writing with more fidelity. It is a well-established fact that it was attended by an indefinite number of belligerent partisans, whose bitter animosity was quelled only by the fiat of Constantine. This sanctimonious despot, after presiding over the refractory Conclave, and controlling its decisions, finally asserted that "what was approved by these bishops could be nothing less than the determination of God himself; since the Holy Spirit residing in such great and worthy souls, unfolded to them the Divine will." (Socrates School Eccl. Hist., b. 1, c. 9.)

Thus we see how flimsy is the foundation on which is based the faith of orthodoxy in the *plenary* inspiration of the Bible; and also, that while there is much in the ancient records tending to corroborate the recital, in "Nature's Divine Revelations," there is at least no testimony in all those ecclasiastical writings by which that statement can be disproved.

What does the investigating world need in order to get at a reasonable estimate of the New Testament?

In order to disabuse the popular mind of the fancy of the infallible inspiration of the four gospels, the world needs a work, without diminishing regard for their real merits, bringing together all the corresponding passages of the four gospels, and pointing out their essential agreements and discrepancies in a fair and candid manner. Such a production would go far, among liberal and thinking minds at least, toward the final solution of the origin of the gospels, as well as determining the spirit in which they were written.

To what conclusion has a certain truth-searcher come?

By pushing investigation* seriously in regard to these books,

* The reader is referred to an extra-valuable inquiry, and as yet unpublished work, by Darius Lyman, jr, of Ohio.

he has come to the conclusion that they are all *didactic romances*, designed by good men to inculcate moral principles by aid of anecdotes and symbols; that they were written after the second terrible overthrow of Jerusalem, A. D. 131, by men who had never seen the person of Jesus, whom they described by aid of traditionary transmission; and the object for which they were written is the same as the object of modern Sunday-school books, that is, for the moral advancement and religious indoctrination of the young catechumens of the church; and that too at a time when (as De Quincey shows, in his essay on the Essenes) the Palestine Church had become temporarily a Secret Association; reserving *one* of its cardinal doctrines — *The Messiahship of Jesus* as a secret mysterion — to be revealed only to the initiated: while the other cardinal doctrine — *The speedy coming of the kingdom* — being esteemed of such universal import, was taught without reservation to the people.

By further investigation, he has also come to the conclusion, that the gospel attributed to St. Mark, not precisely as we now have it, however, was the *original* gospel; that the gospel according to Luke was a copy subsequently taken — an amplification of Mark's; and that the Matthew-gospel was *a copy* of both Mark's and Luke's, with original additions (by the so-called Matthew) of traditionary and genealogical information. John's gospel, on the other hand, as there is much evidence to show, was written for the catechumens of the Ephesian Church, by a presbyter or living elder of that Church, and not by the alleged apostle. This Ephesian presbyter — entertaining many of the doctrines taught by Plato, and afterward by the Essenes — assumed to be an apostle, in order to give a more lively impression of the supposed divine character of the Nazarene. He, therefore, justified himself with *the invention of facts* in the history of Jesus, because his sole purpose was to glorify him, as the master of men, and the Son of God. (This view is in part corroborated by the historical concessions of Dr. Moshiem.) He did this with no evil conscience on his own part, for it was not his purpose to impress upon his young pupils so much what Jesus did, as what Jesus was — a magnification of the individual (so common to all affectionate and poetic devotees) above the common attributes and ways of the earth's inhabitants. In short, the gospels were, as he thinks, the Sunday-school books of the early Church; which sported with the facts of Jesus's real life, as our modern religious tales, written by conscientious adherents of the Christian Church, revel in pictures and anecdotes of lives altogether ideal.*

In "Nature's Divine Revelations" you assert that *two thousand and forty-eight bishops* assembled at the Council of Nice, and that Constantine expelled seventeen hundred and thirty of these, leaving but three hundred and eighteen to compose the Council; is there any history to support this assertion?

"In relation to this statement of Mr. Davis," says G. Smith, "Professor Mahan, in his late work against Spiritualism, on page 22, holds the following language: 'Two thousand and forty-eight bishops never assembled as members of this Council. Nor were seventeen hundred and thirty, nor any other number, forcibly excluded by Constantine. All but three hundred and eighteen, which did sit as members of the Council, were there as mere spectators, on account of the intense interest which was universally felt in the question of doctrine to be acted upon, and this is a well-known fact in history.' But notwithstanding this dogmatic assumption of the Professor, Mr. Davis has asserted nothing more than is supported by history.

"In Dr. Cotton Mather's 'Magnalia Christi Americana,' book vii., page 442, is found the following testimony: 'But that my reader may also may be prepared for the action of the Synod, I would humbly ask him what he thinks of the relation given us of the first Nicene Synod by Eutychius, an author of the first ages, recommended by Seldon and Pocock as one of irreproachable fidelity? That author, whose history in Arabic, never seen, I suppose, by Salmasius or Blondel, is by some thought, in this matter, much more probable than that of Eusebius and Socrates, does relate unto us that, upon the letters of Constantine summoning the Synod, there were no less than two thousand and forty-eight bishops who came to town; but that the most of them by far were so grossly ignorant and erroneous that, upon the recommendation of Alexander, Bishop of

* These suggestive conclusions of Darius Lyman, being the product of a candid investigation, are of the greatest moment to the explorer of theological and christological history. I trust the public will call for his valuable work ere long.

Alexandria, the Emperor singled out but three hundred and eighteen, who were all of them Orthodox children of peace, and none of those contentious blades that put out libels of accusation one against another; and that by the Emperor's happy choosing and weeding of these three hundred and eighteen, the Orthodox religion came to be established.'"

Suppose Harmonial Philosophers shonld resolve to call a Convention of Creeds, appealing to the clergy of all denominations, do you believe that these gentlemen would, regardless of all selfish considerations and *odium theologicum* which might settle upon their reputations, elect their best minds, to represent the cardinal points of each Church?

This question I can not now answer; in fact, I should not prejudge the motives of these many-coated brothers; yet it is wisdom respectfully to say—Gentlemen! you may object to this public method of discussing these important departments of the Christian superstructure. Your archæological evidences, your historical deductions, your classic renderings of the original gospels, will fail, you presume to think, to be duly appreciated by those who might call this Convention. And besides, you affirm that all honestly skeptical minds can not but be persuaded of the miraculous origin, authority, etc., of the Old and New Testaments, by reading Dr. Nelson's, or Paley's, or Watson's replies and evidences. Nay, good sirs, these writers met the question on merely metaphysical and inferential grounds; but the nineteenth century has conveyed the subject to a vastly different position, and the battle has now to be fought on *scientific* and positive principles. And there would doubtless, be a large number at this Convention, who have neither the leisure nor disposition to read your published works, or weigh the evidences which gentlemen of your profession are supposed capable, *ex officio*, of presenting to inquiring minds. Do you think it *right* to let an opportunity escape you of doing good? A *phonographic* reporter might be in attendance to record your argument or defense, and a volume may soon spread the *pro* and *con* fairly before the people. The pride of Protestantism is the right of private judgment on politics and religion; will you not assist to establish still firmer this glorious principle?

The question before such a Convention is entrenched in *sci-*

entific dual positive principles, which all writers against skepticism have utterly failed to refute. One need but read attentively the recent work by Professor Hitchcock, on Geology and Scripture, to be convinced of this vital fact. Even Hugh Miller (who has made as good a plea in behalf of his theological faith as any clergyman could) says: "It is always perilous to under-estimate the strength of an enemy. . . . . The evangelistic Churches can not, in consistency with their character, or with a due regard to the interests of their people, slight or overlook a form of error at once exceedingly plausible and consummately dangerous, and *which is telling so widely on society*, that one can scarcely travel by railway or in a steamboat, or encounter a group of *intelligent mechanics*, without finding decided trace of its ravages." And elsewhere this orthodox author boldly affirms that the "clergy, as a class, suffer themselves to linger far in the rear of an intelligent and accomplished laity—*a full age* behind the requirements of the time. Let them not shut their eyes to the danger which is obviously coming." Gentlemen, I have but discharged a fragment of justice in presenting this matter. It is the nineteenth Century —with its New Truths and awakening Rights of Men—that invites you to this Convention of Creeds.

QUESTIONS ON

THE EVIDENCES OF IMMORTALITY.

THE fundamental religious elements, immanent in man's highest faculties, seem, at first glance, to be *incompatible* with deliberate investigation. There are few minds capable of reasoning while prejudiced. Come to that most high and princely of all emotions — the religious — and forthwith there departeth deliberation, consistency, and vigilance. How few persons there are from whom you expect straightforwardness, reasonableness, charity, temperance in all things. The Modern Church exerts a powerful stultifying influence upon the human conscience. It has forbidden the conscience to reason, to think, to become enlightened. Men may be intelligent concerning the ordinary interests of life; not upon religious questions. No! Men dare not become religiously enlightened. Innumerable attempts have been made, with more or less success, to shackle the human conscience.

What is the consequence of such mental bondage?

The consequence is, that, while men make advancement in science, commerce, merchandise, in all the relations pertaining to our common existence, they stand still in the far past; without illumination upon whatsoever is religious and ecclesiastical. And a vast portion of the world, therefore, have involuntarily gone into extreme skepticism on religion.

How many sources of human knowledge are there?

There are four sources of human knowledge: first, Intuition; second, Reflection; third, Perception; fourth, Testimony. Two are inherent and natural; two are outside and artificial. The reliable sources of knowledge are, Intuition and Reflection; the unreliable and secondary are, Perception and Testimony. Perhaps, these have never been harmoniously consulted.

Do the churches refer men to their own inherent sources of knowledge?

No; The Churches have not allowed mankind to rely upon inward sources of light and illumination. It is but recently that a party, relying upon the inward bosom of truth, has dared to stand out and criticise past religions. But they are quickly counted. All the religious world, daring not to reason upon sacred questions, rests upon Perception and Testimony. Intuition and Reflection are sources of wisdom; not consulted by fearful churchmen. Perception and Testimony are, in the main, the foundation of everything which they believe or hope to realize. The religious element overrides all else when it has once fairly trammelled the intellect. No other fanaticism is more to be feared. Under the *afflatus* of a religious enthusiasm, man loses all idea of self-preservation, disregards family and friends, and plunges, like Peter the Hermit, into the crusade of fanaticism, never so much as reasoning a moment upon the possibilities of self-deception.

Would it not be a beautiful day when men become illuminated in the religious faculties, even as they now are in their social and intellectual departments?

Yes; a beautiful and heavenly day it will be, indeed! when men shall dare universally to exercise Reason concerning the great questions of human Life. When men shall see that it is a rich privilege and prerogative to reason, then will they become, not mere debaters and disputants, but true and serious inquirers concerning man's perpetual continuation.

Do you make a difference between reasoning and debating?

Yes; Reasoning is very different from debating. Logic is no source of plain truth. There is no surer and quicker path to Error than this system of logicalization. Sophists commence with certain premises and jump at conclusions; a species of jugglery, of legerdemain. Commence this, my friend, and you are on the straight road to self-mistake; to self-degradation. No matter how brilliant your faculties, or how much your logical success may go out into the annals of the world, you will possess at the end of life a very small residuum of satisfaction. How many insincere persons there are who bring merely their *perceptive* faculties to bear upon the sublimest questions of human concern! When the question of Deity comes in, such try to comprehend it with the front part of their heads—and failing, begin to doubt, and eventually to repudiate, the Divine existence. Such is not reason; but logic. He alone is altogether reasonable whose soul is harmonized. Mere logical exercise is a prostitution of the faculties. Intellectual perceptions are designed to ascertain the rudiments of all things, to comprehend phenomena and relations. Reason is the flowering out of all the intellectual and love principles in man's nature. Reasoning is *the process;* the method, by which the soul gets exercise. Reason is the full-blown flower of the spirit; its fragrance is Love and knowledge.

Has the race made much progress in acquiring knowledge of future existence?

No; men have made but little progress in knowledge concerning life and immortality. Look through the history of Egypt, through that of Greece and Rome, through all Anglo-Saxon annals, up to the present time, and you will discover a slow increase in the number of evidences. Spiritualism was known to the most ancient races; to the Indians of the East and the West. Whole races have rested solely upon external sources of knowledge concerning immortality. As soon, however, as the intellect gains a predominance, and the conscience is liberated from the thraldom of prejudice, then the externally-convinced mind begins to reconsider these evidences. At first he turns out to be an unhappy skeptic; at last he is delighted, because he sees so clearly that *this life is all;* and that the highest wisdom is to make the best present use of it.

Do you meet persons who sincerely doubt immortality?

Yes; There are persons utterly destitute of any intelligent evidences of immortal existence. I have met minds who inherit a repugnance to the idea of an eternal continuation of their individuality. Others have ventured, after breaking loose from the Church, to read some merely logical authors. Becoming persuaded of the eventual annihilation of man's personality, they have spoken this doctrine to the world. And the Christian Church is accountable for it all.

How is the Church accountable for this skepticism?

It is accountable, because it has for ages denied to Reason the right to investigate and decide upon immortality. Thousands have become *externally*-minded, in consequence. Such have gone out into the senses, and—discovering that animals die and that man is only a higher animal—they reject all spiritual stories and ghostly anecdotes. These become confirmed, and even happy, skeptics; full of logic, with little reason; at the same time, conscientious and willing to sacrifice themselves for their belief.

But have we not an abundance of positive external evidences?

No; were you to exercise your intellectual faculties, on the question of immortality, and ask: "How much positive intellectual evidence have we?" you would be surprised at the small amount. What *appears* to be positive and conclusive, turns out, at last, to be but inferential and uncertain. For instance: it is alleged in general by the Christian world, that nothing is more certain than that Jesus brought life to light; that his existence was the first manifestation of a great and beautiful principle; that his resurrection was a *demonstration* that all regenerate persons will one day come up out of their graves, and bask in the light of an eternal world. The Church is *certain* upon this point. They say, with Paul, that Jesus was seen *after his resurrection*, by over five hundred persons; and from the perception and testimony of these, it is said, all Christendom should believe in life and immortality.

Well, what effect does this evidence exert upon the thinker?

I will explain: The skeptic, who perhaps is learned in logic, comes to the analysis of this evidence. He finds that twelve of the fourteen have not testified at all to the facts asserted; and that, although the testimony of five hundred persons would, in a court of justice, balance off a vast amount of prejudice and skepticism, yet such testimony does not appear. It was never put into the Bible. Men have the assertion of Paul only; not the testimony of five hundred. It appears to the skeptic, therefore, that here is an extraordinary illustration of immortality with *less than ordinary evidence.* Believers are now driven upon inferential grounds. The Church goes searching for what are called "natural evidences" to corroborate the affirmations of revealed religion Historical religion, however, brings out several points of evidence. One is, that almost all seers, prophets, and apostles, have testified to the doctrine of immortality; another is, that this doctrine has been believed by all nations. Here, let us ask:—

Would God have planted in the human soul such a belief, unless there was something answering to it?

Now, skeptics inquire as to the universality of vast superstitions and great errors. Unfortunately, for the Churches, these errors and superstitions are found to run parallel with the conviction of immortality; therefore, the so-called positive evidences of immortal life, drawn from historical religion, departs out of intellectual society. Now cometh the question suggested by natural religion, as to the adequacy of the supply for all man's needs. Is there not a law of this sort in nature? Man's soul asks for personal immortality; therefore, *he will have it;* this is the natural inference. Then arises the question:—

How do you know but your want is educational, instead of natural?

To this question the Church is mute. It has not a word of explanation—only says: "You are an infidel, and captious; unable to be fair and Christian." All that such men need, is: the substantial and ample testimony that this great and desirable doctrine is not a superstition. The skeptic asks: "How shall men know when their wants are natural and when artificial—when acquired, and when innate?" Who knows but this desire for immortality has been implanted by judaistical Christians, who received it from sects still more remote? This doctrine extends back through the Persian into the Egyptian races; and still further even to their primitive ancestors, as is demonstrated by the pyramids. But there are superstitions carved as plainly as this doctrine of immortality.

Would Father-God have implanted Hope in man, unless there was something answering to the faculty?

Man, I reply, can not be a complete contradiction. The skeptic, however, will ask: "Is a belief in immortality a result of the organ, or is the organ a result of the belief? Phrenology discovered that the faculty of Hope, like every other organ, is capable of cultivation; that, although innate, it is under the jurisdiction of its possessor. On a low scale, this faculty never hopes for immortality; but contents itself with hoping for a good day, for a to-morrow, for success in business, for happiness through life. Sometimes it inspires great heroes and small politicians.

"Hope springs eternal in the human breast,
Man never *is* but always *to be* blest."

Hope is considered by the church as the voice of Natural Religion, inducing man to think himself a being of the future; that his success, or his failure, is a result of his present efforts. The skeptic, however, finding that Hope, in its ordinary normal operations, suggests only happiness and success this side of the grave, concludes that it does not prove immortality. There is, he boldly affirms, no *positive* evidence on the question. Now, churches cite the *testimony* of certain ancient seers and itinerant prophets; rejecting, of course, all seers and prophets whose history does not come through canonical channels. But when a careful analysis is made of this branch of evidence, the skeptic pronounces it inadequate and extremely inconclusive. Skeptical persons look into the character of the old seers and wandering prophets, and wherever there is a spot upon it, they will hold it forth to a world's consideration. The church, unable to give back a frank and lucid reply, confirms the skeptic yet more in his skepticism.

Shall we not consider the facts of clairvoyance as good evidence?

It was but a few years ago when clairvoyance was presented to the American public. It was long ago known in France, in Germany; in certain localities in England. In this country it was heard of as a faculty; but, after all, how few experience it! Most people know of it only through the outward sources of perception and testimony. They receive the testimony of those who have interested themselves in the phenomena. And the conclusion is, that clairvoyance—not being a universal human experience—is at best but an *inferential* evidence of immortality.

Have we not positive evidences in the spiritual manifestations?

Yes; one would say that there has been a concert of action between mediums and their spirit friends; to bring out the clearest and most unequivocal proofs that man's soul is not extinguished by the catastrophe of death. Spiritual manifestations, however, are very far from being universal; they are local and special and mostly private. Skeptics say: "There are too many things undignified, not addressing man's highest nature, and injuring proof which otherwise would be clear and indubitable." He who has never seen our Table of Explanations* stands off and makes this report; then this report, invalidating our evidence, gets into influential papers, and becomes the prevailing conviction of America. Although manifestations are now very general, compared with their limitations of six years ago, yet the mass is not convinced that immortality *is not* a mere enthusiastic poem, a religious dream! The Church, when required to give answer to a candid man, finds itself compelled to be mute, or else to use the old vituperations. Should spiritualism become popular, these same churchmen will ask the material forces of Nature to furnish an explanation. But spiritual men and women (of the New Dispensation) have received positive evidences. Without qualification they can affirm, that immortality is approved; that the received evidences are sufficient to settle this question. These evidences, unfortunately, are not universal; not accessible at every table; spirits *can not* act upon every human soul equally; this gives sea-room for immense Doubts of many tons burden. Spiritualists have yet to make *some* discoveries, I think, which will address this class of skeptical persons. Teachers of the New Dispensation are asked by skeptics to bring forward some *positive* demonstrations; as lucid to the intellectual faculties as any sum done by rules mathematical. (I have responded

* See a work by the author entitled, "The present Age and Inner Life."

to this call in a course of lectures, lately delivered, which will probably make the fifth volume of the Great Harmonia.)

What have you seen and developed on this question of immortality?

By intuition and reflection, I have seen that man's immortality, to be of any practical service to him, *must be felt in his religious nature*, and not merely *understood* by his intellectual faculties. I have seen it to be possible for every man and woman, after coming under spirit culture, to feel through all their being this sublime truth: that the perfected human soul can never be extinguished! Evidences which are worth anything, are not outside—are not in the table-manifestations; not in spiritual stories and ghostly anecdotes. True evidences come through the two sources, Intuition and Reflection—through the inward sources of Wisdom. Each human head hath its own evidence. Intuition brings man this treasure in advance. Each human being holds a note on the Bank of Eternal Life. Individual existence is the endorsement; the soul contains the positive proof. The treasures of the future world are lodged in us! If skeptical men could but take leisure out of business relations—if they dared to be candid and truthful to the *inward sources* of knowledge—they would begin to feel positive evidences of immortality. Spiritual manifestations will yet become a hundredfold more desirable; they will not be sought as evidences of immortality, but as illustrations only. Let it be known, positively, that a man contains *in himself* the power of eternal continuation, and he will look naturally for some correspondence with the other world. He is not *surprised* when he gets such communication; nor is he *disappointed* or skeptical if he should not get it. A person who relies upon the *external sources* of knowledge, insensible to the inward fountains, is sure to be swept away when the sensuous evidences disappear. Such must have the testimony now, and under the best circumstances, else they are distressed with irresistible skepticism.

Does not every externally-minded person suffer somewhat from the absence of intuitive knowledge?

Externalists realize a mischievous and lurking suspicion, that all these so-called positive evidences of future existence may be explained eventually by some ordinary principle. Paul was mostly in this condition. Every one acquainted with Paul as a writer, can see, nevertheless, that he was a man truly religious. He undertook to be philosophical upon the question of immortality, but his enthusiasm for the life of Jesus, his indulgence for this branch of the religious sentiment, caused him to affirm that man's resurrection from the dead *was dependent* upon the resurrection of that one individual. Man's individuality was not determined, in Paul's opinion, by any organic qualification—he did not argue that man contained the immortal treasure naturally—but he supposed man to be immortal *in consequence of a miracle:* namely, that Jesus was in reality raised bodily subsequent to passing through the mysterious process of dying.

This extraordinary manifestation was a matter of testimony; did Paul ever seem to cherish doubts on such evidence of immortality?

Paul was frequently very sensitive on the nature of this evidence. He would say: "If Christ *has not risen*, then of all men we are most miserable." Often have men read the fifteenth chapter of Corinthians, so full of beautiful analogies—so full of agricultural arguments and figurative illustrations, but, at the same time, so utterly *destitute* of confidence in man's constitutional immortality. "Now, if Christ be preached that he rose from the dead, how say some among you that there is no resurrection of the dead?" Here he predicates man's resurrection entirely upon the traditionary miraculous resurrection of Jesus. "If there is no resurrection of the dead, then is Christ not risen." Then he turns this rule, makes it to work the other way, and says: "If Christ be not risen, then is our preaching vain, and your faith is also vain. Yea, and we are found false witnesses of God, because *we have testified of God that he raised Christ:* whom he raised not up, if so be that the dead rise not. For if the dead rise not, then is not Christ raised: and if Christ be not raised, your faith is vain; ye are yet in your sins. Then they also which are fallen asleep in Christ are perished. If in this life only we have hope in Christ, we are of all men most miserable."

What does Paul mean to teach by this language?

Paul means to teach that if men consider the life of Jesus valuable as *an example only*, then the whole gospel is worth next to nothing. The great matter in view is, the establishment of man's individual immortality. Although not a philosopher, Paul undertook, as well as his arduous nature would permit, to reason upon the miraculous foundation of his beautiful religion. Paul afterward says: "How can a thing be quickened except it die?" His philosophy of immortality was —that men *must first die* in order to be raised through the miracle; that we are sown in corruption and raised incorruptible; sown a natural body and raised a spiritual body; that we are sown into the grave first, and then, when the harvest-time comes, the spirits who have died down are all raised up. Afterward, however, Paul did not think so; he taught that death was not necessary. Let us read him further: "We which are alive and remain unto the coming of the Lord shall not prevent them which are asleep; for the Lord himself shall descend from heaven with a shout, and the dead in Christ shall rise first, then *we which are alive, and remain, shall be caught up* together with them in the clouds, to meet the Lord in the air, and so shall be ever with the Lord."

Do you mean to affirm that Paul contradicted his own theory of man's resurrection?

Yes: let me prove it. The leading doctrine taught by the apostle was, that it is first necessary for every man to be sown —to die and be buried—in order to be reaped or raised as Christ was; he taught that Jesus was crucified, placed in the grave as one being dead, and rose again in best *status*, to show mankind the dying process which is indispensably necessary *for all to pass through*, in order to secure a resurrection. Yet he elsewhere concluded, that "we who are alive"—without passing through the dying and burying process which before he described as essential—will be "caught up" and live right on just as well.

Does Paul ever appeal to what you term the internal sources of knowledge?

Paul relied for the most part upon miracles, external perception, and traditionary testimony. He was extremely anxious to have it established that Christ after his death *was seen* by reliable witnesses. This was necessary first to every man's belief; an idea which Paul would not have valued had he felt the principle. Jesus was seen by two on the road to Emmaus; then, by twelve; then, by five hundred at once; lastly, spiritually, by Paul himself. The apostle thought that all the evidence a man had of life hereafter, was embodied in an incomprehensible miracle; the physical resurrection of Christ from the state of the dead. The skeptic, in view of such reasoning, says: "This is an extraordinary demonstration with less than ordinary evidence to endorse it."

How can I believe in immortality upon the testimony of a person whom I have never seen?

This question represents the position of the skeptic. How obviously necessary, therefore, that spiritualists, while interested in the excitement of the manifestations, should not fail to seek *internal* evidences of immortality. Axiomatic spiritual principles will save skeptics when the manifestations shall have ceased. No reasonable mind, one who comprehendeth the spiritual law, will believe that these phenomena will continue without variableness. The manifestations, as to their variety, will gradually retire from the world. Behold! the seed is being sown. Already it is time to prepare to reap the harvest of evidences. Let them be garnered into form, and stored into the beautiful temple of spirituality.

Do you mean that spiritual manifestations will become less general?

Yes; this is my irresistible impression. Men must make an intelligent use of these manifestations; else they will go down into history as the tricks of itinerant boys and girls. Look within, my friend, for that principle which causes all effects in the external. When you find an internal conviction that you are immortal, which no sophistry can invalidate or disturb, then you have found *a treasure;* the beauty of which is greatly enhanced by spiritual manifestations. Secure this internal conviction, first; then, add the illustrations. In a few brief years more—when clairvoyant, healing, impressional, and writing mediums only will be known—men will have reaped a harvest of evidence. The testimonials of hundreds of thousands could then be secured. Persons, considered skeptics, will read with earnestness. The Churches will become gradually powerless. Skeptical minds will get their questions answered *outside* of the Churches. Then the Churches will come to you! Be careful, my friend, lest you forget and go to the Churches; do not be absorbed by them. There is danger in becoming *too* popular! Beware, when the Churches begin to consider it profitable to invite you to take a seat in their beautiful compartments. Accept this, and you are on the road to annihilation. Yea, when the Churches consider spiritualism *reputable enough* to endorse you, then consider that you are all on the broad road to certain mischievous prosperity; an easy thriftiness which will turn into conservatism, like all the past, and build up institutions against another dispensation.

Is the spiritual world as solid and as natural as this world?

Yes; I would like to show you how natural and familiar are spiritual things. The other world is as natural, astronomically considered, as the globe which we now inhabit. The spirit-land hath laws, days, nights, stars, suns, firmaments. In that world is treasured up, not the artificial facts of earthly society, but all the elementary facts of mankind. Commence with the most common stones at your feet; watch them; see them ascend through all the gradations of refinement; till they become a physical part of the vast second sphere! The finest particles of all things, not absorbed by this world, go to form a spiritual globe! Like a zone, on the inside of the vast milky-way, is unfolded the second sphere.

Could you indicate the existence of this spirit-world by any laws visible to man's intelligence?

Yes; the existence of a spiritual world is as demonstrable as any proposition in astronomical science. All it requires is, an intellectual inductive ascension, step by step, through the material evidences that lead to it. Mind can be intellectually led to see that *there is a spiritual world* just as readily as it can be taught to perceive that the earth revolves; a fact of which men have no *ocular* demonstration. There are certain facts in nature, as tides, as days and nights, as eclipses of the sun and moon, which require explanation. The astronomer explains all these phenomena by the laws of planetary revolution. And you believe. Why? Because you see that his explanation covers all the facts adequately. So, too, there are facts in human experience which can not be solved upon any other hypothesis save that which admits the existence of spiritual globes. The phenomena of human consciousness, the spiritual experiences of all races, can be explained, I repeat, only by a set of principles which, if legitimately followed out, will lead inferentially, analogically, and positively, to the existence of spiritualized worlds. I am persuaded that six nights of continued investigation, would make the existence of a spiritual world more valuable and familiar than the golden lands of California.

Does a belief in this philosophy give happiness to the mind?

Yes; your ordinary affairs, crowned by this philosophy, would go on with the greatest possible harmony; it becomes, more and more, a strengthening power to the human soul. To allude to my own experience, I would say: It has been a source of inexpressible pleasure (for many years) to live conscientiously in reference to spiritual intercourse. Yet, it is not easily acquired. I have devoted myself to it, studiously and industriously, as an artist to music; as a mechanic to the principles of his occupation. To succeed in anything, a person must be devoted. Such has been my effort, and devotion, and success. Some of my private personal experiences I tremblingly lay upon the altar, that you may see how substantial and replete with consolation are the positive evidences which I have received of the existence of a spiritual world.

It is more than two years ago that Catherine De Wolf, my former companion, went to the Spirit Home. On the morning of the evening of her departure, her father, her mother, her sister, and her nephew—persons who had been in the second Sphere several years—together came near to my house in Hartford. I have become accustomed to the personal presence and spiritual influence of persons: more particularly to the sphere of a spiritualized individual. Thus, I felt their spheres near the house. I went down to the front door, opened it, and invited them up to my studio. As soon as they had entered, I closed the studio door, and composed myself for the interior. In the course of ten minutes I was lost to all externals; was not aware of possessing a physical nature, nor of being in a room; in fact, I was myself A SPIRIT. Still remaining in my body, yet being a spirit, I could see them and hear their words.

Her father said to me: "We have come for our daughter. We think she is going to-night; and we have a special request to make of you that, inasmuch as she has been sick for many months, and thereby fatigued in spirit as well as in body, she be left alone with us, in the spiritual world, for three months; that you do not even *desire* to see her during that time." When I asked why I should not *desire*, he said: "Your desire might reach and rouse her from a required rest; and she be unable to recover as fast as we wish." Therefore, I promised that I would not even *desire* to see her in three months. Her spirit relatives said that they would remain in the vicinity till she (in spirit) was ready to depart.

During that day there were some favorable symptoms; indicating that she might take nourishment and continue a few days longer. But other evidences, toward evening, made it certain that she could not longer remain. About twenty minutes past seven, that evening, she ceased to breathe. Not being in the interior at the time, I did not witness the departure of her spirit. In fact, under the circumstances, I had no opportunity for interior exercises.

Three months passed, and I heard nothing directly from her; nor indirectly, except from two mediums who supposed they had received telegraphic despatches. I had no confidence, however, in anything which I did not receive myself. In the winter I went to the city of Boston, to give a course of lectures. At six o'clock in the evening of my first lecture, I felt her spiritual approach; and that she was somewhere within a hundred miles of that city. My lecture was duly delivered, and I returned to my boarding-house immediately. On going upstairs, I felt she was near. I admitted her by the door, passed up the hall, and went into the superior state. She was now by my side; just like any person in the body. She seemed to have regained about ten years of youth; and in appearance she was not so large as in her physical body. She looked as if she was enjoying her existence; although she was not as enthusiastic as her nature inclined to generally. We conversed pleasantly; face to face. She used her new organs of speech, and gave me portions of her recent experience. She did not know when she would visit me again. I asked her if she came from the spirit world alone; to which she replied, that "she had some one near (the house) who would accompany her." The interview now ended.

Next, I went to Auburn, to deliver lectures. While there, I felt her approach as before. As before I admitted her into my room, and we had another conversation.

When I received her third visit, I was in the city of Hartford, some five months afterward. On that occasion she seemed to have lost about *twenty-five years of age!* She was very brilliant, and filled with emotion. She said that she had "*seen so many beautiful things, and enjoyed so much!*" She wished to tell me something about a "Sunset" she had witnessed in the Spirit Home. She promised, at my request, to be deliberate in her recital, so that I might take it down in writing. While she was standing, with her arm on my shoulder, I wrote the communication which follows: I place it before the reader solely to give him an impression, that no world is more natural than the Second Sphere of human existence.—

A SUNSET IN THE SPIRIT HOME.

THERE are times, my beloved, when I long to speak of my new home.

On the bosom of affection's memory, I voyage back to the happy days when we together trod the earth.

Once, I feared for us both . . now, for both I love and fear not.

Day before yesterday, our family journeyed along the banks of the "Mornia" . . a lake flowing westward.

Accompanied by the dearest ones we know, we ascended the great Mount . . south of the lake . . called "Starnos," being somewhat fashioned after a solar body.

And I yearned for thee, beloved . . yet, my spirit was full of love . . breathed from those around me.

I find in the air of my new home . . the house of the spirits of men . . a something blander, and more pleasant, than in any other atmosphere I ever breathed. . . . There is a joy in it to me. . . . But there are many here who seem not to remark this. . . . And then, our sunsets here!

Oh! I would gaze with you, dear brother, on such a sky as glorified this rose-covered spot day before yesterday!

We visited the summit of Starnos to witness this exhibition. . . . It is likely to occur here once in every *eight* of your weeks . . I mean the setting of the sun on this side of the Spirit Home.

I would bring thee a full description. . . . But I have no words, beloved!

I have looked to see if that was the evening you wrote respecting your visit at High-Rock Tower . . it was!*

Should an artist paint the scene that sunlight gave us, it would be said that he had *exaggerated* the picture. . . . But there is no pencil for such delineation. . . . Art has no hues for such coloring. . . . Language no powers to reveal . . or, if there be words, I feel too much to think them out.

We had been walking around the Lake. . . . The valley was half-viewless and misty with the plenitude of countless odors. . . . And the sea of hills, surrounding Starnos, was half hid by the rainbow-streams of Beauty that were showered down from the sky!

At length, we attained the top of this glorious eminence. . . . We gazed, with unutterable joy, upon the ever-brightening and kindling firmament.

With us, in company, were many you never knew . . some well know and love you . . others you have seen in the earthly home.

My brothers were with us . . and One, whom I will now call my "guardian angel" . . and William's Cornelia . . also their recently married daughter . . and James, too, with a group of his recently-formed acquaintances . . and the blessed *four* you witnessed at High-Rock Tower.

* High-Rock Tower is described in a work by the author entitled "The Present Age and Inner Life.

I sought your hand . . I found *the memory* of your spirit near.

I breathed . . and, the breath I drew was of Life eternal.

And there was no void of existence. . . . Although you did not hold my hand nor administer unto me, yet the fullness of my happiness was all permanent . . all heavenly.

And that sky above us. . . . . It was even more beautiful in the east than in the west. . . . Such a mass of burnished gold. . . . Yet, not all gold . . for here and there a silver edge unrolled . . disclosing the azure sky.

I would that you had seen it, my brother. . . . I can not tell thee of the scene. . . . I can now close my eyes . . and, looking in memory, can see it all again.

There was a glorious cloud . . all clouds are glorious, my brother . . which reflected a far-spreading light upon the sea of hills and the lake below. . . . And Mornia, in consequence, looked like a miniature ocean of liquid gold. . . . The cloud assumed a ruby hue. . . . And, then, the fair flowing Mornia looked like a sea of blood. . . . The light thrown upon the opposite shore, was like a sunny gauze cast over the landscape's emerald green. . . . And the remote habitations of the "Brotherhood of Morlassia" . . the groves of meditation . . appeared as a great City illuminated. . . . And the environing fields, receiving the crimsoned light, looked like a World on Fire!

We gazed . . and gazed . . and, the sun went down. . . . The lights opposite were put out. . . . And the fair flowing Mornia darkened. . . . And the cloud was first a silver gray . . then dark. . . . 'Twas *night* in the Spirit Home!

This is the first time my eyes . . divested of all mortal corruption . . ever gazed upon the sunset.

And I feel that I can no more forget it than I could the event of my new birth here.

Of this, beloved brother, I will hereafter speak.

Our party now descended the rose-covered Mount . . wend ing our way amid green-hilled groves . . serenaded by the birds of the twilight hour. . . . And, as we stepped from spot to spot, *I thought of the glories you had taught me to see with my understanding*. . . . Seeing the FATHER as I now do, I must worship Him in Love. . . . In spirit and in truth I must worship Him!

Beloved brother, HOW MAGNIFICENT IS THE TEMPLE IN WHICH WE DWELL AND WORSHIP!

HOW DO SPIRITS WALK ON THE INVISIBLE AIR?

TO A. J. DAVIS:—VERY DEAR SIR: It is not saying too much to state that I have derived more pleasure in reading your works than all other religious authors, ancient and modern. This is because I have thought that you furnished more philosophical evidence of the soul's immortality than all other writers, "inspired" or profane. But, my dear sir, if there are some things which do not admit of an easy explanation, you will not think me unreasonable in demanding one of you. In your "Philosophy of Spiritual Intercourse," p. 100, you give an interesting account of a "congregation of friendly spirits who from a distance of eighty miles directed a mighty column of vital electricity and magnetism, which current, penetrating all intermediate substances, passed through the roof and walls of the apartment where we were seated, and there, by a process of infiltration, entered the fine particles of matter which composed the table, and raised it several successive times three or four feet from the floor." Now, sir, this would seem very possible were it not that they were above the earth's atmosphere, consequently could not partake of its motions. Now, as long as they maintained their relative position to your little circle in Bridgeport, they had to travel at the rate of something over five hundred miles per hour from west to east, to correspond with the earth's rotary motion; then add to that the rate of sixty-eight thousand miles per hour in the same direction, which would be necessary in order to keep up with the earth's annular motion, and the spirits must move at the rate of sixty-eight thousand five hundred miles per hour! If I am not right, I am nearly so. Now, sir, this seems to me to be an unattainable speed, after being told, on page 141, that "the gentleman closed the door rather too quickly behind him to admit the passage of the spirits of Solon and Pisistratus."

Again, what seems to make it a thing incredible is, you tell us, page 151, that "a stratum of atmosphere, more or less dense, is necessary for the spiritual organism to walk or stand upon." Now if an atmosphere is so rarified as to admit the feet of James Victor Wilson to within eighteen inches of the floor, and not dense enough for the spirits of Solon and Pisistratus to go in at the door, while a spirit in the body could go in, how could that "large congregation of spirits" maintain their distance of eighty miles from the circle in Bridgeport for a moment, and that too without the earth's atmosphere to stand or walk upon? One might suppose that they had rather poor foot-hold to *run* at that rate.

Sir, these inquiries are prompted by no spirit of captiousness; but rather in the hope that you will give them a rational solution. They are made by one who hungers for evidence of his immortality — evidence which he has never been able to get a morsel of from the pulpit, and which he hopes to get alone from the sensuous manifestations which are claimed to be given daily in our country.

I am, sir, very respectfully, AN ANXIOUS INQUIRER.

WILMINGTON, *Mass.*, *Oct.* 3, 1855.

THE QUESTION ANSWERED BY A. J. DAVIS.

TO AN ANXIOUS INQUIRER: Your letter addressed to me contains questions of moment, especially so to all who seek to establish the immortality of the soul by and through scientific facts and philosophical principles. The imaginative poet, the cultured sentimentalist, finds no difficulty where you do; yet such persons — although perhaps satisfied of the soul's indestructibility and endless growth in love and wisdom — can never remove, what *thinkers* consider, philosophic objections to the possibility of man's continued existence in other worlds.

Your mind seems to be impressed — perhaps, I should say, *oppressed* — with two physical conditions which militate against my spiritual disclosures — first, "velocity:" — second, "density." In reply, I am admonished to be brief, but my explanation, I trust, will not be obscure in consequence.

Electricity of immensity is different from that which is so

called on this globe. It is the same, essentially with ours; yet, as I have often said, it is different, because finer and semi-spiritual. This element thus spiritualized, is omnipresent. Its operation is everywhere the same—unbroken, unshorn, indissoluble. It is a positive imponderable reality, which, because of certain functions performed by it in the various sections of the material creation, I sometimes term, "Magnetism." The schools have as yet no reliable intelligence, free from conjecture concerning this beautiful agent of boundless influence. Like the DIVINE SPIRIT which vitalizes it—it is shoreless, trackless, pathless, independent. It never departs from certain principles of uniform action, local and general.

Please, my esteemed Inquirer, remember the foregoing as the fundamentalism—on which, as I think, all your inquiries may find an adequate solution.

You can not understand how the spirits, over the Bridgeport circle, could "maintain their relative position" to that circle, unless they moved, in harmony with earth's rotary motion, at the frightful rate of sixty-eight thousand five hundred miles per hour. I will endeavor to explain:

Electricity, being an omnipresent principle, is the medium through which spirits see and act upon physical objects. This element penetrates and permeates every physical substance; so that an object on the side of the earth, in it, or on the opposite side, would be as clearly seen, and could be as easily acted upon, as if it was on that side nearest the spiritual congregation. The congregated and operating spirits, therefore, have *no need of changing their position* in order to see and act upon terrestrial objects. Next, you inquire:

How can you explain the problem of density?

The question of "density" is here easily answered. It is only when spirits approach the earth's surface that this peculiarity is noticeable—that is, the necessity of some *eighteen inches of nether air as a floor* on which to walk or stand sustained. Solon and Pisistratus did not enter the door. Why not? Because, as I originally explained, the *haste* with which a gentleman closed it, rendered their ingression inconvenient, if not naturally impossible.

Do you mean to teach that spirits are unlike earthly beings with reference to the laws of gravitation?

No; I do not mean to teach such doctrine, but, on the contrary, that spirits are regulated by laws which govern men. That spirits have as much power as we possess to triumph over atmospheric and gravitational conditions—to overcome the laws of friction and comparative *inertia* (which is accomplished each step we take on the bosom of matter)—must be almost self-evident to every careful student of the Harmonial Philosophy. This philosophy provides for all such considerations, by teaching the universality of an element upon which *will* can extensively act with surprising exactitude. By reference to the "Vision at High Rock," dear Inquirer, you will observe the immense Congress above the earth, sustained by atmospheric stratifications—far less dense than those near the globe's surface. I questioned the possibility at the time, but was referred, as you may remember, to the existence of *far heavier bodies* sustained by air-floors still more remote. Upon further research, I was forced to a conclusion that "the laws of gravitation" are not yet comprehended. For example: birds, weighing from three to twelve pounds, ascend through dense strata of air, and move easily in rarer mediums—such as wild ducks, geese, and eagles; and all this is done by *will*, operating upon voluntary muscles—for, as evidence, should a bird suddenly close its wings mid-air, it would fall to earth like a stone or any other involuntary body.

Now, *while it is true that spirits have no wings*, yet do they conform to certain laws of gravitation (not yet understood by mankind), and thereby ascend to any height and travel to remotest populated globes. This is usually accomplished by conforming to the "rivers" of magnetism and electricity which flow, with great swiftness, between all inhabited planets and the contiguous margin of the Spirit Land. (See "Present Age and Inner Life.") Hoping that you will continue the investigation of scientific spiritualism, and be thereby advanced to all happiness and important truth, I subscribe myself,

Your friend, A. J. DAVIS.

BROOKLYN, *Oct.* 13, 1855.

Can you familiarize the life and society of the Spirit Land yet more to the common understanding?

My impression is, notwithstanding the private nature of the words imparted, that I can not familiarize the social facts of the Second Sphere to denizens of earth, unless I introduce the following narrative, which, with much more, was given in a conversation between my former companion and myself; on the night of the 15th, and the morning of the 16th, of August, 1854. Three or four days previous to her visit, I felt, in certain unoccupied moments, her approach. During the evening I had been out walking on "Lord's hill," in the city of Hartford, Conn. As I was returning, she joined me about a dozen rods from the residence of William Green, jr., whose house was then my home. She came home with me—accompanied by her sister, three brothers, and her "guardian angel," as she termed her most cherished associate. They all came together into my room. And, while the party entertained themselves in conversation concerning the diagrams, &c., which were hanging on the wall, we (Catherine and I) began a familiar conversation which continued for nearly two hours.

This is the seventh visit to me since her spiritual departure. From her first, which occurred in Boston, I remarked that she gave me only the *fraternal* recognition.

To her esteemed friends and acquaintances it may be gratifying to know somewhat of her personal appearance. She now appears to be about fifteen years of age—is very enthusiastic and brilliant—and yet, has a depth of expression which indicates strength of character as well as intellectual acumen. Usually she stands by my side, with her arm resting upon my shoulder; or else, moving her hand lovingly and tenderly over and upon my forehead.

Her dress differs considerably from those with her and other female spirits, except her guardian angel's dress, which resembled her habiliments closely; whose appearance is also brilliant, and whose expression is fraught with much sweetness and energy. Blue, white, and a light crimson hue, entered into the colors of her simple garb, which, like the finest gossamer fabric, crossed over her neck, the same on her back as on her breast, confined at the waist with a silver-white girdle, and falling thence gracefully down over the hips, and terminating within two inches of the bend of the knee. Her arms were proportionally covered with the same garment. This dress was, as I observed, only one piece.* Above any earthly fashion, it is best adapted to please the most cultivated taste, and display the grace and beauty of the female form. Although this beautiful habiliment concealed her person in particular, yet the *general outline* of her symmetrical form was visible — resembling a soft snowy shadow — through a fine web of light.

I have written out the result of our conversation, nearly *verbatim*, from my immediate recollection:—

"My Guide! my Protector! my all of life on earth! I did not speak yesterday to thee . . nor last night as I longed to do . . but nearly all my thoughts were of thee.

"Thou hast led me to the mountain where I behold my joys . . from whose blessed height my spirit looks forth on the world where once I strayed . . and, in the fullness of my present happiness, my heart's tongue speaks recall to the sad wanderers there. . . . My grateful soul addresses them . . I can tell of happiness . . I am happy now . . Oh, *so* happy! . . . *Who again can find such joy as I have found?* . . . Can any *other* soul be wedded to its guardian angel? . . . Yes, this may be! . . . God's Kingdom comes. . . . And, it seems to my joyous soul that mine is the happiest . . yes, the happiest . . for *who can feel so happy as I?* . . . Who can be so blest? . . . Who can love like me? . . . And, where is another so worthy to be loved . . another *such guardian angel?*"

Then I asked her this question: "Katie, while with me, you frequently said you could not live without me — why can you now feel so happy away from me?"

"Brother beloved!" she replied, "I will tell you all. . . . Many days after my arrival at my father's *Pavilion* . . situated on a beautiful eminence from whose summit we can see the

* The purest spirits are not clad in artificial dress. The spiritual garments are not manufactured in the Second Sphere, but, as I have observed many times, are "imported," so to speak, from factories on neighboring physical planets. The same is true of certain birds which animate the Spirit-Land.

Seven Lakes of Cylosimar . . I could see no beauty, feel no life, believe in no Immortality, *without* the personal presence and constant companionship of my only earthly guide. . . . 'Without him,' I said, 'I can see no Father . . realize no Heaven . . without him, I can not be comforted.' . . . Even in my dear mother's smile . . in the holy loving touch of my beloved father . . in the soothing music of my dear sister's love . . from Marcus's gleeful words . . I could gather no relief . . I would have *only thee*. . . . But, unexpectedly, one day I was quieted by *the the sound of a voice*, so like thine, that I started . . all trembling, all tearful, and overjoyed . . to meet thee *so soon* in my father's Pavilion. . . . I looked in every direction . . I saw no one near. . . . Presently, I saw . . just by the door, and standing close to Cornelia's* side . . *one so like thee that I flew into his open soul!* . . . 'Are you my Jackson's brother ?' I asked. . . . With deep sweetness, and a look of love, he replied . . 'You shall know me soon.'

"But I could not wait . . no, not a moment . . suspense is such torture. . . . And yet, how easily I did compose myself at his request.

"He departed from my sight. . . . But I felt, *how beautiful is Love*. . . My spirit *sought him* as if 'twere thee. . . . I felt he could tell me of thee . . even, if he were not in reality thy prototype . . thy real brother and counter-image.

"But of this all, my own dear friends would reveal nothing . . to my questionings, replying only that in future I should see him more."

Here I interposed this question: "Katie, did this occur before your first visit to me in Boston ?"

"Yes, dearest brother," she replied, "I had not seen thee . . neither did I know how to find thee. . . . Every day I would impatiently ask for thee, or for *thy brother*† whom I had seen. . . . And then I walked a little. . . . Environing beauty, of which I was often told, was all dead to me. . . . I could only think of thee. . . . Through the love of thy soul *only* I could

* "Cornelia" I understood to mean the ascended wife of William Green, jr.

† When she spoke thus I supposed she had seen the only natural brother I ever had, whose name was "Sylvanus."

gaze upon the SPIRIT HOME. . . . Without a consciousness of your presence, I could see no charm in existence . . no loveliness or grandeur in all that lay spread out before my father's Pavilion. . . . *Oh, I so longed for thee.* . . . Most passionately my soul did yearn for thee . . or, for the *one* I had so fondly embraced . . because I felt that he alone of all others in my father's house could see thee and love thee, and appreciate all my love for thee, while on the earth.

"Dearest brother, 'how can I stay from thee?' . . I would exclaim . . 'How wait thy coming? . . so long a time, perhaps . . How can I wait? . . Thou art not here. . . .

"But I see thy room, and the sweet couch there!
Thy table too, and the dear writing-chair,
The birds they seem to sing, and flowers look fair,
And that which makes it heaven, I see truth there.

"'Could I not better bear this separation,' I asked my father . . 'had I not been personally with Jackson?' . . . . I began to doubt the wisdom of it . . so intensely did I feel your absence. . . . And yet, I would not but have been with him . . I was *so happy* for it . . it makes me happy now. . . . Memory brings thought, and love awakens feelings, which carry me back to our first meeting . . and to the cottage parlor, too, wherein I was so blest. . . . Each day the same fond memories would command my soul's attention . . yea, a thousand times. . . . And yet, at times, I was confused between thee and thy brother . . I knew not which I wished *most* to gaze upon . . for so I loved all that was related to and resembled thee.

"As my strength strengthened . . as my youthfulness returned . . I could not *realize* at times your absence . . neither at times that we had ever met. . . . My existence with thee began to fade out . . I remembered only our first acquaintance . . when I dared not to think of closer nearness.

"But I know we have met. . . . Upon me the deathless record is made . . all here can read it. . . . My soul has expanded . . the mortal vestment confines it not . . and, in all I have of heaven, I see thy work upon my nature. . . . Yes, my Guide . . my best earthly friend . . my only earthly protector. . . .

Yes, thy lessons are not lost. . . . Thy spirit-sister's being has received them all . . all . . and, they shall live in her eternal life. . . . They shall embellish her existence *here*, while they still prepare her spirit for higher homes and purer heavens. . . . Thanks . . thanks . . for thy gentle patience. . . . How sweetly thou hast led me. . . . My ever-grateful soul remembers all . . all . . and, my spirit ceases to be rebellious, when, as now, it senses the chastity and liberty of the Father's Love and Wisdom!

"One morning my dear father came to me, and said: 'Daughter, Arise, go out upon the hills with us . . for *thither* goeth thy Guardian Angel.'

"We prepared . . we went out upon the hills. . . . The Seven Lakes of Cylosimar . . disposed at regular distances, forming a crescent-shaped curve, amid the overfolding margins and beneath the far-off lofty heavens . . appeared like the setting of brilliant diamonds. . . . In all directions, distributed through the landscape, were many groups of beautiful trees . . so beautiful, and so green . . uplifting their emerald boughs at least a thousand feet above the surface of the Lakes. . . . And I flew . . to my Jackson's brother. . . . .

"'Are you not my own Jackson's brother?' . . I asked . . 'I am his brother' . . he replied . . 'and, *together*, we will visit him!'

Here, I inquired: "Katie, did all this occur before your first visit to me?" (She had been gone from earth nearly four months ere I received anything from her.)

"Yes, my own brother . . all this was before I knew where you were . . before I knew how I could ever find the way to the earth again. . . . He told me in beautiful language of your mission . . what he knew of your teachings. . . . For all this I *loved* him very tenderly. . . . 'Thou hast loved well' . . he said to me . . 'but I will teach thee wisdom.' . . . 'Thou shalt teach me love.' . . . 'This world is all love. . . . Unto it the Father hath his love imparted . . the love which knows no recall, no weariness, no change . . illimitable . . infinite . . eternal.' . . . He bade me to see in him my Guardian Angel. . . . But already, before he granted me this holy blessing, my heart had named him thus. . . . Yes, he is my Guardian Angel . . and more . . I love him. . . I do not fear to love, with all my heart, with all my strength, with all my mind, with all my soul. . . . God is no 'Jealous God' . . as error hath taught . . enslaving love. . . . Truth hath *no chains for the soul* . . and, freely loving, I worship God. . . . My love I draw from an inexhaustible treasury . . heaven is our exchequer . . boundless are our riches . . unfathomable the deep fount of Love, whence flows all our wealth. . . . Infinite the beneficence of Him who giveth to us. . . . We will repay him by loving one another!"

(Here Katie remarked that she would now retire with the party, to return early on the following morning. She said she was going to visit the beloved members of her family still on earth, also several of our mutual acquaintances, but would say more to me ere she left for the Spirit Home. Accordingly, on Wednesday morning, at four o'clock, she awoke me by an influence which came through the walls, like a breath. Feeling which I arose, dressed myself, went down to the front door, and found there the entire party as before. Each refused to come in, save Katie—who accompanied me up-stairs—and, resting her hand upon my shoulder affectionately, she said:)

"In a few days, my own dear brother . . we all depart for the Northern Section of the Spirit Home."

Hearing this I inquired: "How far is that Section from where your father resides—from his Pavilion?"

"Many billions of millions of miles," she replied.

"Why," I asked, "do you go so far away?"

"To see new societies and different scenery," she returned, "and besides, my father and my Guardian, and many others, have something to do thither. . . . We go, because lovers are never separated here either by space or circumstances."

"Will you tell me the name of my brother?" I asked.

"My Guardian Angel is not your physical brother . . his name is Cyloneos."*

"His name is almost like mine"—I said.

* She pronounced it thus: Cy-lone-os—meaning the Morning's Ray.

Yes," she replied; "because you both belong, by character, to the same Brotherhood. My name—" she continued, speaking of herself—"is Cylonia;* and yours is 'Silonius'—as you used to write it."

"Does the soul of Cyloneos fill yours as fully as sometimes you used to say mine did?" I asked.

"Without him, my brother, I feel that I could not exist—even in the midst of all this Heaven! He is to me *another* Jackson. I love him—because I have so loved you—because he gives what my soul ceaselessly yearns for—I love him, because—I can not help it! Out of his abundant wisdom, he promised me that your mission will go on without me. He has let me into the benefits of my earth-life . . exhibits it all, its lights and its shades, its storms and its sunshine . . has made me see plainly that I came to him from you as a gift. My soul senses the truth of *all* he says, with deepest gratitude. . . . 'I not only know,' he tells me, 'the jewel the Father placed on earth for me, but also where and how I must wear it.' Oh, I am *so* happy in the knowledge of thy power to go on, unmoved and unchanged, with thy mission without me. In this thought, too, I find rest and heaven. Soul calleth unto soul, and each answereth the other. My love uttereth its voice, and lifteth up its hands on high, in worshipful gratitude for the undivided possession of my Angel's love, which, in all the things of my life, is abundant—making more and more visible the glory and greatness and goodness of our Heavenly Father!"

* * * * * * * *

Thus, ended our seventh interview. Besides those recorded, I asked her a multitude of questions which I do not feel free to publish. I asked her—"if I understood her?" She observed my thoughts, and replied in the affirmative. She could not tell exactly when she, with the large party of friends, would return from the Northern Section.

In closing let me remark that, previous to her marriage with the wise and beautiful "Cyloneos" of the Brotherhood of Morlassia, I had made deep excursions into the very *interior* ter-

*** She says her spiritual name "*Sy-lo-nia,*" means the "Morning's Bride."**

ritories of conjugal science.* From my discoveries in reference to temperamental harmonies—that only certain combinations can eternally cling to each other—I had concluded, although the relation subsisting between us was temporarily wise and fraternally beneficial, that it could not extend beyond the tomb and be crowned with the Harmonial perpetuity. Therefore her narrative, although it had at first somewhat of sadness in it, did not surprise me. And now, as I remember her withdrawal from earth—sustained and enraptured by the strong embrace of her real conjugal Companion—my soul can utter but one affectionate sentence, a true farewell blessing—"Progress, and be happy!"

* * * * * * * *

Astounding contrast! My vision has closed upon the spiritual; the curtain has dropped; my condition is no longer superior. Exhausted by mental activity, and feeling the need of air and exercise, I go out through the public streets. I meet familiar faces; we smile, and quickly separate. My feet tread the brick pavement with rapid succession. The gate of the North Cemetery is open. I walk quietly through its shady avenues. The ground is wet from recent rain; the grass glistens in the sun-ray; the trees drip moisture. This silent place is suggestive; at once of Death and of Life. Against the new iron fence I am leaning. Overhanging boughs cast a veil of thin shade upon the Siberian Hedge. Beneath this pale shadow the earth is gracefully raised. Here are visible a few violets, white lilies, and some mignonette. Here, too, stands a pale record by one of her cherished relatives—a snow-white stone on which are written these mutually significant words—"My sister."

* * * * * * * *

What is the phenomenon of death to the worldly-minded?

To the worldly-minded, the fatal certainty of death is draped in darkness; to such persons the elements of change and alteration pervade all external nature. Mutability and waywardness characterize every form and substance which man's bodily

* The reader is referred to the fourth volume of the Harmonia—"The Reformer"—which contains the author's impressions on this question.

senses can recognise. A birth—a fleeting existence—a certain decay—each following the other in rapid succession. To external observation everything is changing constantly—from budding infancy to blushing youth—from blossoming maturity to decrepit waning and passing away—from a state of life to a state of death. A few hours since, the east was radiant with the newly-arisen sun; now, it shines in the zenith; a few more fleeting hours, and the bright orb is gone, and nature is dressed in the sad and sable habits of night, and darkness drapes the world.

Such may be death to the ungodly and unsanctified; but is it not a more blessed fact to the Bible-believer?

No; the worldly-minded and the receiver of ancient myths are equally terrified by the mystery of death. Jeremy Taylor, the eloquent dignitary of the Church, says: "Man is a bubble. He is born in vanity and sin; he comes into the world like morning mushrooms, soon thrusting their heads into the air, and conversing with their kindred of the same production, and as soon they turn into dust and forgetfulness; some of them without any other interests in the affairs of this world, but that they made their parents a little glad and very sorrowful." And again, the same ecclesiastical teacher and excellent writer says: "So I have seen a rose newly springing from the clefts of its hood, and at first it was as fair as the morning, and full with the dew of Heaven as the lamb's fleece; but when a ruder breath had forced open its virgin modesty, and dismantled its too youthful and unripe retirements, it began to put on darkness, and decline to softness and the symptoms of a sickly age; it bowed its head, and broke its stalk, and at night, having lost some of its leaves, and all its beauty, it fell into the portion of weeds and out-worn faces. So does the fairest beauty change, and it will be as bad with you and me; and then what servants shall we have to wait upon us in the grave? what friends to visit us? what officious people to cleanse away the moist and unwholesome cloud reflected upon our faces from the sides of the weeping vaults, which are the longest weepers at our funerals?" Thus have spoken to us the ministers who should proclaim "glad tidings;" thus has the Church led us to the charnel-house — till its gloom is impressed upon our minds with awful blackness, and earth becomes as a sepulchre for ever yawning beneath our tread — where we walk in gloom, led on by popular theology, whose best consolations are cold, repelling, unspiritual.

But are there not some redemptive elements in the Church system of consolation?

Yes; there are some elements of faith and hope — some sparks of truth illuminating the darkness — which may preserve the Bible-believer from utter despair, and soften the anguish of the bereft. But to the clear, philosophical understanding, there are neither consolations nor wholesome elements in the various systems of religious faith which are now recognised in the world.

What is it that produces so great a change in man's conceptions of life and death — of the present and the future?

This is not the place fully to answer this question, but it may be well to remark, that the *discovery of the existence of interior senses in the human mind* (termed clairvoyance), was the beginning cause of progress in this new region of thought. And subsequent research and meditation has diffused a clear and enthusiastic joy over the entire being of many — imparting that serenity of mind, untinctured with fanaticism, which so beautifully characterizes the truly harmonial man.

Can you explain how the "interios renses" act, superior to the bodily organs, in bringing to light the fact of immortality?

Yes; the interior clairvoyant senses can gaze upon higher worlds, and reveal new worlds within the one we at present dwell upon. These senses address man's inward sources of knowledge; they speak to his Intuition and Reason. As the microscopic and telescopic worlds are hidden, in their prismatic splendors and awful magnitudes, from the powers and penetrations of man's corporeal senses; so, from the same limited vision, are concealed the stupendous magnificence of the spiritual universe, and the kindling skies and indescribable beauties of the eternal spheres. But, to the interior senses, all these worlds are visible. Men, and things, and planets, and angels, and future existence, and the vital laws of Father-God

—all, appear in that consistent order and philosophic precision which distinguish the truth from the dark chaos of mythic Theology. To the interior senses, the changes of Mother-Nature are indications of the ceaseless operations of unchangeable principles—steps from lower to higher—from matter to spirit. A birth, a fleeting existence, a death—these are manifestations of the beautiful Laws of progression and development. When the fair foliage with which summer adorns the forests, and the flowers which garnish earth, are changed—tinted by the breath of the rude autumnal winds—and when the blushing rose and the modest violet shed their leaves upon the frost-covered ground, then the philosophic heart is not saddened. These *obvious* changes diffuse no melancholy vapor over the healthy mind. They mean that a brief period of rest has arrived preparatory to the resurrection of kindred elements in higher forms and other essences; to unfold, if possible, a still more lovely spring and a sweeter summer, when Mother-Nature's domain will again be decked with high-raised foliage and beautiful garlands.

Does the harmonial philosopher find his consolations in objective existence?

No; and yet the true philosopher sees, in every outward process and object, a form of internal truth which is full of unfailing consolation. For example: the sun absorbs its far-spreading radiance, and disappears behind the western hills, and a dark curtain is drawn over the earth; but, lo! the darkness reveals innumerable stars. These royal orbs—robed in garments of essential light, and controlling, like mighty gods, the many planets which traverse the boundless domain of solar systems—are visible only when the sun is unseen. Its light is gone out, yet there is no darkness, no death, no funeral. Although the clouds may temporarily conceal the distant orbs from our view, and a sad gloom settles upon our minds, and a dreamy slumber succeeds it, yet ere we awake, the sun is already arisen in the east, tinging the distant clouds with auroral splendor, and converting the weeping dew into rays of golden light, bathing the mountains and the valleys, the gardens and the fields of Mother-Nature, with a fresher and a lovelier radiance!

You picture the Spirit Land to be one of uniform happiness to all people; now, if this be so, what possible motive can an unhappy earthling have to desist from suicide?

The answer is ample and conclusive. It is always true that, when a body dies on earth, a soul comes out, more or less beautiful, in the angelic land. But a bright beauty and glory can not be obtained there by violation of natural laws, by wrong motives, or by the voluntary extinction of life in this world. No; it is only when Father-God's and Mother-Nature's Laws are permitted their full and complete operations—it is only when the issues of inimitable principles are patiently received and cherished—that glory, happiness, and promotion, are attained through physical dissolution. In the voyage from childhood to maturity, our bark is frequently overtaken by storms—dark clouds hang o'er our heads, weeping sadly, as if some fearful disaster were prepared for us in the next hour—and we, too, mingle our voices with the dirge of mournful sighs, and resign ourselves to the fearful calamity. But the next hour is redolent with sunshine and safety; the elements of Nature have but changed places—inferior conditions are transferred to superior circumstances—our disturbed feelings have but induced a quiet and refreshing slumber; and our waking is into fresh vigor and lasting joy. Such is the ultimate experience of him who, having done all within his power to prevent every description of disaster and discord, yields to the legitimate operations of Nature, and rolls into harmony with God's eternal purposes, as an infant falls asleep on its mother's breast. Such is the death-bed experience of the true student and lover of Mother-Nature, of the true lover and server of Father-God.

What is the great lesson which you mean to teach by the foregoing?

The great lesson which I would have enstamped on men's souls is, that the harmonial formation of character—*in harmony with the principles of Universal Love and Distributive Justice*—is the only security against temporal unhappiness and future disturbances. Let us remember that true valor, true principles, and true motives of action, only, can promote us to the position and glory of the *sun;* while unrighteous ambition and impure intentions, convert us into the pale and powerless satellite which borrows its light—being visible only when the greater and purer radiance of the sun is bathing and beautifying landscapes behind the western hills. Progression is made by a reasonable belief in progress. Harmony of character and loveliness of disposition unfold gradually from unwavering efforts to acquire them. May such faith and such efforts be our crown and adornments—for they are at once the causes and effects of fraternal harmony and personal happiness.

All can not exercise the interior senses; few can realize your experience; what can be said to console such minds?

It is no part of the Harmonial Philosophy to depend solely upon outward evidences—upon perception and testimony; on the contrary, its students are referred each to the fixed principles of universal Nature. This method has been strictly followed by the writer, and the deathbed consolations to my spirit are many and ample. We may weep, but only for joy and gratitude. The dear departed is not in the coffin—is not dead—is not buried in the earth—the sod will not always conceal from your view the hand that has pressed yours; neither the face that has darted its smiles and emotions into your spirits. Nay, not so—the bone-and-muscle-garment which the spirit had worn for years, has been properly conveyed to its appropriate hiding-place; while the eternal INMOST has glided to a fairer country—where friends and acquaintances surround, and pour forth the deep anthems of congratulation. A bud has burst, and a rose is unrolled; the night is passed, and the sun shines bright in the heavens. A light has been extinguished on earth, but the light grows brighter under another sky. Divine elements have proceeded from the centre of the universe—through innumerable forms and combinations of matter—into the organization of a human soul. That soul has struggled with the physical and social world—has lived through the caterpillar stage of existence—has escaped the rudimental form. It now resides in the land of the butterfly; in the home of the spirit. Its pathway is onward and upward—leading the happy pilgrim nearer and nearer to the ETERNAL MAGNET—to the INFINITE MIND!

All who are acquainted with the postulates of the Harmonial Philosophy will remember, among other things, that the anterior part of every human head is *atheistical*, is skeptical, is materialistic; that the highest portion is *deistical*, is a believer, is spiritual; that the posterior portion of every head is *idolatrous*, is loving, is devotional. The cerebellic portion is called "Love;" when inverted it is terrible to contemplate. The front portion is called "Intellect;" when inactive, it is idiotic. The superior portion is called "Spiritual;" when subverted, it induces the inquisitorial cruelties recorded by the blood of thousands.

What do the upper faculties teach the intellect?

When normally exercised, the "spiritual" portion of man's head teacheth not only that his soul hath a God, but that *it is* itself a god; not only that there are spirits beyond the vale, but that his own existence *is a spirit.* But the spiritual portion of man's head — being the highest, the last, and most perfect development of character — is little exercised in this age of the world. Persons are, therefore, devotional through the Love-nature; and skeptical, through the front parts of the head. In churches and out of churches there are skeptics and infidels; to every fundamental principle which underlies this stupendous development. Merchants and ministers, when honest and transparent, appear equally skeptical. They have doubtless heard — "the importance of investigation." Many reasons there are — cogent and startling to men of conscience, to men of intellect, to men of moral and religious aspirations — why spiritualism should be investigated.

What do you consider a sufficient reason?

The most momentous reason why spiritualism should be examined is this: that it numbers already more believers than Christianity gained after three centuries and a half of primitive enterprise! It is extensively wide-spread; if false, it is equally fatal. If true, it should be made universal, beneficent, useful. How necessary, then, that men should be candid and truthful in approaching a question to which are attached such immense and lasting consequences!

Few public minds have treated this question with sincerity; in view of this—what is the scientific exposition of the "rappings"—as satirically given about two years since by the ascended Galen?

Mysterious rappings proceed from the sub-derangement and hyper-effervescence of small conical glandular bodies situated heterogeneously in the rotundum of the inferior *acephalocysts;* which, by coming in unconscious contact with the etherization of the five superior processes of the dorsal vertebræ, also results in "tippings," by giving rise to spontaneous combustion with certain abnormal evacuations of multitudinous *echinorhyncus bicornis*, situated in various abdominal orifices. The *raps* occur from the ebullitions of the former in certain temperamental structures; and the *tips* from the thoracic cartilagineous ducts, whenever their contents are compressed by cerebral inclinations.

What is Galen's scientific report of the affection (or disease) which the prejudiced affirm against mediums?

All rapping media have that extraordinary affection, known by the professsion as *cephalomatous*—being, in common phraseology, an elastic obtuseness of the superior hemispheres of the cerebellosus. Whenever such patients (vulgarly termed "mediums") arrange their *manui* (hands) or cerebellous functions and protuberances in *corpus* juxtaposition with a table or other substance, the *movings* occur as a matter of compulsatory necessity, to wit: by an *ejaculation* of volatile invisible effervential *gases* (*flatulentus cerebelli*), generated by the decomposition of *ascaris lumbricoides;* which, being regular descendants of the *gymnotus electricus*, perambulate miscellaneously through the duodenum and the abdominal viscera generally. The vulgar theories and anti-professional hypotheses of *spiritual spasmodic* action of the muscular system, or of *electrical aura*, in spontaneous dislodgment and preternatural infiltration, we pronounce delusive, gentlemen, and unhesitatingly reject them, *in toto*, as unhealthy excretions and galvanic evolutions of diseased and contused cerebellous glands, called, by the uneducated, phrenological organs or faculties.

It is well known that so-called scientific men pretend to information on this subject which they do not possess; in view of this supercilious profession, what is Galen's ironical definition of the treatment of media?

Observation endorsed by a stupendous array of clinic ex

perience, enables the *scientific* man to pronounce this "spiritual-rapping-and-table-moving" development, to be an irregular and anti-scientific disease, raging among the lower and superstitious classes—affecting by inoculation certain predisposed organisms in higher circles of society. Patients, who realize membraneous and abnormal nervo-excitements by attendance upon *rapping* assemblages, may be considered, by the regular allopathic faculty, as being afflicted with a *hypergenesis* in the pigbaceous cartilage of the medullary processes. The conveniencies of the Hospital should be secured to such patients, as a surgical operation may be correct treatment in chronic cases; and our countless *students* should see such cases scientifically treated by the regular faculty.

What does the satirical Galen say in conclusion?

Furthermore, in conclusion, to enlighten you still more on the pathognomical symptoms of this extraordinary disease, I will state* as a result of my recent three-quarters-of-an-hour investigation, that patients who fancy they hear "raps" and see "tables move" are mostly laboring with a *hyperacusis* in the tympanum cavity, also, very probably, with chronic *hypersthenia*. The symptoms are recognisable by protusion of the visual orbs, irregularly-distended mouth, suspended breathing, with occasional ejaculations, and a morbid exaltation of the sense of touch; treatment should be prompt and allopathic—anti-phlogistic, anti-scolic, anti-spasmodic—with three of our best leeches periodically applied to the patient's purse.

It is well enough known that men in general do not rely upon their own spiritual faculties; therefore will you not give your impressions on the *material* evidences that man is a spirit?

Yes; and I will begin with this proposition: that man's spirit is a product of his organization—that the physical organization of man is designed, by the whole system of Nature, to manufacture the form and structure of the spiritual principle.

How can you substantiate this proposition?

One proof is: man contains within his body a little of all which is to be found out of it. For example: he may employ an allopathic physician, who will feed him upon mineral prepa-

* Galen here speaks like some wordy member of the medical profession.

rations. Minerals can be absorbed by the physical system, because they find acquaintance there. The supercarbonate, the muriatic tincture, and the peroxide of iron, also all the different forms of silver and gold, and other metals from gold to the lowest substance in the mineral world—all find an acquaintance in man's physical organization. Chemists know that there can be no real attraction, no appropriation, without affinity. Man's body could not absorb iron or gold—none of the sixty-four primates which form the physical constitution of Mother-Nature—unless in his organization there resided a spirit of invitation. Iron within *invites* iron without. Give man too much, and his system will try to repel it. It is not the substance, but the quantity. This is the reason why allopathic medicines frequently substitute themselves for diseases which they were given to cure.

Does this proof appear equally obvious in the use of vegetable substances?

Yes; another proof is: that man can take a little of every kind of vegetation, of fruit and berries, which exist upon the face of the earth. The Cicuta plant, belladona, and stramonium, are administered and absorbed. No such absorption could take place without a welcoming affinity. Men eat the muscle of the ox, of the deer, of the lamb, of birds, of fish, and the tortoise; because there is something corresponding in the body which *invites* animals, vegetables, minerals. The main question for dietists is: how to combine food, how much to eat, and when to eat it.

What is the doctrine which you now desire to impress?

The doctrine which I now urge upon your attention, is: that man's body is the *fruition* of all organic nature; that the spirit body is formed by the outer body. I am writing now as if the reader had just begun, in the primary department of the school of the Harmonial Philosophy. The body is the focal concentration of *all substances;* the spirit is the organic combination of *all forces.* The representation of every particle of matter, therefore, is ultimately made by man.

Do you mean to teach that the spirit is *manufactured* by the body?

Nay; I mean to teach that the body of the spirit (the soul) is a result wrought out by the physical organization; not that the spirit is created, but that its *structure* is formed by means of the external body. Mind internally is not a creation or ultimation of matter; but mental *organization* is a result of material refinement. Man's organism is composed of muscles, bones, tissues, membranes, visceral organs: these structures must have some specific purpose.

What uses do these structures subserve in the economy?

The use of a physical bone is to make a spiritual bone; even so the physical muscle makes a spiritual muscle; not the essence, but the *form* thereof. The use of the cerebrum is to make a spiritual front brain; even so the cerebellum makes a spiritual back brain. Inside the visible spine is the spiritual spine invisible; the material lungs contain spiritual organs of respiration. The physical ear is animated by a spiritual ear. In a word, the whole outward body is a *re*-presentation of that which is imperishable. Father-God and Mother-Nature first unfold lungs, eyes, ears, brains, bones, muscles, and tissues. What a stupendous marvel! Throughout all subterranean caverns these structures exist in principle. My investigations lead me to affirm, that there is a spiritual anatomy within this physical anatomy; a spiritual physiology within the physical physiology; that man's physical structures operate, like the wheels and processes of a mill, to manufacture the spirit's external organization. Mother-Nature claims the physical body; and Father-God claims that which is spiritual. Father-God and Mother-Nature, by their celestial copulations, formed these children!

Can you illustrate your impression?

I will try. Plant a peach-pit in the earth. Mother-Nature, by her subtle magnetism, warms and swells it. Presently it breaks through the earth's crust, and comes out. At first, a tuft is only seen. Gradually, however, foot upon foot of wood is added; then come beautiful branches; these branches produce others smaller and better; and lastly, the whole tree is perfected.

Why does that tree exist?

It exists to the end that its whole might bring forth peaches. These peaches go to work, in due course, to reproduce their kind.

Even so all Nature exists to the end that Man may come forth; then, the types being established, the process changes to propagation; and men continue to multiply and replenish the earth.

Do you mean that man's inmost spirit is a substance?

Yes! "Ah, Jackson, you're a materialist!" Nay; I am not. Mind, essentially different from matter, is eternal; so, also, is Matter, essentially distinct from mind, eternal. These principles, as male and female, live together in unchangeable wedlock. One is what I term Father-God; the other, is Mother-Nature.

What do you mean by saying that spirit is substance?

I mean that spirit is the absence of nonentity; that matter, after reaching its highest point of unparticled attenuation, becomes a celestial magnetism; that the spiritual essence takes hold of this material magnetism; that, at this point, the two are married; and a succession of elaborations commence until the whole spiritual structure is completed. First, there is muscle; second, nerve; third, blood; fourth, tissue; fifth, brain; sixth, electricity; seventh, magnetism. When arrived at the highest point, *vital magnetism*, you have reached the seventh degree.

Let us now go further. Motion begins upon magnetism; Life on motion; Sensation upon life; Intelligence upon sensation. Commence at the bone-basis and walk up-stairs. Bone — Muscle — Nerve — Blood — Tissue — Brain — Electricity —Magnetism — Motion — Life — Sensation — Intelligence. Twelve rounds in the upright ladder of existence!

Do you mean to teach that spirit is matter?

No; I mean to teach that *spirit* IS SUBSTANCE. The most definite conception of *nothing* ever given to mankind, is, the theological idea of spirit!

Can you demonstrate that the spirit of man is a substance?

Yes; I can take the method of the scientific world, and affirm, as self-evident, that there can be no motion without force; that no substance can be moved without weight, which implies substance. Every person's experience is a complete demonstration that spirit is a substance; that spirit can move weight. Look into the street yonder: see persons, with bodies, weighing from seventy-five to two hundred pounds. What an immense quantity; in the aggregate, how many tons! Those bodies of weight, solid weight, would not move if the spirits were gone out. No deception; it is real bone, real muscle, real matter. Can there be motion without force? Can substance be moved without weight? Can something be moved by *no*-thing? Can entity be moved by *non*-entity. The fact of your existence, of moving your body about from place to place, is evidence that spirit is substance. It requires intelligence to act upon sensation, sensation to act upon life, life to act upon motion, motion to act upon magnetism, magnetism to act upon the brain, and so on down through the sympathetic system — composed of membranes, blood, nerves, muscles — down until the bone is reached and controlled. Thus you go down the stairs every time you move your hand — down twelve rounds in the ladder of normal consciousness. You even move without thinking. You may produce a gigantic manifestation of muscular power even *without thought*. And why? Because your hidden spirit-principle is composed of all vital forces. It can, therefore, think and do a great many things *at the same moment*. Every time a voluntary muscular manifestation is made, your thoughts pass through several telegraphic depôts — sensation, life, motion, nerves, muscles, &c., as already explained. Thus, telegraphic despatches are sent by the will-force to all departments of the system. Man's spirit demonstrates its own *substantiality;* by means of its own normal manifestations. I appeal to no other Bible than to man's own Life-Book! Let every intelligent person, who doubts that spirit is substance, shut off all foregone conclusions, go into the *Innermost* for ten brief minutes, consider this proposition in the light of his own daily and hourly experience, and quite certain am I that he will require no other or better argument.

You intimated that you had two propositions in view; what is the second?

My second proposition is this: that although the spirit of man is substance and weight, although it hath elasticity and divisibility and the several ultimate qualifications and properties of matter, yet that it (spirit) obeys laws which are superior to ordinary gravitation and superior (not antagonistic) to the known physical forces. Gravitation refers to weight; to rarity, to density; to squares of distances. Physical forces in nature are of various kinds. Some are mechanical, as the lever, the screw, etc.; but the spirit of man obeys naturally, as it should politically, a set of higher laws.

How can you sustain this proposition — with what proof?

The proof is prima facia — that man's being *is double:* twofold throughout. These are signs on the outward structure pointing to the corresponding fountains of causation inward. Man has two eyes, two brains, two hands, two feet, two sides to the lungs; the human heart is double, and so is each part of the system. What does it mean? Merchants put signs without their stores; to indicate what they are doing within.

Do you mean to teach that the body indicates the soul?

Yes; the double visible structures come from double invisible principles; and these are male and female. They operate reciprocally; they regulate all action and all animation. One contracts and the other expands. These two principles cause sensation to flow from the head to the extremities and a return wave to go from the extremities to the centre of the sensorium. When there is harmony there is reciprocation. How could there be such a beautiful compensatory activity in man's system, unless there were some grand correspondential principles underlying and producing it all? One principle, I repeat, is positive; the other is negative — or, one is male, the other is female. These principles together form a unit — uniting the double system in *one* action. This positive and negative Law is that which the mind obeys. Men go and come in obedience to this law. For example: if you feel a power in the Koran more positive than that which influences you to read this work, you will ere long leave these pages and seek those more attractive. Man ever obeys the strongest attraction. That attraction may come through the intellectual, the moral, or the social, nature; whatever the direction whence it comes, it is a manifestation of this double principle. Why not say, then, that Life is ample; that it is a plenarily inspired book?

Can you further explain and illuminate your proposition, that spirit obeys a law higher than common gravitation?

Yes; the heart throws blood to the head. By what law is this done? Is it not higher than that of gravitation? Water has weight, and in consequence will run down hill. But, in man's body, water runs up hill! The heart is constantly sending a mass of blood to the brain. Where now is your physical law? When you come to analyze the spirit, take care lest your analogies be constrained. It is easy to get lost in the intricate mazes of psychology. Men float in a sea of boundless conjecture. Yes; "water will flow down hill." But apply this analogy to the spirit—and say, that if spirit be substance, it can not get beyond the physical gravitation of the earth—and you make a fundamental mistake. If I were to affirm that the spirits of some men, after residing a proper time in the spiritual world, weigh seventy-five pounds, you would reply that such persons would be governed by the law of gravitation—which law would cause a stone of less weight, projected into the air, to fall to the earth again. But I reply that this spirit, unlike inanimate bodies, operates upon a positive and negative principle; by virtue of which, the spirit holds up the body, and the body holds up the spirit.

Will you not restate your two propositions?

Yes; my two propositions are first, that spirit is a substance; second, that this substance, although not unlike matter, obeys *a law higher* than gravitation. The last proposition is illustrated by the heart which throws the blood to the finest ramifications of the vascular system, and magnetically calls it all back again to its primal fountains. The blood runs *up hill* every instant of time. You have heard the analogy, that the heart *is a force-pump*. But the truth is, that this organ, unlike a pump, operates upon positives and negatives—by alternate contractions and expansions.

What enables the physical heart to perform this function?

The visible heart performs this function, because there is a corresponding spiritual heart within it. A spiritual heart performs a material manifestation. The spiritual heart which is something, moves the physical heart which also is something, more external.

Where is the seat or centre of the soul?

The centre of the soul is near the centre of the brain. There is a small nucleus in which is concentrated the vital power of all that constitutes a man. This place, in the lifeless brain, is not larger than a buck-shot. In the living brain it is as large as a frost-grape. Now grant the idea that spirit is substance, and that, nevertheless, it obeys a law higher than gravitation, and you are prepared to comprehend many of the facts of death.

Will you describe the facts of death as seen by clairvoyance?

Yes; death is a continual manifestation. The body is gradually passing into a state of insensibility. Look at it; feel of it. It is just what it was, except that it is cooler. Disagreeable humidity and a chilliness; it hath a look of coming annihilation. Look at it with your bodily eyes!

Is there any sensible evidence that a spirit of substance is ascending from that brain?

No; the sensuous evidence is somewhat otherwise. Weigh the dead body. It will weigh as much as it did before death, probably a little more. Why? Because the absence of action increases specific gravity; by giving a greater advantage to the law of ordinary gravitation. Nevertheless, I affirm, that the spirit's organism is substance; that it weighs something.

How many times have you witnessed the departure of spirit?

I have clairvoyantly observed it about thirty times. In regard to this function of dying I have but one testimony. Outward vision borders upon the thought of nonentity. People called "second-adventists" believe in the annihilation of spirit, except it be saved through the miracle and sufferance of a risen Savior. Unless they be dead in Christ they dare not hope for resurrection. Other church people have modified their views. The substance of all Christian doctrine is, that breath animates the body; this once breathed out, the body is no more; and the spirit *is nothing*, except by virtue of a miracle. This theory in regard to the unsubstantialness of the spirit is very strange; only, however, as all error is strange.

Does the death of a body, and the spiritual liberation, resemble the birth of a child?

Yes; the centre of the head, the seat of the soul, absorbs the life principles from the feet, hands, muscles, bones, nerves, blood. Presently this centre expands. The brain and the skull are porous; and there is an emanation. This emanating substance ascends through the wall, and reaches a place in the atmosphere, higher than clouds and storms. When arrived, there are in readiness many accouchers; men and women, from the Second Sphere, waiting the new birth. It is not larger now than the morning-star; to the eye it is but a radiant point of light. Now it begins to expand; to look more like a human face. A human head begins to round out; yet it is small, light, vapory. The neck and shoulders are slowly built up. It continues to grow more real; now you see the shoulders and arms; and now all the structure complete! The lungs come out there, and the heart; good prototypes of the physical organs. The heart still hath its sensibility. The spirit is like a child, just merging into being. It feels the pressure of a fresh atmosphere; of strange surroundings. It keeps outfolding very light; very like an infant. Presently it is disengaged and complete, above the storm; perhaps, five hundred furlongs away. Thus, the spirit-child is born out of the body: which was its mother!

There was Dr. Webster, who put away Dr. Parkman: will you tell what you witnessed in that instance?

Yes; I had an opportunity to observe the process of death by hanging. I was, at the time, boarding in Cambridge, Mass. While the final trial was proceeding, I prayed to ascertain his mental state. I examined him, therefore, and the knowledge thereof was *good for me;* but what I wish to speak of now, is, the experience of his last moments; of his emergement into a different and better Sphere. At eleven o'clock, one day, I went from the Brattle House to Mount Auburn. Alone there, enveloped by the suggestive solitude of that beautiful place, I passed into the interior. By clairvoyance I looked through the distance of three miles; gazed into the yard of the jail in Leverett street, Boston. Carefully I viewed the spectacle. And I testify to what I observed; to illustrate the soul's immortality.

When the fatal word was given, his body fell. I saw the effect it had upon his spirit. If all the weight of Boston city had been concentrated in one cannon-ball, and if this ball had fallen upon the head of Dr. Webster, he would not have experienced a more instantaneous annihilation of personality. As quick as the telegraph can give one pulse from New York to Boston; so quick was the suspension of all his consciousness. This was the first person I ever saw hung; and I hope the last. Everything was still. Motion, life, sensation, intelligence, magnetism, electricity—all was still as the stillest breath. When he was taken down, I saw him laid in the coffin. They pronounced him dead, but his spirit was not gone out; and it seemed to me that he might have been restored.

Did you watch the departure of his spirit?

Yes; during seven hours and a half—the longest period I ever watched—I observed the process. It took him seven and a half hours to be born into the other Sphere. This was done without his consciousness of having any existence. The soul-centre of the head—which became as a star—ascended about four miles above the streets: at an angle of about thirty degrees. It grew rapidly positive, and began to draw upon the elements still remaining in the body. This little radiant power in the atmosphere was surrounded by five spiritualized personages. It grew more positive, and pulsated. There came out indistinct features, gradually; then the neck and the shoulders; then childlike hands, etc., till the organization was complete (as I have described in previous volumes). He was profoundly and congestively asleep. His consciousness was somewhat between sensation and thought; that is, he had neither thought nor sensation; his state was just between joy and sorrow, heat and cold, harmony and discord. It was temporary annihilation. There were five spirit-persons attending him. By their kindly offices he was carried to the Spirit Home. I saw where he was by them deposited.

How long did he remain in that semi-annihilated state?

He was eight days and a half in that semi-unconscious situation. Every day, at eleven o'clock, I walked out to the retirements of Mt. Auburn, in order to witness that beautiful spectacle beyond the Milky Way! On the ninth day, I saw throughout the spiritual atmosphere, a strange, vibratory pulsation. It seemed to tremble wave-like through the whole heavens. At first, I observed it in the distance. It kept rushing on, swelling out, pulsating round about; until it penetrated Dr. Webster's spiritual brain. As he roused and opened his new organs, I saw upon him certain expressions of agitation, alarm, wonder, somewhat of gratification. He made an effort at memory—"What! is this Boston?—Is this a dream?—Have I been asleep?—I was hung.—No! this is not Boston." Thus, he was awakened by music, to a knowledge of his future work.

Do you mean that man's spirit grows in the Second Sphere, and increaseth in substance and weight?

Yes; spirit grows in the spiritual world—as children grow in the natural—by inspiration, aggregation, and secretion.

Can you offer some illustration?

Yes; plant a young peach-tree in a half ton of earth: placed in wooden or earthen enclosure, with a few holes only to admit moisture. Previous to planting, weigh the earth to an ounce. We will suppose that you have half a ton, plus twenty-eight pounds. Now let the tree grow in its own beautiful way, year after year, till it hath brought forth peaches. This matured tree will now weigh, perhaps, one hundred and fifty pounds. Then weigh the earth, and you will not miss more that *two or three ounces!* How can you account for the peach-tree, while the supporting earth beneath weighs no less? This question answers the other. The spiritual body which, when it escapes the material body, does not weigh more than the sixteenth of a pound, continues to absorb from the elements of the invisible air, until it becomes comparatively weighty, acquiring not only a power of gravitation, but also a power to overcome it.

What may be said about the unity of causes?

The unity and fixity of truth presupposes and determines the unity of causes. That is to say, whatever caused vegetation to grow on the plains of Judea four thousand years ago, produces the identical effect in the State of New York to-day. And our next affirmation is equally plain and irresistible, viz.: whatever law will explain the manifestations of the nineteenth century, will adequately solve the manifestations of past ages; and throw off, thus, all the mystery and incomprehensibility which have hitherto lurked over the regions of miracle and supernaturalism.

What does the Apostle Paul say concerning Spiritualism?

Paul said there were in his day diversities of gifts, and diversities of operations. But the manifestation of the Spirit is given to every man to profit. For to one is given by the Spirit the word of wisdom; to another the word of knowledge by the same Spirit; to another faith, by the same Spirit; to another the gift of healing, by the same Spirit; to another the working of miracles; to another prophesy; to another discerning of spirits; to another diverse kinds of tongues; to another the interpretation of tongues; but all these are by one and the self-same Spirit, dividing to every man severally as he will.

Is the Apostle's account based upon theology or philosophy?

Paul's words are mostly theological, yet there is profound philosophy lurking in these few passages. In the first place, Paul affirms that every person is a medium. Instead of "gifts," however, I would have said endowments, qualifications; a faculty, an ability, not imparted to the mind, but an element latent in mind, which invites and produces manifestation. Upon examination, I think the reader would change this word "gift," to "endowment," implying an inherent and organic ability. Had Paul spoken philosophically, rather than theologically, he would have said: "There are diversities of *qualifications*, brethren, of which I would not have you ignorant."

What did the Apostle mean when he said that these diverse manifestations are all by the same spirit?

The word "spirit" signifies *animus;* that which unites, energizes, and gives vitality. There are different qualifications, but *by the same principle.* Truth, I repeat, is a unit: and like effects are never referable to different causes. Whatever principle explains the manifestations of the nineteenth century, must, of necessity, account for all similar manifestations in days of yore.

How many varieties of media were there in the days of Paul?

Paul describes nine different kinds of manifestations, viz.: the word of wisdom, the word of knowledge, faith, healing, the working of miracles (that is, effects incomprehensible at that age), prophesy, discerning of spirits, divers kinds of tongues, and interpretation of tongues. There were, therefore, nine different kinds of media. These signify differences, not of gifts, but of mental qualifications. Whatever principle it was which unfolded nine types of mediumship in the days of Paul, is the same which has produced twenty-four* types of mediumship in the days of President Pierce and Queen Victoria. It is of no consequence whether men believe in Paul's theology or not. History is uniform in her testimony, that *that principle*, operating in Nature and the human soul, which brought nine mediums in the period of Paul, is sufficiently progressive and potent to develop twenty-four different classes in the course of eighteen hundred years.

What does the Douay Bible relate concerning the mediumship attributed to St John

It says that John, the son of Zebedee and Siloam, brother to James the Greater, was called the Beloved Disciple; that he wrote his Gospel, not from observation or experience, but *sixty-three years after everything occurred about which he wrote.* From this we are constrained to conclude that John—the beloved, the earnest, the enthusiastic—was compelled to take *memory*, or tradition, or inspiration. Which do you say? Will you take memory for sixty-three years? Will you trust tradition for sixty-three years? Human experience, in the main, is identical. And such experience proves that *memory* is defective in sixty-three hours; and *tradition* is seldom trustworthy sixty-three days from the date of its tale. You are driven, then, to the last ground: to assume for the Apostle a sort of revelation or inspiration. If John's Gospel is to be taken as authentic, then you must find some *explanation* of the mode of his getting at correct information. If he received his ideas by

* See the classification in the "Present Age and Inner Life."

inspiration, then what law regulated that inspiration? The Douay Bible says that John *supplied* many things which the evangelists omitted. If he supplied conversations and ideas omitted by Matthew, Mark, and Luke, then arises this question:

What was the principle whereby St. John acquired such information?

Saint Jerome states in the preface to John's Gospel, that when he (John) was earnestly requested by the brethren to write the Gospel, he answered that "he would do so." Remember this was sixty-three years after the occurrence of the events and conversations to be written! But what were the conditions? They were these:—"After ordering a common fast, they put up their prayers to the Almighty." Here, then, are two primary conditions: abstaining from food, and becoming reverent in soul; which "being complied with," says Saint Jerome, "replenished with the clearest and fullest revelation coming from heaven, he burst forth in that preface, 'In the beginning was the word,'" etc. Suppose a medium, in the Nineteenth Century, no less physically and mentally prepared for manifestation, should be moved to write, "In the beginning was the Word," etc., you would perhaps say, "it is incredible." The idea I would urge, is—the unity of truth; the oneness of explanation. As progressive philosophers, we are unconcerned whether you stamp our experience "psychology," or "magnetism," or "hallucination." We can hold up to the Christian world the same explanation of all they hold to be sacred. Our experience should be conscientiously examined. Because whatever will explain *our* experience, will explain similar antecedents, and force the Bible to its true position, as a relic or history of mediumistic literature.

Are the modern effects of spiritualism superior to those of ancient days?

Yes; the superiority of our manifestations, over those of the past, can be easily traced and demonstrated. Taking modern mediumistic revelations, all in all, we find a variety of superior results. Many mediums of to-day are far better than many of ancient periods. Let me report a case: "Now when Jesus was risen the first day of the week, he appeared first" . . . . . . to one of the most talented and unimpeachable characters? No! to a person about whom nothing of wrong or evil could be said? No! . . . . . . Have ye not heard it said that the manifestations of to-day can not be *divine* because they do not come through ladies and gentlemen of an unimpeachable character, and through persons of commanding social positions? This has been asserted in the Churches. Churchmen assert that the persons selected as media are those in whom little or no confidence can be reposed. "Jane," "Bridget," "Susan," "Tom," "Dick," "Harry"—indifferent persons, about whom community can know nothing. And yet, I am now reporting a case where, when Jesus spiritually arose, he appeared first—not to one of the most unimpeachable characters—not to one of the celebrated doctors of the Church, but—only to *Mary Magdalene*, out of whom he had cast seven discords. Think of it! The Church believes that a *detachment* of the God of the Universe makes his first appearance to Mary Magdalene out of whom he had cast seven (D) evils. When this medium told what she had seen "they believed her not;" perhaps, because her character for truth was not well enough established. Jesus subsequently appeared, in another form to two on the way to Emmaus; and the Apostles believed them not. Afterward, however, he appeared unto the eleven as they sat at meat and upbraided them because they believed not the testimony of Mary and of the two on the way to Emmaus. A most extraordinary circumstance when isolated and considered by itself, but, viewed through our ample and superior experiences, it seemeth familiar as household words. If the character of our mediums reflect upon their manifestations, the same is not less true of the past.

What relation does modern spiritualism sustain to the ancient bible?

The bible stands or falls upon that *verdict* which will be eventually brought in by impartial investigators. The mythological past is to be tested by the experience and intelligence of the present. I affirm the unadulterated spiritual origin of forty per cent. of all our experience. The bible is good as a history of spiritualities—is valuable as a history of hallucinations—just as our experiences may determine. It is no benefit to a Harmonial Philosopher that the Bible teaches spiritualism.

But to the world it may be important, that the psychological department of our experience turns out to be spiritual, so that the Bible may be retained in confidence as a truthful historical relic. It is of great importance to the Churches, and not to us, as to the explanation of our experiences.

Should spiritualists endeavor to persuade the people that spiritualism is Scriptural?

No; it is of little advantage to spiritualists to *Christianize* their experience. It is important to churchmen to know that Daniel, who had a vision (see ch. x.) ate no pleasant bread for three whole weeks; drank no tea, no coffee; smoked no cigars; chewed no tobacco; ate no pork or beef-steaks; but devoted himself body and soul, for three whole weeks, in order to receive a manifestation! How many plethoric persons are there who would go without food three days to get a manifestation? Full of pork and potatoes, full of corruption and excess, they stand up — maintaining commanding positions in the pulpit or through the press — and sneer at the experience of him who is willing to forego all luxuries for spiritual insight. If they would but try the methods adopted by John or by Daniel, they would soon discover that spiritualism is a truth to be strengthened by scientific investigation. No! There is no positive advantage to accrue from Christianizing spiritualism. The Universalist, once the most liberal, is now anxious to avoid the name "infidel." We have *Christian* Universalists, *Christian* Unitarians, *Christian* Wakemanites, *Christian* Shakers, *Christian* Spiritualists. Does the spiritualist need *the past* to endorse him? Far from it. The worst disadvantages would result from the adoption of spiritualism by the churches. Let churches discover that it is their safest policy to invite you in, in order to preach their spiritualism to you; then accept, and you will become incrustated amid the consolidations of time-serving institutions. In fifty short years our spiritualism would have a sectarian encasement. Forbid it, O Genius of Progression! Spiritualists! stand positive; do not go backward. Go up into the resplendent Temple of Father-God and Mother Nature; stand ye firmly there; and into yourselves welcome the spiritual testimony.

"And they that tell us of these glorious things—
The blessed visitants from happier spheres,
Whose presence felt from gently-wafting wings,
Is known more often in these later years—
How shall we thank these shining angel-hosts
For all their loving patience shown to us?
How bless these wanderers from the heavenly coasts
Who journey here to love and labor thus?

"For they unseal the eyes that long have been
Shut out from Truth by what the Preacher saith,
And are proclaiming to the sons of men
That God is Love and that *there is no death!*
May we not join them in their choral song,
That swells an anthem through the fields of space
To spheres beyond, where, radiant and strong,
Is felt the glory from the Father's face?

"Oh God! we thank THEE, that the time has come
To melt the shadow of this vast eclipse.
It rolls away—and lo! from those long dumb,
Hosannahs rise, and praise is on their lips!
The purple morning breaketh—grand and sweet.
It brings a day the Earth may not forget.
Its airy streamers flow before the feet
Of that glad sun which rises not to set!"*

People complain of deceiving spirits; can you explain why spirits deceive?

In addition to ample explanations to be found in preceding volumes, I will reply through a suggestive incident.

While residing in the city of Hartford, there called upon me a lady, a member of a church, but who, unexpectedly to herself, became a medium for impressions. These impressions were (to her own mind) clear, definite, and every way satisfactory. From word to word she wrote on, with great assurance, and always with a praise to God on her tongue. She was devotional; and believed the Bible to be an emanation from the Divine. Therefore, on the doctrine that like cleaves to like—that Spirits in the other world seek their counterpart here—she should have attracted a Bible believer—or, persons entertaining sentiments identical with hers. Did such spirits visit her? Let us see. There was a beautiful radiance all over her countenance; it was a deep, settled, and almost frightful

* These excellent words are taken from a poem written by Franklin L. Burr, of Hartford, Conn.

excess of enthusiasm. I have often seen such expression. It is the sure sign of the lack of true investigation.

Immediately on entering the hall, she said: "Mr. Davis, I understand that you have impressions from the spiritual world. Did you ever hear of any person getting a communication from God?" "Certainly," I replied. Then I brought to mind the whole Bible history — the historical development of religion — — which is ever good to contemplate.

"Do you ever get anything from God yourself?" "Certainly," I replied; "I communicate with him every time I breathe. In fact, I have never supposed — since I have had any reasonable consciousness — that I could exist without a Divine emanation. Therefore I live and move and exist in him." "No, No," exclaimed she, "I mean, did you ever receive into your mind words directly from God?" "Never," I answered. "Well, I have a communication; and it is signed 'God.'"

She took out her communication and read it. It was very sensible indeed; and it was of importance in her view. Its purport was, that the Bible was written by chosen penmen, imparting truths deeper than those penmen supposed, in order to meet the mental wants of the century in which it was written, and those of all the succeeding centuries — up to the very middle of the nineteenth; but the race had, by a natural operation (which was not described) suddenly *outgrown the whole letter*, and much of the spirit, of the Bible; yet the Lord wished to preserve the book from annihilation. He said science had outstripped it; and philosophy had seen beyond it. He had appointed her (the medium) to come to me and say, that from the high throne of Heaven he had chosen me out of all the inhabitants of the earth to re-write the Bible, and adapt it to the wants of the nineteenth century — and for two thousand years to come. He gave many reasons why I was qualified especially to take hold of the translation, and go on with it. Well: I considered a few moments. The communication was signed "God," and she believed it. I resolve to run the risk of shocking all her religious prejudices at once — for I sometimes discover, as the surgeon does, that amputation *is better* than any temporizing palliative methods — in order to save the whole body from corruption. So, I thought, I would amputate even our friendship, perhaps; for a *principle* is higher to me than friendship. Therefore I told her the next time she got in communication with god to tell him that, in my conscience, I believed that there were already too many Bibles for the world's good; that any more would be adding insult to injury; and, lastly, that I was too much engaged in other matters to undertake any such commission.

She was shocked, of course. Her enthusiasm was changed into a sort of abhorrence of the blasphemy of a man in whom she expected to find instantaneous approbation, and a cheerful acceptance of the distinguished office. She said, demurely, that she would comply with my request.

In ten days she returned. She had given my message to god. "Well; what did he say?" I asked. "Why, he said that he was not the God of the universe, and never pretended to be." She then opened a spiritual correspondence with the apocraphal "god." I asked: "Why do you sign your name 'God'?" "Because," he replied, "I am all the god this *my charge* can comprehend." "Do you take this method to *deceive* her?" "No," he exclaimed. "Why, then, did you give her that message?" "Because," he answered, "I saw no other way to bring her to visit with you — to bring about the conversation that has passed between you — and the results to grow out of it." "Do you mean that you are a very high and illustrious Spirit, and a God over many?" "Not at all; I am only a god in the sense of administering to the needs of my charge, helping her into a new dispensation. I am her guardian angel — I do not believe in her doctrines — I wish to convert her from them — I have not been deceiving — I gave her that message to secure your conversation — to turn her mind into new channels." "Do you mean to go on with her now?" I asked. "Yes; I have her confidence; and I will go on with her development."

I saw her about three months afterward. She was unfolded greater than all the churches; she was happier; was further from creed, but not less devotional. Her mind was entirely divested of the idea of great importance attaching to her, be-cause she was an agent in the hand of her guardian-god.

How does spiritualism compare with Christianity in its beneficial effect on mankind?

To give a just answer to this question I must first state the fact, that Christianity has been in the world nearly two thousand years while modern spiritual intercourse is only a little more than eight years old. Now Christianity *has never suggested a single scientific fact*—has never developed a single broad scheme for the practical relief of a suffering humanity; but, instead, the system has wielded its *entire might* in opposition to almost every new development—has slandered and denounced as "infidel" each one who has wrought, *independent of Sectarianism*, to correct abuses in high and low places—has set its power against every leading philanthropist who has labored to abolish slavery and capital punishment, to reform the misdirected voluptuary, and to introduce that *practical religion* which looks to the moral and intellectual regeneration of our race, instead of fashionable preaching and praying. The pioneers in the cause of the Slave have encountered such opposition from popular religionists as did all the first teachers of Astronomy, Geology, and Phrenology. Spiritualism, on the contrary, has already discovered to the world a multitude of the most momentous and practical truths. In the fields of science and philosophy, especially in *mental* philosophy (which is foremost with all intelligent, cultured minds) it has revealed fresh facts and demonstrated several great general principles. The sciences of magnetism, electricity, chemistry, psychology, clairvoyance, psychometry, &c., have each received valuable additional illustrations and highly suggestive principles from some of the departments of spiritualism.

Does the world refuse such new information?

Yes; such information is superciliously rejected by the devotees of sectarianism—contemptuously repudiated by the advocates of expensive churches and the defenders of a paid priesthoood.

But what shall we consider of "practical benefit to mankind?"

Whatever increases the sum of human knowledge, and

augments the joys of the human soul, is beneficial to the world.

Does spiritualism have this effect on humanity?

Yes; spiritualism, in addition to its scientific benefits, has brought to light many important religious truths, among which are the following:—

1. It proves that man is an organized substantial spirit;
2. It proves that his organized spirit is immortal;
3. It proves that his immortality consists of an infinite series of social, moral, and intellectual progressions;
4. It proves that all spirits advance from lower to higher degrees of existence;
5. It proves that this world is not a providentially probationary "vale of tears"—that it is not a fleeting show, for man's illusion given—but that it is the *beginning* of his eternal and more blessed career;
6. It proves that the popular doctrine of "total depravity," is false; that mankind as well as all Nature is progressive—ascending from every kind and shade of imperfection;
7. It proves that the popular doctrine of "Hell punishments," is false; that, instead, each individual is obliged, by a law of his own being, to work out either in this life or the next, his own salvation from error and all manner of sinfulness. No vicarious atonement; because punishment or pain is the legitimate and inevitable result of transgression.

These are a few of the prominent "practical benefits" of spiritualism. How unspeakably superior is *all this* to modern theology! Modern theology *can not* prove the immortality of the soul; nor can it demonstrate anything to the satisfaction of intelligent minds except this—that it originated in the East, in the darkest recesses of tradition and superstition, and that, in its present form, it has proved itself quite *incapable* of blessing and harmonizing mankind.

What is spiritualism in the estimation of some of its advocates?

Some define spiritualism to be, "the principle, the essence, the science of life." They say that "it reaches down through the various gradations of animal, vegetable, and mineral nature to the most elementary forms, and up through the various spheres of human development to the Divine Being."

Is this definition correct?

No; inasmuch as the term spiritualism is used to represent a certain state of religious development, it can not be made so all-embracing in its scope. Were it so, every subject would necessarily "arrange itself under the head of spiritualism," and every human being, of whatever belief, profession, or condition, would be a spiritualist. There are three great articles of faith, and three only, which (without forming a creed) are generally adopted by all who are willing to be considered spiritualists.

What is the first of these three articles of faith?

That man, as to his internal, is an organized spirit.

What is the second?

That after the event called physical death, his spirit, preserving its individuality, and all its endowments, goes forward and gains a higher and better state of existence.

What is the third?

That after having become acclimated, so to say, to that world, and acquainted with its customs, and with the great recent discovery that a communication can be had with remaining relatives, that spirit can come back and demonstrate its existence; dispensing not only social harmony but also occasional moral and intellectual feasts at spiritual tables.

Will the adoption of this faith prepare the mind for general reform?

Yes; spiritualism is the fourth, the grandest, the most important movement of the nineteenth century. It is breaking up the creeds and institutions of the land, and sending their former devotees out into the fields of investigation, to seek for principles of interpretation by which to understand the remarkable facts which are pressing upon the attention of mankind. At the same time there is a lack of that unity of effort, which I yearn to see in the minds of all who adopt its three principles of faith.

How can this be remedied?

Owing to the recent development of many and various progressive ideas which demand interchange of thought and free discussion, I deem it to be wisdom to adopt new and improved methods for the acquisition and impartation of knowledge. And since I believe that *true inspiration* is universal and perpetual, and confined to no particular age or personage, but received by the *representative* minds of both sexes in Science, Literature, Art, Philosophy, Spiritualism, History, and Reform; and also that the PUBLIC ROSTRUM should and will in due time supercede the private pulpit as a channel of transmitting instruction to the masses; I would therefore recommend the establishment of *free platforms* on which lectures can be given, by those inspired to do so, on everything to be thought of in the whole realm of human interest. Thus can we fraternize with the progressive and spiritualized talent of all countries, and while avoiding the dead sea of sectarianism, become instrumental in the discovery and dissemination of *all facts* both physical and spiritual, and in the promulgation of universal *truths* both terrestrial and heavenly.

QUESTIONS ON

THE EFFECTS OF UTILITARIANISM.

EVERY dispensation, like a globe, is susceptible of a thousand different interpretations. But it will serve our present purpose to adopt that classification which is confirmed by all experience. The first dispensation was the "impulsive;" with which was associated the principle of perception. The back-brain was principally developed; mostly over the eyes, and between the ears. This age of impulse and perception culminated in the Mosaic period. The second age was that of "intellect" and reflection. The superior portions of the front-brain began to be developed. The intellectual faculties observed the earth; and that man must act upon and subdue it, through instrumentalities. Coupled with this discovery, was the disposition to inhale ideas, to absorb truths, to feel out, as by instinct, the great principles governing Nature and regulating the soul. This age culminated about the time when Christianity had fairly had an exposition. Its author and primitive founder foreshadowed the age of intellect or reflection. After this there began to appear, in different parts of the world, another age, which I call "wisdom," including the rudimental manifestations of impulse, intuition, reflection, and perception. Coupled with this wisdom age was a principle which I call "utilitarianism," or the disposition to work out and embody a thought once conceived.

At last we arrive at a development of the race, called the "practical," which is the beginning of wisdom.

Do you think that history will corroborate this classification?

Yes; the history of man represents, first, the age of childhood, which is the age of Feeling; second, the age of manhood, which is the age of Thinking; third, the age of bloomed-out manhood, which is the age of Action. There are persons, at all times, in each of these stages. Some minds represent the age of "impulse" and perception; that is, they *per*ceive vastly more than they can *con*ceive. There are others who represent "intuition;" such have the power to absorb more ideas than they could, under the best of circumstances, embody. Then there are yet other minds, who represent the scientific wisdom age—the disposition to embody and put directly into practice every thought which they can conceive.

What do you mean by the wisdom age?

The first manifestation of the principle of wisdom, IS USE; the second, is Justice; the third, Power; the fourth, Beauty; the fifth, Aspiration; the sixth, Harmony. The race has taken the first step upon the threshold of the great temple of Wisdom. Use is the doctrine of the Nineteenth Century. It will not be long in coming to great perfection in Anglo-Saxon achievements. Utilitarianism is in the ascendant; it is the principle supreme; the Gospel, of all in all, to the world at present. Men do not ask, in these days, what relation is there between "prophet" and "seer"—but, tell us of the mystic relation between "Profit" and "Loss." The question once was: "What shall we do to be saved?"—now: "What shall we do to make it pay?" The nativity of the god of the Nineteeth Century can be traced, far back through multitudinous genealogies, to the threshold of the furnace of Aaron. The "Golden Calf," manufactured by that skilful mechanic, is our god. Yet this is not depravity; it gives us no cause for discouragement.

What is the effect of this utilitarian principle?

The first manifestation of the principle of wisdom, is Use. Through this principle, it is coming to be seen, that physical improvement, that organizational reform, lies at the very foundation of all spiritual progression. Men must be physically well situated, physically developed, physically prepared, before they can have an influx of the high, the beautiful, and the good. Use hath its every eye fixed upon that which is external, fundamental, elemental. Spiritualism has come, as a kind of side inspiration, to augment mechanical constructions; to improve man's physical circumstances; to give men leisure for spiritual growth. The gospel of Use is the doctrine of weighing, measuring, gauging. It is a development which will come, eventually, to every man; telling him whether he is a disciple of the past, of the present, or of the future; telling him that he has been weighed in the balance; telling him that his ideas have been gauged; telling him that his place in the universe has already been described. Scientific suggestions will be made as to how man shall dispose of his ideas and occupations. Utilitarianism will see what are the useful, the beautiful, the beneficial. The doctrine of Use will work directly into the vitals of the church; into the vitals of all other departments of human life; into the State; into the family; into those relations which constitute "Home." No department can shut itself against the onward march of this principle of investigation.

What is the most prominent feature on the face of this century?

If you think of Christendom, I reply—Utility. There never was a century so utilitarian. USE is the sovereign of men and nations. There is now no safety in anything which is not absolutely, and supposed to be immediately, practical. People have no time to lose; the cars are just ready to start. Every one is contriving to accomplish a vast deal in little time and less space. Use and economy walk hand in hand. The fine arts are considerably neglected.

"Now sawmills grate in every forest nook,
Now spindles hum beside each mountain brook;
Through virgin forests locomotives wail,
And prairie flowers are crushed beneath the rail;
Where ocean rolled, so trackless once and free,
The age of prose stalks forth and maps the sea;
And the swift lightning—once celestial fire—
Does drudgery in harness—on a wire;
While patents fill the air, bestride the wave,
And dog us from the cradle to the grave.

Machines that rock asleep our infant cry,
Machines that wait upon our latest sigh;
We waft by telegraph our love's young dream,
Live by machinery, and die by steam."

But poetry is altogether too impracticable. The Promethean fire is worthless, to be set aside as a luxury, unless it can be made to warm dwellings and feed the igneous stomach of an ocean-steamer. Some semi-believers think the golden floor of heaven should be mined out, and wrought into eagles endowed with wings, to keep up the spirit and balance of commerce. Several oriental ideas—of the lake burning with fire and brimstone—are repudiated; as being altogether too expensive as well as impracticable. In short, the Anglo-Saxon wants nothing which "don't pay." He studies prices; not pictures: loves policy; not poetry: wants facts; not fancies. His friendships, and his marriage even, are measured by profit and loss. His standard is compounded of money, history, fashion, selfishness. He is anxious to possess a large share of business gratitude and of business friendship; but any gratitude or any friendship outside of business relations, is wholly useless—"It don't pay"—it is too poetic and sentimental.

Is not such utilitarian selfishness deplorable?

Yes; it is a great grief that the money-grasping propensities of the Anglo-Saxon should so hold in check the growth of his his higher nature; counting the emotions of his inward spirit as merchandise, to be used as business (and only as business) demands their combined exercise. The motto of the age is—"Go ahead." "It don't pay" to linger in the rear; to be outdone by your neighbor. If you manufacture any useful commodity, let no man excel you; not even do as well; for your customers will leave you and seek the other whose goods are preferable.

What is the immediate consequence?

The consequence is, the selfish, isolated competition of the age is unparalleled. There is an individual race for Success! The most useful, the most economical, the most saleable article, is *the thing* which all Christendom is striving to obtain, by individual effort; and all advantages surround him who has "the means" to his order. There is a wish to invent a "perpetual motion" which shall be self-feeding, self-regulating, generous-hearted enough to furnish itself with all requisite motive power, and to perform the extra work men may desire. But inasmuch as the universe is as yet the only perpetual motion, and the only one possible to exist, I think nearly all dreaming and toil on this scheme will prove unprofitable. And yet every effort at invention is useful, because:—

"This is true — that you can never
Seek to know, and fail in finding;
Seek an End, and it will ever
Grow *more* near, and be *less* blinding."

But will there no good come out of utilitarianism ?

Yes; because, although it is true that the utilitarian tendency of the age leads unfortunately to the degradation, temporarily, of many of the best impulses of our common nature, yet will there surely grow of it a class of circumstances exceedingly beneficial to the lower and middle portions of society.

Can you explain how such "good" will come ?

I will try. The motto of all go-a-head-men is — "Multum in parvo" — or, much in little. The law is, *use* with *economy*. With such an impulse, and with such a law, I think it is not difficult to anticipate a variety of permanent blessings. For instance: the energetic men of this century, having assumed great and numerous mercantile responsibilities, requiring constant vigilance and extraordinary despatch, must have recourse to more economical systems of spelling and writing the English language. It costs too much time to learn at school the system now so popular; it takes too much labor to write a long explanatory business letter under the present plan. Consequently, "it don't pay." This is a sufficient discovery! The next step, therefore, will be a prospective reformation in the art of spelling and writing. There will be a general orthographic, chirographic, and phonographic reform; making it far easier to communicate thought, take less time, and with greater perfection, than can be attained under the popular system.

"I have just received," says Rev. D. D. Wheedon, of Long Island, "from a friend in Cincinnati, a mysterious epistle, which may form a small text for a large discourse. It is a letter of so tiny a magnitude that the full sheet, single fold, is not larger than the envelop which enshrines it. Its weird and winding chirography looks like an Arabian spell, and its dainty dimensions might make you think it a missive from the king of the dwarfs. Yet brief as is its apparent length, and written, as it was, with a telegraphic rapidity, it really embraces as much matter as an ordinary well-filled sheet of note-paper. I read [rĕd] with the ease of fairly-written text, and feel a sort of *gratified sense of power* in the fact that the same feat of compressed performance is accomplished in written correspondence, that M'Cormick's reaper wins in the harvest, or the steam locomotive in our travel. Those cabalistic stringlets on that diamond little page, my fair friend, is Phonography; and you and Phonography ought to be better acquainted."

"Our living flocks of thought," says Henry Sutton, "need no longer trudge it slowly and wearily down the pen and along the paper, hindering each other, as they struggle through the strait gate of the old hand-writing; our troops of feelings need no more crawl, as snails crawl, to their station on the page; regiment after regiment may now trot briskly forward, to fill paragraph after paragraph; and writing, once a trouble, is now at breathing ease. Our kind and loving thoughts, warm and transparent, liquid as melted from the hot heart, shall no longer grow opaque, and freeze with a tedious dribbling from the pen, but the whole soul may now pour itself forth in a sweet shower of words. Phonotypy and Phonography will be of use in the world not dreamed of but by few. Ay, and shake your heads as ye will, they will uproot the old spelling; they will yet triumph over the absurdities of the dead age."

What shall be done to annihilate the distance between the Producer and the Consumer?

In the midst of *utilitarian* developments, I think there stands a relic of feudal times, which needs the genius of Use and Economy applied to it. Time and space, in commerce, have been comparatively destroyed by steam and lightning. The road to prosperity, or to bankruptcy, is shortened by countless business facilities. No man need spend more than *five* minutes of his valuable time to calculate the number of miles between any two cities, countries, or continents. The "Traveller's Guide" tells him the whole for a shilling, even to all the dollars and cents the journey will cost, together with the hours and minutes necessary to its accomplishment. If he can't spare the time to go, then he can command the nation to convey his letter thither; or send the fleet lightning instead, to make an apology and do the business.

Intelligence is not confined to particular localities. Telegraphic wires stretch along the principal roads, and sketch the world's news upon your breakfast-table. The locomotive's whistle may be heard from every hill. The morning paper, fed by the intelligence of the country, informs the whole family of everything incidental, literary, or commercial, which has transpired in any portion of the preceding twenty-four hours. The road to learning is not royal, yet it is difficult to remain ignorant. "It don't pay." Each and everything is "done up" with railroad speed—even to jumping the yawning chasm of a draw-bridge, shattering cars and passengers into shapeless fragments. The speed, and excitment, and feverishness, and chicanery, of mercantile and commercial avocations, are equalled by nothing *outside* the brazen gates that close upon the dungeons of perdition. Meanwhile, let us inquire:—

What progress has society made toward the abolition of the antagonisms between the interests of producers and consumers?

I have space allotted only to brief answers. The world would do well to read Charles Knight's recent "View of the Productive Forces of Modern Society, and the Results of Labor, Capital, and Skill." Working-men and working-women are the most afflicted portion of our race. They work, for the most part, under the most depressing circumstances. They live and have their being at a great disadvantage. Unless capricious Fortune seems to smile especially upon their efforts, laboring people, in the present social disorder, are most likely to be kept down in the cess-pools of *poverty*, simply by the antagonism between labor and capital. He who, by industry and personal integrity, has rescued his family from ignorance, wretchedness, and crime, deserves the gratitude of all his fel low-men; because, under the antagonistic interests of our present social construction, it is unspeakably difficult for a laboring man to earn enough to meet the current expenses of his family, and at the same time avoid debt and dishonesty. If he does this in cities, he must forego almost every species of comforting luxury, and all cultivated amusements.

What are the poor man's disadvantages?

His disadvantages are very numerous. If he be a mechanic, then there are, probably, certain months in each year when his services are not required. But his house-rent and family expenses go on just the same as when his labor is in demand. The wealthy man can pay cash for his drygoods and groceries, can purchase them at wholesale prices, which gives him the advantage. But the poor man must buy in small quantities, must pay high interest for credit, and so lives at a perpetual loss. When he goes to the market, he pays the butchers and stall-keepers 50 per cent. more than the original cost of the articles. When he goes to the grocer, he must defray the accumulated and combined profits upon, tea, sugar, soap, molasses, etc.: first, of the producer; second, of the wholesale merchant; third, of the retailer. Here is a mass of profits which the consumer must pay, and he must work hard, and live very economically, to do it. Again, when he wants muslin, cloth, and calico, for his family, he must pay sufficient, *over and above* the actual cost and value of these fabrics originally, to support the manufacturer, the various second-handers and wholesale go-betweens, and lastly, the merchant of whom the goods are purchased. Now this is all wrong; it don't pay. The laboring-classes—who produce all the wealth there is in the country—are the constant and only real sufferers under this system.

What is a prominent injustice of this system?

While the manufacturer, the wholesale merchant, and the flourishing retailer, can live in fifty-thousand-dollar houses, environed with all the comforts and privileges thereof, the poor, hard-working man and woman, with a large family of children to feed, and clothe, and educate, are compelled to occupy un comfortable rooms (for which they pay a high rent), and toil perpetually on, ofttimes without the least glimmering of a hope that their circumstances will ever improve. Again we ask—

What shall be done to annihilate the distance between Labor and Capital—between Producer and Consumer?

I might give you *my* reply to this question; but you should find the true answer by reflection. All the multitudinous complications of the mercantile world must be supported. Between the Producer and the Consumer there now exist, in all kinds of industry, numerous intermediates. These produce nothing. They add nothing valuable to the world. They serve as speculating go-betweens. But they must all be fed, clothed, and enriched; and the laboring-classes must do it all. These must support all non-producers. But how? By direct taxation? No. How otherwise? In this way: Producers support non-producers by paying higher prices for everything they purchase, and by paying rents to landlords, who out of it pay the taxes. This popular speculating, this fashionable subsisting upon the labor of the servants of Poverty, is becoming well-nigh intolerable. The homage that Capital requires of Labor is beginning to be insupportable and detestable. Industrial communities are seeking the remedy. Some efficient plan must soon be instituted to relieve the poor man from his manifold oppressive disadvantages—to give him a fair and equal chance to enjoy his existence—to emancipate him from the mountainous interests and antagonisms that now oppress and keep him in bondage to Poverty—or, we shall experience rebellions, and turmoils, and revolutions, in our social and judicial departments, which neither riches nor eloquence can prevent or allay?

Is American Slavery sanctioned by the American Priesthood?

Yes; there is a cotton-thread, extending from Maine to Louisiana, which, being more profoundly revered than the principle of Justice, is allowed to hold together the United States and the United Churches. Among Churches I know of some glorious exceptions. In business the agitation of the Slavery question "don't pay;" so the Churches furnish a "Thus saith the Lord" in favor of the institution. Hundreds of laymen have most nobly withdrawn from the Churches solely on this account. And now, when the clergy begin to make the discovery that such seceding from sectarianism "don't pay"—that it sets a bad example to godless persons who have never joined it—they begin very complacently to preach its "ultimate extinction," that Slavery will finally die out, and say "the genius of Christianity does not warrant its perpetuation." And so it is, in this as in everything else, the human mind—the people—*outgrow* certain discords and errors, and *first* remonstrate against them from the rostrum and the press, and make new discoveries, labor to spread comfort and civilization around, and, by persistent inquiry and invincible energy, finally succeed in converting an ignorant priesthood to the measures of practical reform.

Do you mean to affirm that the Priesthood is intentionally utilitarian in its opposition?

Yes; printing, for example, the chief agent and angel of civilization, was opposed. Why? Because it would enlighten the people on ecclesiastical matters. This would interfere with the *monopoly* of the priesthood. The people, who, they say, have no rights, would begin to discuss the merits of the so-called infallible dogmas. So the glorious art of Printing was once denounced as an invention of the devil. But these blessings are now enjoyed equally by saint and sinner; in spite of all bigotry and venerable superstition. The present race of clergymen would laugh, should it be seriously urged that printing and the sciences were projections from the devil. But they are far from being healed of the old malady. In our very midst, they raise the cry of "Infidelity and demonism," at every fresh revealment. Every new revelation is from the devil. Why? Because "it don't pay;" and, merchant-like, they repel it. But, thank God! there are always outcasts and anathematized persons who will entertain the "stranger"—the new-comer—and when the *new thing* proves itself to be an angel, and becomes popular and pays well, then the Churc' throws wide open its doors, invites it to a cushioned seat in the synagogue, and proclaims it "ours"—a blessing "brought by Christianity"—while, in truth, the blessing came of human progress, forcing its way through every species of ignorance and aristocratic bigotry.

Does utilitarianism look into prisons and criminals ?

Yes; the people, especially those who have thought on the subject, begin to discover this important fact—that prisons and capital punishments are exceedingly defective methods of defending the morals and protecting the interests of society. This is a business age. Everything must be looked at and judged by the mercantile standard of "profit and loss." And there are things which do, and things which do not, pay. Among others, it is beginning to be seen that the money which is now expended to arrest, to condemn, to imprison, and to punish, *a single criminal*, is sufficient, when judiciously and at the right time appropriated, to educate twenty poor children, and to place them in circumstances above the sphere of temptation to crime. It will "cost" far less to save fifty human beings from crime than it now costs to punish ten without improving them. But let me ask:—

Does the Church propose any reformation in this direction ?

Not at all. It will oppose the measure until opposition no longer pays. When the people announce their determination to carry through this reform—then, as they always have, the sponsors of theology will jump upon the platform, and exclaim, "*Oh, we always thought so!*"

Will you specify some of the material improvements of utilitarianism ?

Yes; the first material improvement, which I have carefully contemplated, will pertain to the atmosphere. Several mediums have foreshadowed this fact. Through the semi-satisfactory developments of John M. Spear, of Boston, men have heard of "electricizers" and "magnetizers"—names of a class of sentimental and semi-practical spirits, anxious to bring about physical improvements, as stepping-stones to mankind's spiritual advancement. Atmospheric improvements will come within the area and dominion of man's inventions. A harmonious relation between the planet and the sun will not accomplish it. Climatological reforms will be brought about by human investigations and systematic industry. The investigations of Humboldt, and those of Lieutenant Maury, are helps, whereby many shipmasters have been enabled to navigate the sea with unusual safety. Certain currents of wind may be anticipated. These researches show that the atmosphere is regulated by *certain fixed laws*, which, when understood, come within man's immediate use. Meriam, on the heights of Brooklyn, is calculating the circles of cold and heat. He is showing that the changes of the atmosphere may be calculated, as eclipses are; and mapped out, as men put down the weeks and months of the year. The different aerial phenomena are to be classified under fixed Laws. Through the instrumentality of machinery, man will control aerial currents, and produce that state of climate and temperature which will augment the soil's productiveness. By arrangements of electricity and magnetism, he may prevent extreme heat or cold; also, drouths and disastrous storms. Man's power is limited by nothing save infinity and omnipotence. If man can comprehend the laws of the atmosphere, his knowledge foreshadows the ability to control their phenomena. Laws which govern the propagation and existence of human beings, once enveloped in mystery, are now within man's control. Having ascertained these laws, the children of men will soon improve before as well as after birth, and will feel themselves one day but "little lower than the angels."

Will the principle of Use bring agricultural improvements?

Yes; progress in agriculture will come upon the world. But too many agriculturists, like men in the churches, have worn the thinking-caps of their forefathers. However, as such minds increase in spiritual knowledge, there will be agricultural improvements. Farmers will be able to double, treble, and quadruple the crops of their fields; and, by machinery, to store up every season two or three times the quantity they now do, and with much less trouble to either head or hand. Just in proportion as population increases the demand for food, so will there be an increase of machinery to do the labor of the hands: giving the head leisure to make more progress in spiritual and higher departments. The Anglo-Saxon is certain to make his head save his hands; he will combine both, to save the heart. The expansion and distribution of benefits, growing out of agricultural reforms, will be commensurate with the increase of population. At the present rate of increase, without the discount of war and epidemics, there will be nearly a hundred millions of people in the United States fifty years hence, and possibly eleven millions of slaves! Therefore, in the year 1900 there will be a greater demand upon the soil and sea. But I think that improvements in agriculture will be numerous and absolute: and all people will surely have an abundance. Although there will then be three times the present number of individuals, yet methinks each will have more leisure to improve, and hold intercourse with the spiritual.

What effect will such farm-work exert upon the merchant?

Machinery will increase the value of farms so much, and the use of magnetism in combination with electricity will so beautify and multiply the crops, that farming will be considered more popular and profitable than storekeeping. Men of youth and means will associate and form vast farming and industrial monopolies. And were it not for the distribution of property, the result of our limitation laws, we should have the old feudal system temporarily established in the United States. Little, selfish farmers, unable to compete, would be swallowed by the great ones; farming associations would multiply, and become popular; but the results would be every way beneficial to mechanics and the skilful professions. Such improvements will exert an effect upon the inhabitants of cities; to draw them out into the far-off countries. People now rushing from the country to the city will then be drawn back into farming districts; and cities, as now existing, shall be changed. There will be more Brotherhood—better opportunities for enjoyment—such as now exist upon Mars, Jupiter, and Saturn.

Will there be still greater utilitarian improvements in factories?

Yes; in the year 1808, the first piece of broadcloth was made in the United States, by Arthur Scofield.* He was from

* The following advertisement appeared in the Pittsfield "Sun," November 2, 1800:—

"Arthur Scofield respectfully informs the inhabitants of Pittsfield and vicinity that he has a Carding-Machine, half a mile west of the meeting-house, where they may have their wool carded into rolls for 12½ cts. per pound; mixed, 15½ cts. per pound. If they find the grease, and pick and grease it, it will be 10

Berkshire, Massachusetts. He presented, I think, his first piece of broadcloth to James Madison, who was the first President inaugurated in American broadcloth. That was just forty seven years ago. Since that time, observe the increase of woollen-factories. What a superabundance of improvements! Do you not behold reasons to believe that improvements will be no less active, sure, and progressive, in other departments? From the time that Samuel Slater introduced the system of carding into this country, to the present, there has been a race of inventions and steady progression. This increase is in itself a vast and surprising manifestation. There are men lying upon their backs, keeping vigils all the night long—between sleeping and waking—inventing a new factory-wheel, altering the spinning-jenny, by which human heads may save human hands, and do in a day the work which before required scores of men and women. At a glance, you perceive the increase of this labor-saving machinery will work no injury to the human race. It is the natural result of utilitarianism. Machines will furnish you with clothing; will labor, and lay at your feet all you need; will prepare your food; and, sometimes, they may do your eating.

Will there be any improvement in materials for garments?

Yes; flax and the cotton-plant already furnish much. But there are other herbs, in the forests of North America, which, when cultivated by machines invented for the purpose, will render considerable slave-work unprofitable. These plants of North America—to be found in Pennsylvania and in the State of Maine—will be cultivated to some extent, and men will be using new materials for garments. Great trees will be wrought up into beautiful fabrics! Scientific discovery is on the increase; she will invoke all Nature. Everything of which she asks a question gives back a satisfactory reply. She will ask herbs, and grass, and trees, "Can you not give us raiment?" and she will receive an answer, and human society will also find a response in clothing equal to anything now pro-

cts. per pound, and 12½ for mixed. They are requested to send their wool in sheets, as it will serve to bind up the rolls when done. Also, a small assortment of woollens for sale. Pittsfield, Nov. 2, 1800."

cured from the sheep's back, or from the cotton-fields of the South. For Science is the doctrine of Use—of Perception, Calculation, Constructiveness, and Ideality. There will be so much ease in acquiring a beautiful dress, that a poor family may, by ten days' labor, obtain clothing enough to last through a whole year.

Will utilitarianism bring a reform in the locomotive world?

Yes; there is to be great improvement in motive-forces; also a method for travelling upon dry land and through the air. There are persons mentally capable of receiving inspiration upon this subject from the Spiritual world. Such inspiration will bring *a new motive force;* by which talented minds may increase the speed of travel and the safety thereof. Cars may be constructed so that no accident, not even a collision, would be dangerous to either passengers or baggage. We shall have new and more commodious methods of constructing railroad-cars, as soon as the mass of working-travellers can afford to pay for luxuries. The most useful will become the most agreeable. Every person now wishes for as much as possible in little space, even if the concentration is disagreeable. But more thriftiness will bring more wealth, this more luxury, and this will widen our railroads. Instead of the present gallery-looking cars, we will have spacious Saloons, almost portable dwellings, moving with such speed, that perhaps there will be advertisements—"Through to California in four days!" These hotel-cars will be of beautiful architectural proportions, two stories high, with staterooms and saloons for converse, plays, parties, balls, and concerts. These travelling-establishments will be as wide as modern dwelling-houses, and provided with all the most desirable comforts. Railroads must first be straightened through the country, and a new motive-power introduced. In presence of these beautiful Saloons, it will be difficult to get the cows of the year 1900 to take passage upon cars which men now consider so excellent, utilitarian, and convenient.

Will utilitarianism make any discoveries in other locomotive directions?

Yes; in the almanac language, "look out about these days" for carriages and travelling-saloons on country-roads—sans horses, sans steam, sans any visible motive-power — moving with greater speed and far more safety than at present. Carriages will be moved by a strange, and beautiful, and simple admixture of aqueous and atmospheric gases — so easily condensed, so simply ignited, and so imparted by a machine somewhat resembling our engines, as to be entirely concealed and manageable between the forward wheels. These vehicles will prevent many embarrassments now experienced by persons living in thinly-populated territories. The first requisite for these land-locomotives will be good roads, upon which, with your engine, without your horses, you may travel with great rapidity. These carriages seem (to me) of uncomplicated construction. We will one day ventilate, and light, and spiritualize our dwelling-houses, by a very simple admixture of water and atmospheric gases — from which combination will also spring the new motive-power under present anticipation.

What progress will men make in atmospheric navigation?

I find only one thing necessary in order to have aerial navigation, viz.: the application of this contemplated superior motive-power, which is even now in process of discovery and elimination. Deeply impressed am I that the necessary mechanism — to transcend the adverse currents of air, so that we may sail as easily, and safely, and pleasantly, as birds — is dependent upon a new motive-power. This power will come. It will not only move the locomotive on the rail, and the carriage on the country-road, but the *aerial cars* also, which will move through the sky from country to country; and their beautiful influence will produce a universal brotherhood of acquaintance. Nations await only this: to become closely and intimately fraternized. Persons once estranged, when brought in contact, face to face, feel the throbbings of a new friendship — or an old pure one awakened — which has in itself blessings and promises of brotherhood. Apply this fragment of morality to the influence which aerial navigation will exert upon the world, and you will at once see how vast must be the national benefits growing out of such familiarity. There are many inventive spirits who, acting upon the willing faculties of John M. Spear, gave the world to understand that a new motive-power was possible.

Any impartial and intelligent person, who will investigate the lectures which preceded and gave rise to the mechanism at High Rock Tower, will be at once surprised at the profundity of the suggestions, and chagrined not less at the inconsistency of the metallic application. There was the obvious mixture of the divine with the human. Divine principles can scarcely descend into the strictly human sphere without misapprehension. Deep and thorough scientific knowledge, spiritually derived, was dissipated by the human instruments. The received theory was *unique*, although based upon the human structure: the absorption of electricity from the atmosphere, and the incorporation of that subtle element, by the polar organization of a metallic Idol. Inventive Spirits had their minds earnestly at work to develop a new motive-force; and the principles divulged, although so sadly misapplied in the first experiment, foreshadowed the great era of utilitarian discovery.

What effect will the farming associations exert upon producer and consumer?

These combinations will make a vast alteration in our mercantile arrangement, so that the difference now existing between producer and consumer will be well-nigh annihilated. There is, I repeat, altogether too great distance between them, too many go-betweens, and too much expensive clerical manipulation. There will be agricultural and industrial combinations. They will have large common storehouses for certain wards. The fraternal principle will come into action; and harmony will be the manifestation of utilitarianism. We shall have fraternal combinations in villages and cities. These will remove the unnecessary expenses now incurred by poor families: giving them more leisure for the development of spiritual faculties, and for the enjoyment of spiritual joys.

Will utilitarianism do something to harmonize manual labor and machinery?

Yes; this is another thing in the Structure of Society which needs attention and improvement—the conflict between poor men and labor-saving inventions. It don't pay the laboring-man to see a few bars of iron and shafts of steel, moved by unconscious steam, doing more and better work in one day than he can do in twenty! All our manufacturers must resort to Machinery. This is right, and I glory in every new invention. But I think a change is necessary—so that every new labor-saving invention shall not fall into the hands of Manufacturers, and every laboring-man be driven into new fields for subsistence, in absolute competition with Machinery. As Society is now constructed, there is no harmony between the poor classes and labor-saving Machinery. This fact will lead hereafter to great changes. While the conflict continues between human beings and the invention of machines for the manufacturing of certain kinds of goods—while there continues an antagonism between Labor and Capital—so long will the preaching of "peace and good-will on earth" be measurably useless. To love the neighbor, under present arrangements, don't pay. To be a *practical Christian* is to be unpopular. An honest man must leave the business-world, in some departments, or the business-world will leave him. In the present Structure of Society, in the midst of selfishness, it is absurd to expect a manifestation of true religion. Loving your neighbor as you love yourself is now little else but a sacred poem—so revered, that we pay gentlemen to preach it—but "it don't pay" to attempt to live to its requirements. Not long since a man was being tried, on the charge of insanity, in the city of Hartford. When he was asked to make his own statement, he began by saying that "he was a follower of Jesus Christ." He went on with the rest of his story very rationally; and it was afterward remarked that everything he said was sane, *except his introduction.*

Can we expect good to result from a well-defined Social Science?

Yes; Social Science will exert that effect between consumer and producer which the inventions of Electrical Science have already had between cities and continents—namely, the destruction of distance, estrangement, and isolation. Telegraphing is so complete in its operations, that the yesterday's news of a whole nation may be heralded to your fireside. So, too, the benefits of farms and countries will be brought to you scarcely without a thought of expense. We shall have somewhat to fear from Excess of Luxury. Years hence, look back to this hour, contemplate those who are now called popular, and you will see that a man is measured by the length of his purse! One day, however, material wealth will not be fashionable; but, instead, he will be most popular who is fraternal and harmonious. The tendency of the utilitarian element is, to teach man's perceptive faculties the *use* of implements and instruments, the use of tools: by which all material departments of Nature and Society are to be subdued, and brought into systematic harmony with man's immediate spiritual advancement. The head is working to save the hands: and both to save the heart. The consequence will be — harmony of hands, head, and heart, with the Spiritual World. Let men put confidence in this doctrine of invention, of progress in the material world, as the first and lowest necessity. Look through the United States, and see *shafts* of inspiring light let down into minds, dwelling in obscure places! The world can not know of the results just now. Unconsciously there are persons absorbing light from the Spiritual World. These may invent a machine for reaping, for sowing, for harvesting, and for thrashing, the grains; they may perceive improvements for the advancement of commerce; or, may see a new method for the lighting, heating, ventilating, and spiritualizing, human habitations! Never was there a period when all the faculties circumjacent to the front and superior brains were in such a state of utilitarian activity and corresponding inspiration. The eventual result will be — leisure throughout America, and the development of those intuitive faculties in man which are now supposed to be merely possibilities.

Do you see any improvements in human habitations?

Yes; the ideas of the Middle Ages, and those of the Nineteenth Century, are to be united in our architecture. Dwelling-houses of the future will be built in reference to the symmetrical development of their inmates. It is not Utopian to expect this. Men will find that the cottage, the palace, the castle, and several of the intermediate styles, will one day be accumulated into the Humanitarian Edifices. These magnificent edifices will cost far less than so many independent, selfish homes. One of these edificial hotels will cost no more than a modern dwelling, while it will be incomparably more beautiful, and not less calculated to improve both the physical character and the spiritual faculties. Personal character is benefited, or impaired temporarily, according to the *shape* of its accustomed habitation. Place a strong-minded man in a perfectly circular room, where the eye can fix itself upon not a single angle, and two weeks will be sufficient time to produce the madness of insanity. The first effect would be a sort of agonized bewilderment, which would quickly superinduce a savage aberration. Pause, then, and meditate upon the marvellous psychological influence of external structures.

Do you expect other utilitarian improvements to precede these reform habitations?

Yes; subsequent to the improvements of controlling air and culturing soil, it will be more easy to build a brace of these combined unitary Edifices, for sixty families, than three of the fashionable domicils of country-towns and cities. It will be a great proud beauty to have such establishments heated and lighted by an admixture of aqueous and atmospheric gases—the same utilitarian admixture which will produce the *motive power* of land-carriages, railroad vehicles, and aerial ships. How beautiful to have such concentration! Men will unite in fraternal embrace and build temples of harmony upon which their children can ascend to physical strength and spiritual contemplation. No, it is no dream! I do not describe the millennium! All this is no more wonderful than improvements in cotton and woollen factories since the year 1808. In the representations of the Future will be represented the structural arrangements and architectural analogies furnished by the body and soul—a sort of correspondential edificialism, so to speak, cellar-rooms, nutritive departments, social saloons, educational cabinets, spiritual recesses, harmonious dormitories, and pavilions for contemplation, each in correspondence with intestines, with digestion functions, with affectional departments, with perceptive organs, with spiritual functions, and with the intellectual faculties—each and all parts of an Edifice being represented in the physical and mental organization of a human being.

Will the building materials of the future differ from those in present use?

Yes; we will not go as at present into forests to find the

best materials. Humanitarian habitations will be constructed of a lithologic composition which may be readily manufactured. And men will perceive new uses for gutta-percha in combination with iron and artificial marble. Such materials will be employed for portable dwellings. For example: here are two persons to be married this very night, upon the best principles of conjugal harmony. To-morrow morning they will visit places where portable houses may be ordered; they look over the architectural fashions; they issue an order for a house to be built in the country: everything to be ready for housekeeping, furniture and all arranged, in two weeks from date! Remember the first manifestation of the principle of wisdom, in Use. Use condenses and harmonizes, so that, ultimately, the fortunes and misfortunes of modern selfish house-building will be no more. Most easy will it be to have a home! Mankind may one day see that a habitation, composed of artificial lithologic materials, will shelter but a small part of that which in reality constitutes "a home." Because the true home is composed of, and is dependent upon, the existence and the continuation of a most blessed harmonial marriage. Having "one to love and one to love us" is a haven far better than a house composed of gutta-percha, iron, or any artificial substance.

May we expect a more utilitarian method of acquiring knowledge?

Yes; we are not always to have this tedious method of learning to spell and write the English language; this external system of imparting and enforcing the shadows of ideas. Many constitutions are "ruined" by the different irksome and unnatural methods of imparting what is called an *education*. If the United States Constitution had not been stronger than that of many Yankee children now born, it would have been "ruined" the first two weeks by the tyrannical plan of its ecclesiastical and political schooling. Improvements in education will be so great that between the ninth and twelfth year—the ninth being the true time for children to commence—young minds will obtain more knowledge than they now acquire with much trouble between the ninth and twentieth. Yes; there will be a beautiful reform in the whole present barbarous system of thinking and acquiring thoughts. We have a Harmonial Philosophy to teach: that *ideas* are not to be put into the mind, but elicited; that *the divine character* is to be progressively carved out of that which we find constitutionally within the unfolding child. Wisdom is not to be superinduced, but developed; and the educational systems of the humanitarian Future will have this object to accomplish. Improvement must begin in our alphabet; next in our orthography; then in our chirography; then in our phraseology; and lastly, in some parts of our theology. Phonography has discovered how many elemental sounds there are, and has made an appropriation of a letter to every such sound. This utilitarian plan will lead to easy spelling; to the most spontaneous and inevitable spelling; and, finally, also to the most natural scheme of penmanship. All this will be easier and better and every way more harmonious—entirely abolishing the present discordant system of fretting and storming, which is the usual concomitant of the little arbitrary learning men acquire between babyhood and their twentieth year.

Will you detail some of the utilitarian advantages of the phonetic system ?

Yes; there are (as given in a Synopsis by Andrew J. Graham*) eleven specific advantages:—

1. Phonetic Spelling will render reading easy. The art of reading with a phonetic orthography can be acquired in about forty hours.

2. It will render spelling easy.

3. It enables the student, as soon as he has learned the Phonetic Alphabet thoroughly, to spell any word with the same accuracy that he can pronounce it.

4. It enables the student, as soon as he has learned the Phonetic Alphabet thoroughly, to give any printed word the precise pronunciation of the author.

* Andrew J. Graham has recently opened a Phonetic Academy at the office of "The Working Farmer," in Fulton street, New York. This individual is a thorough and Cosmopolitan Reformer; in the phonetic department of utilitarian progress. He works sincerely for the elevation of his important science, and, so far as possible, has simplified and universalized the phonetic orthography. His exemplary devotion and industry, and his skilfulness in following the most rapid speaker as reporter, will not go unrewarded.

5. It will consequently tend to remove the present ignorance by opening a ready means for acquiring knowledge; and millions now unable to read may enjoy the benefits flowing from a knowledge of reading and writing.

6. It will render the business of reducing unwritten languages to written form, sure and easy.

7. It will be of essential service to the student of languages, in showing him the exact state of a language at a given time.

8. It will tend most effectually to the general diffusion of our language among foreigners, and may complete the numerous claims which our idiom can already advance, to be used as a universal medium of communication between nation and nation.

9. It will save much of that time, money, and labor, now lost in merely learning to read and write. The school-days of the child will be virtually lengthened by it, and the sphere of his studies enlarged; the teacher will be saved from a vast amount of drudgery, and his profession ennobled.

10. It will result in perfect uniformity of pronunciation.

11. It will save millions of dollars in the expense of books, etc., annually.*

Do you perceive any plan by which to expedite the art of writing?

Yes; I am almost moved to invent an automatic psychographer; that is, an artificial soul-writer. It may be constructed something like a piano; one brace or scale of keys to represent the elementary sounds; another and lower tier, to represent a combination; and still another, for a rapid recombination; so that a person, instead of playing a piece of music, may touch off a sermon or a poem! Every note, while discoursing sweet sounds, may catch the type and put it in its place; so that, instead of going through the inevitable mechanical drudgery of the superior short and beautiful phonetic method, ideas may be printed upon the surface of paper pre-

* "The present writer is prepared with facts by which he could verify the following position: — that if a child were taught at first on the phonetic principle, and, by graduated lessons brought up to a comprehension of the present orthography, his reading would be taught at half the time, half the trouble — and consequently half the risk of having a distaste for learning engendered by the difficulties of his first studies — involved in the present system."—[Dr. Latham.]

pared for publication. There will then be but little time necessary, and little physical labor required, for a man to tell all he knows, and more too! Men of utilitarian habits will soon have confidence in this Psychographer; it is not more surprising than daguerrotyping, or photographing, or ambrotyping. These are within the domain of utilitarian discoveries which will awaken the Psychographer.

Will all these inventions aid the spiritual development of the race?

Yes; these improvements and discoveries will refresh the soul, give it leisure and prepare it for a natural voyage to post-mundane climes. A glorious period is before mankind. It will be a kind of material heaven—a preparation for the Spiritual Harmonium. In the principles already divulged, in the progress of agricultural knowledge, in the new motive-force, in the use of implements, in all the chivalric achievements of the Nineteenth Century, you may behold foreshadowings of developments higher and better. By mere anticipation, we participate in the benefits of an improved and happier race. The Spiritual Harmonium is now enjoyed by the elder planets, Jupiter and Saturn. Their inhabitants, centuries since, passed through what we are just beginning to experience. By virtue of analogical reasoning, you may believe that everything, foretold in the past regarding man's physical and spiritual happiness, will be realized. Believe through your intuitive knowledge and radical desires. Fall in love with the new dispensation, through Wisdom. Have intelligent confidence in the advancement of the material world. Feel that every science which comes, through the industry of the human intellect, is another manifestation of eternal principles. Shafts of light are being let down upon human faculties. The material world is awake, utilitarianism is fortunately in the ascendant, and the spiritual world makes a correspondential manifestation.

Will utilitarianism act beneficially upon American government?

This question is not easily answered. American politics inevitably generate hostile parties. These parties do not attempt to disseminate the divine principles which underlie and control humanity. Political principles are drawn from the experience of Europe—from the experience of Greece and Rome—in order to establish precedents whereby to legislate for the day, the hour, and the circumstance. Political action does not spring from the souls of reasonable men and conscientious women. Once there existed "Scribes and Pharisees:" now, instead, "Whigs and Democrats." Once there were "Publicans and Sinners:" now, instead, "*Re*publicans and Know-Nothings." Here is evidence of revolution; perhaps, also, of progress. Politics have brought a quartette of parties into the world; and every one is planted upon "the best policies"—not upon that which consults the gigantic interests of universal mankind. True Religion, Justice, is never once consulted. It is a primate American doctrine to have no religion in existing politics. Hence, the elements of a time-fostered despotism and atheism are lurking in our Democracy.

Is this temporary despotism wrong?

Who will affirm that it is right? Perhaps, it can not be avoided. Perhaps, it is consistent with the progressive development of mankind, that despotism should be asserted with democracy. Can we have them separated? There seems to be a natural principle which determines that absolute freedom and absolute slavery shall abound in the same latitude. Despotism is the first governmental principle of every nation; but, by social development and spiritual progress, the race arouses and does battle for equal rights and Liberty. Thus, despotism becomes eventually *negative;* while individual freedom and national democracy become positive! The two principles, however, are asserted in the same governmental latitude. Therefore while we have the highest liberty, in the United States, we also have in them the lowest slavery. The greatest successes run parallel with the greatest reverses. The most splendid days are coupled with the darkest nights. There is no sudden way to escape this twofold action of Nature.

Do you mean to teach that the conservative principle is just as utilitarian as the progressive principle?

Yes; it was one day discovered, by scientific railroad-builders, that the troublesome law of friction is the very best friend of safety and locomotion. Friction renders motion possible. So, too, were it not for this principle of *conservatism*, we should not have that on which to adhere, over which to pass, and in consequence of which to triumph! We should not, therefore, be merely oppositional reformers. We will achieve much Freedom by virtue of the *opposition* set up by the despotic principles of Slavery.

You said that religion is divorced, in this country, from politics: what do you mean?

I mean that the natural principle of universal Justice is not to be found in our governmental departments. Pure morality in politics would be like a star, ascending higher in the firmament of Nations. The Roman Catholic Church hath a stronghold in criticising American political institutions. Political parties do not consult the constitution of man, but the constitution of the United States. Party politics have, therefore, a principle of atheism. The people of the United States, in their political arrangements, do not enough contemplate distributive Justice. The Catholic Church stands as a skeptical critic. It is supported by talented men, true to their principles. They feel called in conscience to oppose all Constitutions which do not look to a supernatural source for political and ecclesiastical arrangements. While we preach and proclaim Liberty, we practise and sustain Slavery. Unless our politics become founded in true religion — in a system which is endorsed by the Constitution of Nature — there is nothing to counteract the influence of the criticisms emanating from the Romish Church. "Your government is godless," they say; "you do not consult the spiritual." We are not enough utilitarian to consult the most high in Man, nor yet the Most High in the Spiritual Universe.

What do you consider the principal enemies to America's perpetuity?

American dangers are twofold: one is *the spirit of Slavery;* the other is *the spirit of War.* War and Slavery are advocated by the American people; the primary rocks these on which our ship is most likely to be stranded. Now we are sailing directly between them — the spirit of war or retaliation on one side, and the spirit of slavery or despotism on the other; but there are good and healthy minds in the United States who have no sympathy with either. Few persons have attained that royal, spiritual summit from which they can perceive that universal Peace is the only doctrine of safety on the one hand, and that unconditional Freedom is the only doctrine of safety on the other. Few can see this, and a less number dare to affirm it openly. We have reason to believe that the influence of the Spirit-Land will be felt by the American people; and that, by virtue of much inspiration, they will judge statutes and institutions in the light of human nature! Not the perpetuity of the American nation merely, but that of all nations, is to be considered in the light of Father-God and Mother-Nature. Better conceptions of Father-God will bring us a higher system of government. Not to advance ourselves as a selfish nation, but to give an example of strength and righteousness to all people. We are not to consider ourselves a nation of superior military strength, born to achieve triumphs, and gain laurels on the field of blood—to drive all opposing nations away, as the Red Man from his native forests. No! If we desire to perpetuate our nation, we must go on in a different spirit. These political rulers must be interiorly opened and expanded, so that they may be recipients of better and higher inspirations. There is something else in this universe to appeal to besides the utilitarian affections of merchants and commercialists. Yet the utilitarian element is furtively working good in this department; and we may begin to expect that the politics of the United States will manifest, ere long, something of the principle of universal religion. The hidden spirit of War and the open spirit of Slavery, are the two dangers which menace our nation's perpetuity. Nothing will enable us to avert these two dangers save a utilitarian principle, full of Love and Wisdom for all human kind.

What do you think of the United States ecclesiastically?

In the Church I perceive just what is most obvious in the State: the State is Godless, and the Church is Christless. We preach Jesus, and practise Moses. Men preach that the dispensation of Jesus must prevail, in order to have peace on earth and good-will among men. But almost every law, code, or institution, has in it the spirit of Moses. They are stamped with the seal of power, not with love; with force and coercion, not with the doctrine of universal Justice. Religion in the Churches is like politics in the State; and, I repeat it, one is Godless and the other is Christless. The Church is preaching love, but practising *force;* and the Government is preaching God, but practising something which strongly suggests the opposite personage! Two incompatible elements animate the American people—absolute Tyranny and absolute Freedom. Roman Catholicity represents absolute Despotism, and Harmonial Philosophy represents absolute Liberty. The first holds that institutions are god-originated; the other, that institutions spring out of a progressive humanity. Harmonial Philosophy teaches that Liberty is the common inheritance of all men; the Church, that Liberty is dangerous, except when granted as a temporary privilege. The Romish Church regards the spirit of unconditional Liberty as its strongest antagonist.

Will these opposite forces continue to agitate each other until they reach dissolution?

Yes; and then will arrive a period of utilitarian discussion and warlike collision. The spirit of force will spring fearfully out of the Church, and the spirit of resistance will start out of the people. Between these two antagonisms the American people will be involved in civil difficulties; and established Churches will experience severe paroxysms and numerous ecclesiastical convulsions. The great mass of Protestants will cling passionately to the spirit of Freedom. But a large minority, considering that ecclesiastical "authority" is safer than the doctrine of individual sovereignty and extreme radicalism, will bow before and embrace the neck of the Mother Church. Conservatives always have more fear than perception of principles, and will militate against progressive doctrines by going back into the maternal embraces of the Catholic Church. One great struggle in America will grow out of a theological question: "Whether God rules the human soul through the church, or the church through the human soul?" This question, methinks, will one day be put to all the inhabitants of America. This will be a Day of Judgment. Tyranny? or Freedom? Shall we consider ourselves wedded to a Church system? or shall we convert these Churches into Lyceums, and make them subserve the utilitarian development of the people? Utilitarianism will put these questions, and the people will be obliged to decide. The decision of one party will bring out a stupendous resistance; and the United States, having political and ecclesiastical troubles at the same time, will be strangely convulsed.

What plan would you suggest whereby to avert these national troubles?

The nation should pass directly through all this wilderness of conflict into the Promised Land. It is now only about half-past nine o'clock to the American government, and half-past eight in regard to American ecclesiastical progression. This question, I repeat, will be put to every soul: "Are you in favor of Roman Catholicity, or of Harmonial Philosophy?" In other words: "Are you a friend of the universal and unconditional control of human souls by institutions, or of the unconditional and unrestricted control of institutions by human souls?" This question will bring a day of great trial to the American people. Fearful conservatives will call to mind the fleeting republics of Greece; the little Italian democracies, also, that flashed out and bloomed for a day! Utilitarianism is full of encouragement for the American people; that, as a nation, we will bask in eternal wealth and distributed luxuries. Such encouragements, to certain temperaments, look like Utopian dreams. They remember the republics of Italy—the evanescent democracies of past times.

What do you think of the conscience of the American Church?

It is not above the conscience of the Old Testament. They preach Jesus, but endorse the enormities of Moses. Love is highest right, but force is ordinary good. The American Church believes that Liberty is good for all White nations, yet Slavery is considered the best state for the advancement of the African! Churches, therefore, have a vital difficulty—bordering rapidly upon consumption—afflicting all departments of the constitution, which interferes with the breathing, the digestion, and the spiritual locomotion, of the American people. There is not a State, in the whole system of American government, but is more or less implicated by this terrible disease, viz.: lack of God in the State, lack of Christ in the Church.

16

Yet no one can doubt but that there are conscientious men and women in the Churches. The Church's conscience is scarcely igher than the country's godless politics. Between the two we find that which every reformer should be alarmed at, namely—a systematic disease, permitting the steady encroachment of War and Slavery. Most people, therefore, believe that partial Slavery is the true way of the world. We deserve a system of religion which will not generate false ideas of man, of Father-God, and Mother-Nature. In the American Church, let it be remembered, there are Unitarians, Universalists, and Quakers, preaching a higher class of negative truths. But their influence is hemmed in, and absolutely debilitated, by the encroachments of institutional authority. Unitarians are fearful of being considered too infidel; therefore, they work themselves deeper and farther into popular ecclesiasticisms. Liberal Christians fear lest they may transcend the wisdom of the past times, and become wise above what is written. Certain Unitarian gentlemen may be seen, with white gloves and sugar-tongs, touching Slavery very gracefully, and very beautifully alluding to Intemperance. The American Church does not appeal intelligently to the topmost human faculties.

In what is the American Church most deficient?

The American Church is most defective in its doctrines concerning Man and the Divine Existence. Universalists have done much to bring in a system of natural ecclesiasticism, favorable to man, and promulgating a higher report of Deity. The principal mischief of the Church arises from its barbarous opinions. It has no complete conception of a Divine Being. Its conceptions of God are well-nigh satanic, and its ideas of man are extremely subversive. Under the influence of the American Church, a man sees himself to be worthless. The God of the American Church is not half as good as the Devil who was elaborated by Zoroaster! It is eloquently preaching whatsoever is lovely, beautiful, poetical, magnificent; but, at the same time, it is practising much which is forcible, hateful, insignificant, and opposed to the doctrines of Distributive Justice. The doctrine, "Let no one call God his Father who calls not man his brother," has been intimated in all ages of the world. I put my ear to the key-hole of human history, and can hear the beatings of the heart of Confucius, all the way across the centuries. This doctrine was first uttered by the man who rose to the summit of humanity. But listen to the American Church, and you will hear no such universal principle advocated. It is poetic, elocutionary, overflowing with symbols and magnificent pictures. But the slaves of "the peculiar institution" are not "Brethren" in the light of the American Church. Even liberal Churches are not free from this prejudice. This fact amply demonstrates that American Churchianity is not willing to endorse the doctrine of universal relationship—the doctrine, "Let no one call God his Father who calls not man his brother." It is good to preach the golden rule, but the time has not come to practise it! Utilitarian policy is paramount to principle. The conscience of the State is endorsed by the conscience of the Church. Whenever the State enacts a law, even though it be against the freedom of all African people, the Church, as a general fact, will silently endorse it.

Will utilitarianism develop a new theology?

Yes; a practical age will bring a new conception of Deity, and a new conception of man. The laws written upon man's inmost nature are more utilitarian than the ten commandments. These are the laws of Deity. Reverence for the principles of human nature is more utilitarian than adhesion to the enactments of institutions. Yes; we are on the threshold of an era when a new God is to be introduced to mankind.

What will utilitarianism demand in order to inaugurate this new God?

It will call for Teachers to protest against bad laws and speak in favor of good ones. Religion must preside over political movements. Matrimonial association, of the new State with the new Church, is to be contemplated. Harmonial political movements will be divinely influential in moulding and regulating humanity. The great thing to be expected from the religious element of utilitarianism is: a new God to regulate the world, and a new Idea of man by which humanity will be elevated and encouraged. This Harmonial religion will not contemplate creeds and organizations, but only whatsoever will serve as stepping-stones to distributive Justice. Universal Justice is the highest manifestation of religion; and morality is the practice of it. A proximate manifestation of true religion will result from the utilitarian movements of the Nineteenth Century. This harmonial dispensation of Justice will ultimately override all distinction of races, all organizations, institutions, and all that in them is; at once revealing to individual man that he embosoms a pure imperishable angel; that Father-God liveth throughout all the domains of Mother-Nature; and that the earth's inhabitants may for ever love, worship, labor, and be happy.

Will anything rescue us from plunging hopelessly into one or both of those great errors, War and Slavery?

We may be measurably rescued by extending the American utilitarian idea of politics, and unfolding and enlarging the American Conscience. The rostrum should supersede the pulpit; and teaching should supersede preaching.

Will utilitarianism influence modern spiritualists?

Yes; but their present danger is twofold: external and organal. In spiritualism we find the utilitarian tendency to externalism and organization; both of which will measurably interfere with progression. Spiritualists will experience the contact of a *Godless* system of politics on one side and a *Christless* system of religion on the other. Utilitarianism will discover that spiritualism is subserving a great development. Use points toward a reform of Church and State. Spiritual utilitarianism works for a new idea of God and a better conception of man. Mankind must rub their eyes and obtain a clear perception of their relations as men and women, as husbands and wives, as brothers and sisters, as post-mortem delegates to the spiritual world.

Does utilitarianism welcome the Spiritual Dispensation?

Yes; it is coming to be seen that it don't pay to shut one's eyes against the incoming LIGHT. The new dispensation, like a star in the cloudless horizon, already shines upon man's pathway. That star shall glow and broaden, "until it hangs divine and beautiful in the proud zenith," filled with angels' faces; the loving companions of his pilgrimage, shedding new light upon men at every turn in the path of life. The old heavens, the old earth, the old theology and its god, shall be destroyed by the light of Harmonial Truths. "For, behold," says an oriental medium, "the day cometh that shall burn as an oven — and the proud, yea, and all that do wickedly, shall be stubble." Hence theologians and politicians will find at last that it don't pay to shut their eyes against the higher law of Truth and Justice. To every faithful progressionist, to all hospitable friends of the Harmonial Dispensation, the Sun of Righteousness will arise with healing in his wings, and myriad spirits will joyfully become their fellow-workmen. Most grateful am I for the utilitarian proclivities of the age. They will help to destroy all fictions. The doctrine of "profit and loss" will eventually put each thing—in church and state, in man and society — to the test of Use and Economy. And thousands of absurdities will be abandoned: because they don't pay.

Will the doctrine of utility be applied to modern law and government?

Yes; although we have the best country in the world, with the best government, yet are we very far from that harmonial condition of reciprocal interests in which Law and Liberty will be synonymous. As a nation we need less government and more growth. Our laws should be more comprehensive and harmonial. Mankind will create laws, I think, as long as they remain *beneath* the plane of Wisdom. In fact, laws are natural and necessary to transitional stages. But, in our progressed condition, it won't pay to have Laws enforced which do not subserve the welfare of the individual as well as the whole. Our laws, as I shall hereafter show, are now against the rights of Individuals. The African race have no rights under our laws. Our laws grant but few liberties and fewer rights to women. Our laws favor the Capitalist. The legal rights of those persons are protected who have money to pay for them. Our laws seek the imprisonment, not the improvement, of the unfortunate offender. The offender is regarded as a wilful foe to society; not as a misdirected member of a common Brotherhood. Hence, our laws seek his punishment; not his development. Viewed in a utilitarian light, there is much in such laws which don't pay.

Do we entertain ideas of Liberty which don't pay?

Yes; there are many minds who imagine that individual Liberty means, or ought to mean, unrestrained license or recklessness. Whereas Liberty is a sacred Principle—a power unto salvation—a flower, blooming with an immortal beauty. At first, like everything else, it comes from the soil. It springs up in the midst of thorns and thistles. But moved forward by the powers of progression, it transcendeth all terrestrial hindrances, and towereth grandly above: spreading its branches in all directions, like the kingly oak on the mountain's summit.

Is Liberty a radical law of the human mind?

Yes; Liberty, as a radical law of mind, has struggled and labored on the tides of ages: as a ship with waves and storms. Amid the consolidations of monarchy—amid rocks and sand-bars thrown up, in the sea of human experience, by Caracalla and Tiberius, Nero, Commodus, Caligula, and the nocturnal workers of modern days—amid all, LIBERTY has marched steadily onward: with the strength of Justice and the fearlessness of Truth. Although feloniously assaulted now and then, and well nigh wrecked upon the blood-stained coasts of tyranny, yet has Liberty gained, in safety and with a glorious triumph, new and better continents: ladened with divinest blessings.

Have men never lost confidence in the idea of Liberty becoming universal?

No; the Greek democracies, the Roman Laws of suffrage, the Italian Republics of the middle ages, the efforts of different races, evolved by Liberty from the very womb of darkness and despotism itself, have conserved the high purpose of keeping man's faith alive in the potentiality and divinity of the Principle. High above the thundering uproar and clashing tumult of the semi-barbarian age, stood the natural apostles of humanity—Dante, Petrarch, Tasso, Raphael, Michael Angelo, Galileo, and others—flinging a luminous beauty o'er the tragedy of the times: foreshadowing an era of refinement, of science, of civilization, and Universal Liberty! And all the friends of humanity still press forward to that Era. The continent of real organic Freedom is still in the future: to be discovered and peopled.

When was the doctrine of human Brotherhood first proclaimed?

The ship of human Brotherhood, with all nations on board, was launched countless centuries since. At first, it was but a rude sailing vessel, illy constructed and equipped, managed by kings and tyrants, with recurring signs of mutiny and revolt; the crew against the masters; left often thus to struggle with the storms of ignorance, passion, avarice, and superstition, barely escaping the perils of utter destruction. Finally, however, in a propitious hour, this eternal ship, leaking and damaged at all points, will be drawn upon the stocks of Reason—examined, and converted by the aid of new material, into a magnificent ocean steamer, freighted with the best interests of all men, and piloted no more by priests and kings, but by the Father-God and Mother-Nature. Thus circumstanced, we will joyfully glide away, with the highest hopes and fullest confidence of all on board: believing that, in accordance with the working of immutable Laws, our ship will eventually reach the Plymouth Rock of a Harmonial United States—the haven of a new world—where Love and Light and Law and Liberty will be integral—flowing on through human affairs, musically, like the voice of many waters. O Liberty! Thou speakest, from the fountain-centres of the Universe, to the heart of universal Man. Liberty! Thou thrillest the bosom of the world. Liberty! In true souls thou kindlest a fire of boundless Love. Liberty! The ages have borne sublime witness to thy divine majesty. Liberty! There is an immortal melody in thy Thought. Liberty! Hearest thou the echo of thy voice through upper Spheres?

One effulgent day my immortal Preacher* read from his radiant altar the following notice: "This happy congregation is urgently requested to take part in a Utilitarian Convention which will commence its sessions in this consecrated Sanctuary to-morrow morning." Accordingly, at the appointed hour,

* See a chapter in the Great Harmonia, second volume, entitled, "My Preacher and his Church."

the fraternal members reverently assembled themselves together; when, unexpectedly to him, my blessed Preacher was by acclamation appointed Chairman, and the convention then peacefully proceeded to business. Any report, of the questions propounded or record of the speeches delivered, is deemed wholly unnecessary. But the honored Chairman offered a set of *fourteen* remarkable Resolutions—plenarily inspired with the very essence of Utilitarian reform—which I submit as being worthy the reader's consideration.

What was the first Resolution?

First: Resolved, That it is the constitutional prerogative of the Human Mind freely and fearlessly and dispassionately to examine into and investigate each and everything to be formed in the Bible as well as out of it; that the Old and New Testaments are our friends and teachers, but not our guides or masters; that any theory, hypothesis, philosophy, sect, creed, or institution, that fears investigation, openly manifests its own weakness and implies its own error.

What was the second Resolution?

Second: Resolved, That all true Liberty and Happiness are predicated upon the twofold principle of Individual sovereignty and Collective reciprocity; therefore, that all religious systems and all forms of government, opposed to the practical enjoyment of such self sovereignty as the basis, are essentially barbarous and vitally antagonistic to the real needs of the man and woman of the Nineteenth Century.

What was the third Resolution?

Third: Resolved, That Religion is Justice; that Heaven is Harmony; that Love is the Life of the Universe; that Wisdom is the Order of the Universe; that distributive Liberty is the natural result of Nature's Laws in exercise.

What was the fourth Resolution?

Fourth: Resolved, That every form of theological sectarianism is anti-progressive, and practically retards the development of brotherly Love among men, and militates not less against the expansion of the eternal principle of Distributive Justice; and that, therefore, all sectarian distinctions and local attachments to creeds should henceforward be abandoned, as worse than useless, by *every teacher* of individual Development, by every lover of social Harmony, and by every friend of political and religious Liberty.

What was the fifth Resolution?

Fifth: Resolved, That, whereas in the constitution of our government it is an essential or fundamental principle that "all men (in the generic sense) are created equal . . . . . with certain inalienable Rights" . . . . . to secure which "governments are instituted among men, deriving their just powers from the *consent* of the governed;" and whereas our government *practically denies* not only the right of Liberty to the slave, but likewise practically denies the right of Suffrage to women; therefore resolved that our government, though the best known on earth, is in effect despotic and opposed to the principles of equal Justice and universal Liberty.

What was the sixth Resolution?

Sixth: Resolved, That America is now but the representative of *Transitional* Republicanism and *sentimental* Liberty; that political antagonism and local monopolizations are natural to this form of civilization; that the Harmonial Philosophy points the pathway to organic and constitutional Freedom; and, therefore, that every Harmonial Philosopher should use his political influence to put in office only such minds as will legislate according to Nature and Reason, and work for equal Justice and universal Liberty.

What was the seventh Resolution?

Seventh: Resolved, That in accordance with repeated ocular demonstrations, and the coincidental attestation of thousands of worthy and intelligent minds in the United States and in Europe, we believe, first, in the sympathetic Nearness of the spiritual world (the Second Sphere) to the natural world (the First Sphere); second, in the possibility of an intellectual and impressional Intercourse between the dwellers of these two worlds; third, that the varieties and gradations of human character extend and continue indefinitely beyond the chemical event of physical death; fourth, and in the special providence, general guardianship, and local ministrations, of those who have passed from earth in advance of us; fifth, in accordance with the accumulative evidence, we believe that these ascended personages are earnest in their associated and combined endeavors to assist mankind toward a practical realization of the "Kingdom of Heaven on Earth"—in the form of a higher social Order wherein each Individual, male and female, without complexional distinctions or intellectual or moral differences, will enjoy an *equal* right to Liberty—inducing all to be good and wise and happy.

What was the eighth Resolution?

Eighth: Resolved, That modern Spiritualism is not antagonistic to, but is essentially in harmony with, the Spiritualism of antecedent centuries.

What was the ninth Resolution?

Ninth: Resolved, That the Harmonial Philosophy is the best and most rational exposition yet known of the immutable Laws of Father-God and Mother-Nature; a philosophy which can rescue modern Spiritualism from eventuating, as almost all ancient has done, in superstitious ignorance and localized bigotry, in bondage to external authorities, and in sectarian organizations detrimental to mankind's advancement.

What was the tenth Resolution?

Tenth: Resolved, That the Mosaic Dispensation (the past) was an age of FORCE, or Compulsion; that the Christian Dispensation (the present) is an age of LOVE, or Impulse; that the Harmonial Dispensation (the future) will be an age of WISDOM, or Harmony. Accordant with the intuitional experience of all illuminated minds, and with the testimony of nations as found in their several maxims and sacred scriptures, we believe that an exercise of WISDOM (*which embraces the totality of man's intuitional and intellectual consciousness*) is necessary in order to harmonize the elements of Force and Love—the Lion and the Lamb—and bring these elements of mankind practically to bear upon the physical, political, and spiritual interests of the race—in a word, to harmonize Man with Himself, with his Neighbor, with Father-God, and with Mother-Nature.

What was the eleventh Resolution?

Eleventh: Resolved, That the human mind, while it is the

master of one set of circumstances, is no less the *subject* of another set which is positive to it; that man is not absolutely but comparatively "a free agent;" that man's character is formed favorably or unfavorably in exact correspondence with the character of the influences which surround and act upon him before as well as after birth; therefore, that individual redemption from, or progress out of, social error and relative imperfections is possible only through the instrumentality of a higher Societary Construction, which shall, by its concordances of interest, destroy all motives for the perpetuation of commercial antagonisms, destroy all conflict between producer and consumer, all incompatibilities between interest and duty, and provide with equal justice for the inception, for the gestation, for the birth, for the training, for the education, and for the spiritual development, of every son and daughter of the Brotherhood of Humanity.

What was the twelfth Resolution?

Twelfth: Resolved, That "evil," so called, is not a transgression of any Law, either physical or moral; but that evil (and sin) arise from internal conditions and from external circumstances over which *individuals* have no absolute control; therefore, that the Harmonial Philosophy teaches universal Charity toward both the agents and the victims of crime; and points to the progressive improvement and harmonization of those conditions and those circumstances which mould and influence the human character prior as well as subsequent to the event of birth.

What was the thirteenth Resolution?

Thirteenth: Resolved, That the commercial and mercantile relations instituted among men, and perpetuated by the present social disorder, are those of *extreme selfishness*, leading directly and inevitably to Indigence, Larceny, Oppressive Monopolies, War, Slavery, Disease, Delusive Doctrines, Professional Drones, and to the development of diversal Unproductive Classes, the effects of which can not be removed and prevented by any change short of a HARMONIAL DISPENSATION—overthrowing, by its mighty power, all superstitions, *liberating equally man's affections and his reason from the slavery of error and fear*—harmonizing the law of Self-Sovereignty with the parallel law of Social Reciprocity—securing to Woman an equally free career with Man, and resulting in good, in wise, and in happy neighborhoods, which will honor human nature by living, as the inhabitants of higher planets do, in strict and natural accord with the Divine Laws of Existence—fulfilling the spirit of the prayer uttered by our Elder Brother, the gentle Nazarene.

What was the fourteenth Resolution?

Fourteenth: Resolved, That we heartily rejoice in the efforts which benevolent men in all civilized nations are making to ameliorate the condition of their fellows—the poor, the ignorant, the enslaved, and the criminal; and that, while we encourage Reformers, Teachers, Missionaries, Statesmen, and Ministers of every shade and degree, we at the same time very fraternally and earnestly and conscientiously urge upon them the necessity of a better acquaintance with the Harmonial Philosophy; to the end that they may be more correct in their estimations of Man, in their reports of Deity, and in their contemplations of Nature—rendering them more efficient in devising the adaptation of instrumentalities to the development of those humane and universal objects which all true reformers and benevolent minds design to accomplish by their associated efforts.

QUESTIONS ON THE

ORIGIN AND PERPETUITY OF CHARACTER.

A CERTAIN band of questions and answers appeared to me just now as divine and redemptive in their influence upon human character. In presenting them, I am actuated by that conviction which the poet thus embodied :—

> "He that hath a truth and keeps it,
> Keeps what not to him belongs—
> But performs a selfish action,
> And a fellow-mortal wrongs."

The term "Character" is usually employed to discriminate reputation. It is used to signify that for which an individual is either popular or unpopular, famous or infamous. When a person is understood to be "a wit," a powerful "logician," a notorious "gambler," a masterly "actor," or an imaginative "writer," this term is commonly made to follow an adjective, by which to define his characteristics. Hence it is said that certain *traits*, or peculiarities, or dispositions, go to make up character.

Do you employ this word with the meaning which is usually attached to it?

No; I define character, on the contrary, to be "the medium" through which the soul expresses itself openly—the form by which the whole mind declareth and maketh its manifestations. Most distinctly do I affirm that men do not understand the real nature of the soul of a man by his character.

What do you mean by this language?

I mean by this to affirm that "character" adheres to a man only; that it does not *in*here, nor form a part of his inmost. Character is a mirror, so to speak, by which the soul looks at itself; the lever upon which it acts; a door through which it passes in and out of the temple. Character is the way, the fashion, the manner, the expression, the fulcrum, as well as the lever, by and through which the soul announceth and declareth itself to the External World.

Do you mean by this that character is not the soul's real expression?

Yes; character *is not the soul;* neither is it an expression of man's inward nature. You are never more mistaken than when you believe you *know* a person's spirit by its characteristic manifestations. The inward nature is compelled to express itself through a "form;" but that form may be the creation of an unfortunate parentage or education. Consider well, and you will discover that "character" *ad*heres, but does not *in*here; that it *pertains* to the individual, but does not constitute the inmost interior Reality.

Are human beings essentially the same?

Yes; one principle animates all races of men. Mankind are essentially the same in Nova Zembla as in Patagonia; in the far-off wilderness as in the city of New York. Two principles only are capable of infinite permutations: they explain the infinite varieties of character which swarm the mystic realms of Existence. This principle is essentially *monotheistic;* it is all God, and is panoramic in its immutable operations. By interior examination I discerned this Principle, and I term it THE GREAT HARMONIA—a divine principle which animates intelligently the boundless system of Nature. When I mount from the anterior regions of "Knowledge" into the superior "Wisdom" faculties, I call this animating principle the "Spirit of Father-God."

Do you mean to teach that God is distinct from Nature?

No; Mother-Nature is not essentially different from Father-God. Nature is a negative part of the Positive Principle—even as man's body is the negative part of his Mind. There is not one thing which is body, and another which is spirit;

neither is there one thing which is Nature, and another which is God. No; there is but One Harmonium, illimitable: in its positive aspects, "Father-God"—in its negative departments, "Mother-Nature." Between Father-God and Mother-Nature, as I have affirmed, mankind come into existence. Hence man is legitimately and truly a child of both Nature and God. Nature is the WIFE of the Divine Principle, and the Divine Principle is the HUSBAND of Nature!

Where do you begin to trace the origin of human character?

There are three origins and degrees to human character: first, that which is inherited from Father-God and Mother-Nature; second, that which we inherit from our immediate father and mother; third, that which is manipulated upon us by our private habits, or by those with whom we are in sympathy and social communication. There is, therefore, a foundational character, which is innately divine and for ever beautiful. It is never tarnished, for it is untarnishable. It is Godlike, because it is an individualized detachment of the monotheistic Principle. It is pure and immaculate, the same in essence as in conformation.

Do you mean to teach that man's spirit is crowned with three characters?

Yes; there is a *primary* character, a *secondary* character, and a *tertiary* character; and each is built upon and folded over the other. The most radical or innermost character—the divine, the imperishable—is seldom manifested in this rudimental life. The second progenitary character—which man inherits from man—is almost always visible. A child inherits a body, and a head on the top of it; and the future man must live in the thus-bequeathed habitation. He has inherited somewhat of his father and his mother; and his "character" will be manifested concordantly therewith. The shape and quality of his ordinary character will resemble the shape and quality of his immediate inheritance.

Are man's trifold characters equally beyond his control?

There are two characters beyond man's absolute control: first, that which was inherited from God and from Nature; second, that which was derived from his individualizing progenitors. Nevertheless, there is a *third* character which ever comes within the circle of individual responsibility. Man's body, I affirm, is inherited like a dwelling-house; and he must live in it, whether he likes the shape of it or not. The faculties are the furniture — also inherited with the habitation. It is impossible radically to change a single faculty. In fact, in this world it is hard even superficially to make alterations. Every chair and every sofa, every item of furniture, bequeathed to man by his earthly progenitors, was placed in his rudimental house, and he can scarcely move them. He must sit low or stand upright, must breathe, and feel, and think, in accordance with the structure of his habitation and the arrangement of his furniture. He begins the business of life with the top faculties: these are his chambers and libraries. Also with the lower faculties: these are his drawing-rooms. And with inferior propensities: these are his kitchen and furniture. With the body: this is a cellar for the reception of garden-vegetables and various substances. And beneath all are locomotive appendages: these are the agents by which he moves over the earth's surface.

Does man get a third character by contact with his fellows?

Man's character is evidently threefold; or, it may be said that he has three characters: first, the innermost, which is seldom manifested; second, that which he parentally inherits; third, that which is superinduced by the church or state, by society, or the family, into which he is born; or, still more externally, by persons with whom he habitually associates. Varieties of disposition and contrarieties of temperament, in individuals with whom a man lives in contact, go directly toward the formation of a superficial character. And this is the "character" which is mainly sustained and manifested by mankind.

What is the true method by which to control and modify character?

Man needs to become acquainted with well-known psychological principles of self-development. These will put into his possession the greatest amount of power, by which he can control and modify, not only his superficial character, but also, to a considerable extent, the secondary character derived from his individualizing progenitors. When a man knows how he obtained a superficial character, through which his spirit is forced to express and misrepresent itself, his knowledge is equivalent to a psychological power by which to modify it. It is undeniably plain that the more men increase their knowledge and wisdom, the more do they acquire an ability by which to undermine and eradicate the superficial. Grant that the spirits of all men are composed of the same essential elements, and we have at once established a universal Democracy. Go deep into human character, and you will find a diamond inheritance, pure and imperishable. There is no other basis upon which to predicate humanitarian Reforms. If you can see, deeper into the nature of Man, an essence and a character strictly incorruptible, then will you approach him as a being whose inmost can disclose the celestial structure.

Are there not persons who possess double characters?

Yes; you meet persons manifesting, at once or alternately, both the acquired and the inherited character. About four generations contribute to the formation of every individual. Hence, children will resemble their immediate father or mother, or else their grandfather or grandmother, or generations even more remote, until the fourth generation is reproduced and represented. Children of some families indicate neither father nor mother; but remote ancestors come forth in their leading characteristics. Characteristics continue to fold themselves over and over, but seldom reach farther back than the fourth generation. Now, all these conditions originate and construct individual character; and the spirit is compelled to harmonize therewith for a term of rudimental years. If it has inherited a large back-brain, or a large front-brain, or any other peculiarity, the spiritual manifestation must be accordant. Most self-evident is it that a Spirit is constrained to manifest itself in accordance with that character which was given to it without consultation or consent. The character is built up, subsequent to birth, by father and mother. After this there cometh the tertiary formation. This is the work of the ten thousand social circumstances which, like so many potters, have power over the clay to "fashion one vessel to honor and another to dishonor." If you had been born in another portion of the globe, what, think you, would have followed? This: the physical, the geographical, the meteorological, the political, the ecclesiastical, the social, and all the other yet subtler influences pertaining to that latitude, would have, like master-masons and constrúctive carpenters, laid the outer walls and put up the timbers in your Character. From such causes you might have been a Turk, a Mongolian, a Chinese, or a Hindoo: just the same as, by living the life of New York, you may obtain a *concrete* character, and get familiarized more or less with a little of all the world. It is to the rectification of this external, outside character, to which men should direct their immediate attention. If we wish to grow harmonial, let us begin by analyzing and removing those causes which retard the development of that divine character inherited from Father-God and Mother-Nature.

Would some associative method propitiate the inmost development?

Yes; deeply impressed am I that mankind, as a Brotherhood, needs a cosmopolitan or world-wide Association, which contemplates modifying the Church, the State, the Family, Society, and even other departments of human interest, with direct reference to the harmonial formation of this third character. Human character is affected so deeply by ecclesiastical institutions, that nothing can require of reformers more investigation. A religion of forms, of ceremonies, of rituals, is not the religion of manhood. Men need a religion which, when defined, means Universal Justice. Institutions have a powerful effect upon those who keep out of them as well as upon those who are absorbed by their mighty magnetism. Impoverished citizens of New York, who have never entered a church, who live perhaps beneath the walks or in cellars, are affected nevertheless by the nature of the pervading theologies. The most positive type of doctrine acts through all the interstices of consciousness, until it reaches the remotest soul. We need a Religion of Justice, which contemplates the harmonial development of character. Popular religious institutions exert a powerful influence upon character, more especially upon that portion which is called "conscience." How many there are who sincerely believe it "wrong" to attempt theological progression!

They cherish a conscientious conservatism, and the Church has magnetized them into it. The conscience of such persons, I would say, is educational—an acquired idea of right and wrong. These ideas are susceptible of various modifications. Hence persons alter their minds upon all kinds of questions. That is right this week; next week, it is wrong. Alterations are perpetually going on in the superficial conscience, and progress is the result.

Is the tertiary character formed unconsciously?

Measurably so. Suppose, for example, you attend Church next Sunday. By the Monday following you will be more affected by your memory of the prayer, sermon, and music, than by the spirit of the music, the spirit of the sermon, or the spirit of the prayer. It is the *form* which strikes deepest into the soil of the outer character. You remember to have been in the Church, but the spirit of the day hath departed. The outer *form* remains in your memory, which influences your spirit insensibly to manifest itself in like manner. Should you meditate upon God, you will think in your preacher's peculiar language. Think of music, and your thought will be in accordance with that tune which lingers strongest upon your memory. You remember the music's form, and your spirit flows insensibly into that. You know how it was with the "Marseilles Hymn;" it was impressed upon all France. Its form became a part of the memory. Joyful natures would sing and dance it; to them, there was sublime courage and hope in the very form of that hymn. Is it not also true that our own memorable "Hail Columbia," and our still more familiar "Yankee Doodle," has been sung and drummed and blowed and whistled by hundreds of thousands who have simply heard the tune and remembered the words? In order to illustrate how insensibly man acquires his tertiary character, I will tell you an experiment: One Sabbath I saw a man, the keeper of a livery stable, at a revival meeting. The broad-breasted and muscular-mouthed minister used his most emphatic language. He terrifically described the terrors of the Lord, and the not more terrible attributes of the Devil. With all the stirring language at his command, he delineated the fate of the impenitent and unredeemed. Well do I remember how he raised himself up in the old red-upholstered desk, and said: "God will damn to hell every uncontrite heart, every unregenerate soul." At length the meeting closed and the proprietor returned to his stable. As he entered, he was informed that one of his best horses was down and floundering in the stall. Several attempts were made to raise the animal, but he would fall back almost in the same spot. Presently, the livery-man became exceeding wroth; he strongly resembled the minister! And lo, in a manner quite minister-like, he raised his powerful voice, and—"damned the horse to hell." You perceive that the proprietor's spirit rushed through the very words which the clergyman had stamped upon his brain.

Would you attempt to trace all profanity to the pulpit?

No; and yet I do affirm that the pulpit has done much toward giving a morose tertiary character to many, even to profanely-inclined persons who have never been inside the Church. From the Church they learn, first, a provoking idea of "God" —second, "will"—third, "damn"—fourth, "your"—fifth, "soul"—sixth, "to hell;" and, in a retentive and intentive memory, it is a very easy matter to ring the changes on these profane and suggestive words. Let a person with an irascible temperament, who has never been within an orthodox Church, hear for the first time such atrocious expressions; and quite sure am I that he will transmit them to a whole crowd of excitable minds before twelve o'clock the next day! Then each individual of this crowd transmits "God will damn your soul" to another individual: and so the innoculation goes forward; and in ten days, from the date of the sermon, they become abbreviated and changed and stereotyped expressions through that village or part of the country. Now, who will say that the popular pulpit is not responsible for much profanity? A universal religion of Justice, on the contrary, would contemplate the Harmony of every individual. It can not be disguised that every individual, whether a member or not, is affected and characterized by those institutions of his country which are called "ecclesiastical."

Is character also influenced by the existing political institutions?

Yes; it would be interesting to detail what has been done in different countries—in all Europe and in America—to stamp new political ideas, through certain legal enactments, whereby hundreds of thousands have received tertiary characters. You remember a certain powerful magician of our country! He once stood up before all the crowned heads in his nation's capitol, with a deal of learning, and with a mystic rod in his hand, called up from shadow-land a "Fugitive Slave Law." He threw it to the earth, frightened at his own skill, and lo, it became a Serpent! How many lesser magicians have labored to imitate him! Sometimes these political imitators achieve temporary triumphs, but their several "compromises," on being thrown down to the earth, have each become a serpent; but the Fugitive Slave Law, being a Mosaic invention and greater than the others, has swallowed them all! You see how this political contrivance operates in America: do you not? The Fugitive Slave Law will continue for a quarter of a century, after its repeal, to affect the tertiary character of the American people. Repeal it in the next twenty-four hours, and the effect of that Law will remain enstamped upon the American spirit. That is to say, the people will continue to put confidence in compromises and expedients. Yes; the influence of a political institution is stamped upon the tertiary character; and the nation, as well as the individual, is compelled in some insensible way to wade through every inch of the popular channel.

But is it not true that every disease brings its own remedy?

We shall see: it is true that social confusion develops social architects; and that each presents different schemes, or remedies, by which to escape from or cure the injustice and inequalities of present disorders. Of course, the world has never been without these Social Architects. We have had the generalizing scientific Fourier, and the humanitarian Owen. Different industrial combinations have come forth, and societary communities have essayed to work out the gigantic problem, to abolish inequalities and overcome injustices. But the inmost character alone can apprehend and appreciate the better and the best.

Society, like a piece of utilitarian machinery, is full of wheels, of bands, of pulleys; and we pray for a John Fitch, or a Fulton, for some person, skilled in moulding the tertiary character. Shafts and wheels now wabbling, in the social structure, could be brought into harmonious movement. Men should unite those influences which go toward the creation of social simplification; the simplification of commerce and merchandise, of farming and manufacturing. Truth is always simple. This is that for which the inner character constantly yearns. There are persons who, getting fatigued with religious corruptions and the wabblings of the wheels of the social machinery, go away into side conditions. They take some established central principle as the divine *animus* of their movement, and organize themselves around that. If they fail to harmonize all human relations, then decomposition is certain to steal into their organization, and a decay of effort is inevitable. But, feeling at times a deeper character and a radical attraction toward better states, these Social Physicians do not despair one day of administering the perfect Remedy.

Do you contemplate the application of Justice to every human relation?

Yes; there is a religion of Justice which may be applied first and foremost to the Family relations. That is to say: to the relation of man to woman, to the relation of lover and beloved, to the relation of husband and wife, to the relation of parent and child, to the relation of friend and enemy, and to the stranger which is without thy gate. Man's tertiary character should be formed by a religion which contemplates Universal Justice. Character is formed for the individual; in accordance with the family and country and religion into which he is born. It depends upon the influences which the human soul encounters before as well as after its emergement into this world, as to whether it will be discordant or harmonious, or, take the middle track, and exhibit somewhat of both the secondary and tertiary.

Can this Justice be applied by the individual to himself?

Yes; to a certain extent. As nearly as possible, each man should be a practical exemplification of his Harmonial Philosophy. Aim at a proportionate development of character—at the exhumation of the Inmost—to get the fullest and best expression. This can be done, not by individual effort alone, but by combination; through association with those who have the same object in view, and the same plan of accomplishment.

How can this association be arranged?

It would not be difficult for a limited number of persons—say six or twelve—to meet together once each week; to come together, from different parts of the town or country, for the purpose of a normal development. Let them continue to meet and get into sympathy—feeling each other's affections and intellects—and so harmonize each with the other's mind. Such a harmonial association would invite higher and diviner influences—would receive showers and benedictions from unseen sources—until the whole circle would be of one accord, and each individual member would become a positive power unto Salvation. This is the way to commence a system of harmonial reform—in spite of all adverse social influences—whereby you may modify and improve the characters which you have inherited and acquired. Suppose, for illustration, you have acquired a habit of drinking, of smoking, of swearing, of loose thinking, or of indulging passional excesses—and suppose you join the circle with the understanding and intention of emancipating your soul from these defective characteristics—in such case, the effect of the association would be manifested in an insensible diversion of your thoughts into higher channels, and, subsequently, a new tertiary character would be formed for a better expression of your true spirit. There is no church, no sanctuary, so desirable as a well-balanced body and soul; but it can not be erected, nor consecrated, without fraternal assistance; there must be a continual contribution of sympathy, from those who have the same glorious blessing in prayer. Remember, such circles should be formed not to invite outward phenomena—calculated to impress the mind with awe and astonishment—but for the interblending, energization, and harmony of those faculties, or characters, through which the soul must express itself. The primal end to be attained is, the development of individual mind in strict obedience to its own most internal character and proclivities. Mind must be rounded out in accordance with its own most interior tendencies. The ideal character must be your own ideal: of what you would be! Such should be your aspiration, your god, your guardian angel. Around this ideal character, your inmost, will cluster a thousand energizing and friendly forces; and you will surely obtain rest and satisfaction.

What do you say concerning the perpetuity of character?

I affirm that the primary character, derived from Father-God and Mother-Nature, is permanent and immortal. The secondary character, imparted by mundane progenitors, is built over the deepest and inmost. This hereditary possession continues through this world, and may continue for centuries in the next; but it is capable, under self-control, of wholesome harmonial modification. The tertiary character, formed and fixed by habits, has a duration which is determined—first, by the strength of your aspiration to outgrow it—second, by the associations which aspiration attracts about you. You should associate with those who are sure and steadfast in their efforts to obtain righteousness. The perpetuity of the tertiary or superficial character is a question of time. Its perpetuation is not a question for eternity. You may strive to overcome, and may experience defeat; but each defeat is but Nature's affirmation, that nothing absolute can be done without co-operation. It is necessary not only to have the assistance of friends in this world, but we need also to receive the spiritualizing aid of our neighbors in the Spirit Land. On one occasion I met a fine looking literary man, with a bad tertiary character, who was quite satirical and severe upon mankind. I recollect his quoting a passage from Byron, which suited his inverted characteristics:—

"The time hath been when no harsh sound would fall
From lips that now would seem imbued with gall,
Nor fools nor follies tempt me to despise
The meanest thing that crawled beneath mine eyes.
But now, so callous grown—so changed since youth,
I've learned to think and sternly speak the truth—
Learned to deride the critic's starch decree
And break him on the wheel he meant for me—
To spurn the rod a scribbler bids me kiss,
Nor care if courts or crowds applaud or hiss."

He said that this was the most agreeable passage he ever found in Byron! His filial and universal loves were inverted. By reference to the fourth volume of the Great Harmonia you can see the difference between a harmonious character, and one which is oppressed with tertiary deformities or secondary tendencies derived from mismated progenitors. It is a great consolation to know, that all this which we condemn in human nature — this evil and sin — adheres only to those strata of character which are of temporal duration. The human spirit must express itself through forms; hence we get bad representations of the inward nature which is essentially pure. Theologians have endeavored to trouble humanitarians with this question:

How can man be outwardly so evil and sinful, and inwardly so pure and divine?

To which I reply, that "character" is the *form* through which the soul expresses itself. The expression and the form will correspond. If a man should impress bad words upon your mind, your character will flow out through them. If the windows of your house were of blue glass, you would see everything beyond or outside of them as tinged or draped in a color corresponding. If there were interposed between your eye and the pure, white, shining light of the sun, a red, saffron, or green, its light would appear to your mind to be colored accordingly. So the character which is interposed between the world and your spirit. That which is within, like the sun's pure light, is divine and untarnishable. The spirit is not marred or injured in its inner essence by contact with the body or the world, although its manifestations may be crude and painfully discordant. Spirit is unparticled and unchangeable; but character changes perpetually. Hence a man may acquire and represent a multitude of characteristics, while his spirit remaineth essentially unchanged. Yes, it is a vast pleasure to know that "character" is not the exponent of man's spirit. It is but the habitation in which he is compelled by circumstance temporarily to live. Therefore, men must commence with the improvement of those social conditions out of which arise human character.

Do you mean to teach that man's spirit is not to be judged by the appearance of his character?

Yes; character, I reaffirm, is not the man or the woman, but is merely the soul's fragmentary declarations. It is not *the soul*, but its compelled expression. It is interposed between the innermost and the outermost. It is the framework of the spirit—the setting of the gem of immortal life. If the frame is beautiful, it reflects beauty upon the picture; but if the framing be disproportionate and unbeautiful, who will say that the work of the Divine Artist is therefore imperfect? The first character is *natural*, the second is *superficial*, and the third is *artificial*. The first is a *sub* or under-structure; the second is an *inter* or mediatorial structure; the third is a *super* or temporary structure, built over and outside of its predecessors. To the spiritual perceptions of the clairvoyant, or to a person with the clairvoyance of a clear intellect, it is undeniably plain that one character is built over another, until the spirit-essence is well-nigh disguised, *incognito*. The first character, the substructure, is inherited. Its parents, as before said, are Father-God and Mother-Nature. The second character is inherited from our immediate parents, in whom exist the contributions of three or four previous generations. This progenitary character is the interstructure, through which the spirit of man is obliged to express itself. He must follow out the positive proclivities of his immediate parents. External character is acquired by habits, and, to a great extent, from influential surroundings.

Can you illustrate how the secondary and tertiary characters are formed?

Yes; here, for illustration, is an architect. He designs a public edifice. He calls together carpenters and masons, and furnishes them with tools and appropriate materials. In due course of time, the structure is reared. But did you ever know a progressive architect who was satisfied with his elaboration? The archetypal ideas of the architect were the first parents of that building; and the workmen were the immediate parents, by whom come several interpolations. The original plan did not contemplate a window there, nor a door or closet yonder. These new suggestions are introduced. A hall is opened in one place, and a flight of stairs is erected in another. These, I say, are interpolations or interstructures. But now come the superficial workers—that is to say, men with brushes and pots of paint—who add ornaments and external embellishment. This is the acquired character. But the seasons come and go, and the paint, and embellishments, and ornaments, all slowly disappear—all which the carpenters, and masons, and painters, had brought into expression. The edifice itself realizes innovation, which runs parallel with renovation. Finally, the whole is reduced: the character which the masons and carpenters imparted disappears: and the idea of the original architect remains unexpressed. But, on the very foundation on which that building was erected, a class of men bring out his idea in all its proportions. Thus: Father-God and Mother-Nature conceive the idea of a man. They summon together all the carpenters and masons; and their names are Legion. There are nine hundred millions of vegetables, and one hundred and fifty millions of animals—fish, birds, reptiles, marsupials, mammalials, and quadrumanals—engaged, as carpenters and masons, to express the archetypal idea by the production of a Man. It is Nature's idea. Nature works through all these materials and spiritual forces in order to bring out what is represented by you and I. Last of all, instrumental intermediates engaged in the production of a human being, are our father and mother. They impart to the children individualized existence. Then come the painters and ornamental workmen, who have much of stucco-work to do; that is, the embellishments, and ornaments, and accomplishments, and influences, impressed by society.

What do you mean by this language?

I mean that a man may take himself apart, and understand the machinery of a human being; and thus acquire a power of self-rectification—and, without any unnecessary procrastination, polish away and remove all acquired peculiarities which militate against the ample expression of his innermost characteristics, inherited from Father-God and Mother-Nature. The architect's divine Idea is alone immortal; not the house which he builds, nor the paint with which artisans embellish it. Even so, are the imperfections of your acquired character, and of the character which you parentally inherited, ultimately to pass away. Whether your parentage be Caucasian or African, Mongolian or Indian, Celtic or Teutonic, it is all the same. Nature will do her work, and you will experience at last a complete realization of her original Idea.

Do you mean that Nature's idea of a man may be realized in this life?

Yes; nevertheless, your inherited and acquired characters, unless they be duly overcome and cleansed away, will survive the desperate energy of death, and accompany you when you enter the drawing-rooms and supernal chambers of the Eternal Mansion. And there you will not lose your individuality: you will be known as you were known by your father and mother; you will be recognised by the principle of Universal Sympathy. Neither death, with all its mysterious chemical energies combined, nor the grave, though it weeps on all sides for months and years together, can cleanse the spirit of certain characteristics which adhere to it, as a consequence of its rudimental existence and organal development.

Does the mind see the world only through its own characteristics?

Yes; man sees everything according to his mental state. For example: a master-mind goes into the world, and begins an examination of what he calls the Word of God. We will suppose that this mind is Martin Luther. He therefore looks through his own mental characteristics, sees the Word of God, and *Lutherizes* it from the beginning to the concluding sentence. Again: take the man called John Calvin. He owns an imperious, positive, hereditary character. Taking that, with his acquired abilities, he sets his mind conscientiously to a religious work. His twofold character, interposed between his most interior spirit and the letter of the Bible, compels him to see and render new translations to every chapter, verse, and word. In short, the book is logically *Calvinized* from beginning to end; and it depends upon your inherited and acquired characters whether you become a Lutheran or a Calvinist. After a time, we hear of another man—perhaps John Wesley. You all know how well he *Wesleyized* the whole Book! He was compelled to look through his character: he saw a new

God, and read a new revelation. He saw, as he supposed, that Luther and Calvin were much mistaken. He was astonished that intelligent minds could see anything but Methodism in the Bible. Having inherited an imperious and positive nature, his thoughts could not be controlled by surrounding minds. Again, who has not heard of Emanuel Swedenborg? Who would not like to be in his place for twenty-four hours? Examine the Word from his stand-point, and you will be surprised that any mind could be content with Calvin or Luther. You would perceive a natural, a spiritual, and a celestial sense—would see a new scheme, a new Providence, a new Church, and a new law establishing the cohesion of ideas—spreading far and wide through the heavens like an Aurora Borealis! You are let into the language of correspondences; and you come out *correspondentialized* from head to foot, just as the Bible is *Swedenborgianized* from Genesis to Revelation. If the structure of your acquired character comes within that of Calvin, you will be Calvinized; if within that of Luther, you will be Lutherized; if it comes within the generalizations and minutiæ of Swedenborg, you will be Swedenborgianized. Thus, like the edifice of the architect, you would be painted, embellished, ornamented, and artificialized, in your exterior character. Again: here is John Murray. Now, every receiver of his gospel is astonished, when once thoroughly *Murrayized*, that intelligent minds can see anything in the Bible against the doctrine of universal restoration. This principle of explaining character will impart to your mind an interpreting, a generalizing, and a fraternizing spirit toward religious sects—to all of which you will have the advantage of being positive. What a grand joy it is to stand upon a mountain, and see all the meeting-houses and sectarian hamlets in the valley far below; to feel that, spiritually, you are monarch of all you survey! Every one, at some period of life, goes upon the mountain of Contemplation: and when the mind comes down out of that mountain, what would it not give to remember all it had seen and acquired during those moments of comprehension!

What would you do to bring out the innate or divine character?

This question will be more fully answered hereafter. I

would simply elicit that which I know to be integral—the natural image or harmonial character—which is beneath all which you may have inherited or acquired. Bring *that* positively out, and you are saved, not only from influences which flow from your immediate surroundings, but you are rescued not less from ecclesiastical and political organizations. We always get what we give. If man runs up an account with himself, he is sure to be called one day to settle every farthing of it. If a man be a *Christian* of the Lutheran stamp, or of the Calvinistic sort, a Wesleyan, a follower of Murray, of Swedenborg, or of any other leader, and if so be that he passes to the Spirit-Home in such faith, then he has not only the character *inherited* from his father and mother to overcome, but he has to remove an acquired character also, which was superinduced upon his mind by the painters, the artists, the embellishers, and ornamenters, of the religious organization.

Will this explain why different religious sects, during revivals, suppose the Lord cometh to their aid?

Yes; I have witnessed those phenomena called "revival-meetings." There are no manifestations better calculated to illustrate this doctrine—that a man's outward characteristics follow him to the Spirit-Land. Go into a Methodist camp-meeting, for example, and proceed to analyze a certain mysterious, pervading excitement. There is, first, an artificial excitement, arising from the energetic, psychological minister. Then the people, by virtue of combination and oneness of purpose, effect another, which is the second phase of psychology. The third psychological excitement is based upon the passions; that is, the nervous susceptibilities are prayed for and addressed by exhortation. Perhaps, you never witnessed a Methodist minister indulging a philosophical reflection. The consequence is, the people begin to *feel*, not to think. They are drawn into the region where love is in the ascendant. They inspire a love of spiritual excitement: mingled, perhaps, with a love for the Supreme. Now, the religious sensibilities begin to be uncontrollably excited. They are venerable, then prayerful, then convicted of sin: of a thousand things they feel guilty, for which they never imagined themselves to be guilty before!

Then they are psychologically excited to a yet higher degree. Plenty there are who have had this "religious" experience. These can remember how they prayed in the tents, over in the enchanting woods—the many lamps at night lighting up the trees—and the most nervo-excitable persons in the anxious-seats receiving a mysterious afflatus! At this crisis, with still greater tribulation, there cometh a newer experience. They behold startling visions! They gaze upon a Methodistic hell, and into a Methodistic heaven. They affirm the Bible to be the Word of God; and that the doctrine of the forgiveness of sins is also true. Of all which my explanation is brief: that a certain small per-centage of a camp-meeting excitement is spiritually derived. The acquired Methodistic character is perpetuated into the Spirit-Home, and reacts upon sympathizing minds. Methodistic spirits come back to earth at times, and so are kept up religious excitements which are supposed to be ight in the sight of God.

Will your explanations extend over the revivals of other sects?

Yes; the unity of truth fixes the unity of causes. See! there is another strange phenomenon. It is a Presbyterian excitement. This is far more thoughtful; the opposite of Methodism. A Presbyterian must be somewhat logical. You are obliged to take the "premises" upon authority; the rest is completely logical and legitimate. History does not know a lawyer from the time of Luther with a power of intellectual skill better than that possessed by Calvin. John Calvin was thoughtful and logical; hence, Presbyterians are logical and thoughtful. Methodists are, therefore, characteristically different from Presbyterians. And, according to my observations, the Presbyterian's acquired character, unless modified by new truth, is also carried into the Spirit-Home. And when there exists a revival in a Presbyterian church, there is a certain small percentage of spiritual influx manifested. This inspires the members with a conviction of at least doctrinal righteousness; that truth is written through the works of Calvin; and that the Bible is the *plenum* of Divine Revelation. I have heard the logical minister inform the audience that they were all sinners, which I presume no one doubted; and that the deacons especially were guilty of lukewarmness, and of still more heinous sins: and I found that I entertained the same opinion. A revival-meeting is a spiritual phenomenon. Such meetings are measurably inspired, and stimulated, and perpetuated, by the return-wave of minds beyond the grave, who have not progressed sufficiently to disgorge their sectarian characteristics.

Is the post-mundane perpetuity of acquired characteristics demonstrated in armies?

Yes; it was interesting to witness, by aid of clairvoyance, how the allied forces were stimulated by certain liberty-loving Russians who had been shot into the Spirit Home. They obeyed their rulers and generals while in the army, because circumstances compelled obedience. But those same brave-hearted warriors, after existing in the Spirit Home, certainly not more than forty or fifty days, returned to inspire and encourage the men who would break down the spirit of Despotism. It was blessed to behold the visitations to those field-camps wherein reposed the soldiers of freedom. But the Leaders entertained no such belief. Thus, certain soldiers were aided by those who came from the Spirit Home. They brought to the warriors an energy, and a wild enthusiasm; which caused them to pant for an opportunity to cut down whole battalions of opponents! Once I heard the following words, pronounced by a spirit who had been a Russian soldier, who—by being shot (not down, but) up into the Spirit Home—felt the language wherewith to express his innate love of Liberty: "We listen, Russia! for one note of harmony from thy places, but we hear the loud roaring of the practising warrior. Thy soldiers will fail thee in battle; their hearts shall beat for the down-trodden. Thy officers shall fall in death before thine eyes; and thy cunning shall depart. Russians! noblemen of the north! spurn thy glittering swords, and commence the education of thy youth. Ignorance lowers heavily o'er thy habitations. Crime hath sealed thy despotisms; hath consigned them to decay." (See the exordia in the "Present Age and Inner Life.")

Have you any different case whereby to illustrate the continuation of character?

Yes; while residing in the city of Hartford, I was visited

by a gentleman who came to inquire concerning spiritual manifestations. He asserted that he had not conversed with any one on the subject; that he had heard and read but little concerning it; but that, recently, he had certain very startling experiences which troubled him exceedingly. About four weeks ago, after retiring for the night, when he knew that no mortal but himself and wife was in the room, the door seemed to open, and a self-possessed stranger entered. He could not discern the features or the garments of his visiter; but, before he had time to spring from his bed, he heard his name pronounced in a calm yet penetrative voice, and, immediately, the following words were spoken: "Provide for thy slaves homes on thy plantations, give them opportunities to read and write, and you shall be happy." On hearing these words he sprang upon the floor, lighted a lamp, but no visiter could be found. The door had been unlocked. . . . . . Next night, just as he was between sleeping and waking—in the dreamy twilight of slumber—the door again opened, and in walked the same personage. The same words were spoken, and the same disappearance was accomplished. After searching the chamber and finding no one, the gentleman concluded that some abolition trick was being played upon him; he therefore resolved to have a lighted candle, and to remain awake in the capacity of private watchman. He mused a long time, when the candle had burned down to the socket, and he forgot himself in sleep. The door again opened, the same imperturbable personage entered, and the same ominous words were slowly but distinctly reiterated. The gentleman acknowledged that he owned about two hundred and thirty-five slaves; that his possessions embraced two large plantations; that he was about to inherit more slaves and fields; and that his father and grandfather had been extensive slaveholders. Said he: "I don't understand it; but, as I was coming North, I concluded to visit Hartford and obtain your opinion." I had some candid conversation with him; but the sequel I can not now disclose. Now, let the reader remember, that this visitation occurred just three months to a day after "Isaac T. Hopper" had entered the Spirit Home!

If character is continued into the Spirit Land, what shall we conclude in the case of Daniel Webster?

My answer is, that man's intermediate and superinduced characters are perpetuated, or not, in accordance with the progress he has made toward their rectification or removal. Daniel Webster's last earthly deed was the cause of a rapid alteration in the superficial stratum of his character. The Fugitive Slave Law rose up, and became a serpent of fire to the people of the North. Webster's acquired character went with him into the Spirit Home, but his inmost inheritance soon gained the ascendency. Hence, in a speech delivered for the friends of the slave, he gave the following exordium: "We speak, O ye suffering sons of Africa, from the clear sky; and our voices shall be heard. Mammon was the god who first led thee to bondage; so shall it be the god of thy deliverance. We will open the catalogue of national crimes to the world. The nation that perpetuates slavery shall become a by-word; and its people be counted odious as Appius Claudius, the tyrant of ancient Rome, who condemned Virginia as a slave! The people who enslave thee shall prove thy eternal benefactors. There is a Law of Justice which evermore overcomes evil with good. We will inspire thy masters to worship at the shrine of Justice. This is the Great God before whom Mammon shall bow in eternal subserviency! The honest man shall rise in overawing majesty before the doer of wrong deeds. The soil now tilled by enslaved hands, the plants now moistened by the tears of suffering exiles, shall yet be thine, O sons of Africa, to work in the sunshine of gladness, to barter with consumers as thine own. Thou shalt become an *independent* nation! [No amalgamation you perceive, and no immediate emancipation, but that money is finally to settle the whole question.] This shall come [that is the formation of an independent nationality] of thy free-will and choice! We will bring an overpowering light to all oppressors: and the everywhere Oppressed shall go free."

As you are now on the question of slavery, and as William Lloyd Garrison is a prominent leader in the cause of freedom, will you delineate his characteristics?

Yes; he is a fine example: the most extraordinary political

phenomenon. William Lloyd Garrison, is the only individual who is thoroughly *Garrisonized* in the United States. Let him to-morrow reject the outward body, and let all which characterizes and distinguishes the man, both inherited and the acquired, go on with him into the Spirit Home. Now, for the sake of illustration, let us be blasphemous enough to imagine—what the whole orthodox world accepts as solemn truth—a *literal hell* and a *literal heaven!* Picture an orthodox elysium on one side, and an orthodox pandemonium on the other. Day after to-morrow, fancy that this imperturbed Garrison makes an application at the gate of Paradise. (I am illustrating on the supposition, that this man has not thrown off either his intermediate or superinduced characteristics.) Accordingly he knocks at the gate, and the gate is opened. The gatekeeper asks: "What faith?" The prompt Garrison replies: "*I believe in absolute human freedom; no fellowship with slaveholders.*" "What religion?—what Church?" inquires the gatekeeper—"there are Catholics, Lutherans, Calvinists, Methodists, Unitarians, Universalists, in yonder amphitheatre: to which of these parties do you belong?" "Don't belong to any," returns the applicant.—"Unconditional emancipation is my doctrine; no union with slaveholders." The astonished Peter bows respectfully, and replies: "Walk in, sir—help yourself to a seat."

Now William Lloyd Garrison, as I before remarked, is a political phenomenon.* He walks cheerfully through the courts of the orthodox Elysium. Seeing different sects so comfortably seated, amid a plenitude of splendors, he feels very much interested. Although not particularly pleased with the several heavenly divisions, yet he says nothing—seeing a kind of conceded difference among them without misunderstandings or dispute. He spends many pleasant hours in a promenade of observation; for he has the liberty of the domain. Presently, he approaches one of the mountainous walls—lined with that metal which is so congenial to utilitarians, and perceives a mass of fleecy, interlined, and interfused clouds: something

* A psychometric reading of his innate and inherited character may be seen in the last pages of this volume.

dark, smoky, curling up, and sulphurous! It seems to have "torment" in it; it don't smell like the fragrance of Freedom. These repulsive nebula seem to emanate from an empire of immense depth and magnitude. The penetrative Garrison draws closer, and, scorning to notice that the wall is of solid gold, he climbs independently up, looks over, and beholds *an orthodox hell thickly-populated!* One such vision is enough. He turns back to look upon the thinly-populated orthodox heaven. What are the sects all about? O, they are all looking at the orthodox god; the lower part of whose face is bathed with eternal sunshine, while the brow seems circled with frowns and with condemnatory thoughts in number beyond computation. The fearless Garrison readily apprehends the ecclesiastical conditions. He turns firmly and respectfully toward the orthodox god, and inquires—first, whether *the platform is free to all?*—second, whether a speech from him would be considered out of order? After considerable consultation among the chief rulers, he is informed that, by standing on one of the steps leading to the Throne, and preserving himself free from any personalities, he might address the religious audience! . . . . . Just picture to your minds this man, Garrison—with his positive hereditary character, united to his acquired political and anti-slavery characteristics—standing up, alone and unaided, to address such a peculiar aristocratic congregation! No, I will not attempt to imagine a word he might utter. But I venture to assert that he would kindle a red-hot fire of purely moral adjectives, which would burn and blister the lukewarm devotees, until each would feel as if the kingdom of heaven was on the very point of political disunion and ecclesiastical decomposition! Calmly, he rebukes them for their indolence, and deplores their unacquaintance with the urgent demands of Humanity. Most earnestly he points to the neighboring land of blackness, *in which unutterable suffering and slavery abounds*, and fearlessly tells them that they are unpardonably *recreant* to every obvious principle of human happiness. Sitting there day after day, cherishing selfish sympathies for each other, apparently unmindful of the fact that millions are suffering every instant of time!

Well: the speech is delivered, and the speaker is unable to perceive the first appearance of sympathy. Observing which he proceeds to the gatekeeper, and says: "Let me out into freedom; I find no sympathy here."

But where, think you, would duty lead this man?

I will tell you: With his characteristics, duty would direct him to go on a mission of mercy to the population of the orthodox pandemonium. There, doubtless, he would find a free platform! Seconded by minds whom he had somewhat *Garrisonized*, he would, in three days, institute an Anti-Hell-fire Society! Yes, this candid man is so full of organic liberty and of "no union with slaveholders," that he would fix minute-men all along the track; and, methinks, I do not exaggerate when I say that, in three days from the time of his first speech in Pandemonium, there would be a fine-working *underground railroad* all the way up to the Kingdom of Heaven!

In all the foregoing you have employed an unallowable supposition: will you not describe his characteristics through a natural hypothesis?

Without indulging any unnatural hypothesis, then, I can assure you that, should Mr. Garrison go to the Spirit Home, he would be interested in the scheme of universal anti-slavery; and certain individuals at the South, although without interest in Spiritualism, would surely receive many troublesome dreams and waking forebodings.

Would the New-England Yankee's character be perpetuated?

Nothing can be more certain. It hath been said that, if the real genuine Yankee was cast away on a desert Island, he would, on the next morning, amuse himself by selling maps to the inhabitants! Suppose a utilitarian man should enter the Spirit Home, do you imagine that he would be long in acquiring the art of moving a chair or the whole baggage-train of spiritual manifestations?

Are natural characteristics perpetuated into the Spirit Home?

Yes; for example, the true native Irishman does not loose, in this life, any of his national or individual peculiarities. The Irish race is continued into the Spirit World. So with the Germanic, and the French, and the different races; they preserve a momentum; and, for many periods, continue to run the race of a national progression. Ultimately, however, by a closer approximation of tendencies and interchange of sympathies, all overarched and beautified by system, the divergent races begin to converge and assimilate, whereupon the acquired characteristics are dropped, then the parental characteristics are dropped; and, lastly, there alone shines forth the innate and beautiful, the divine and celestial, character which was derived from Father-God and Mother-Nature. But I heard of the case of an Irishman who had carried into the Spirit Home both his acquired and his constitutional wit. At a circle he was very civilly asked respecting his nativity, and he replied: "I was born on the corner of West Broadway and Lispenard street, while my mother was travelling in Europe!" Thus, the mass of mankind resemble the home, the institution, or nation, from which they emanate. Some children, the moment they meet their street-companions, will indicate the last conversation heard at the table. Insensibly to itself the outside character gets formed, deformed, or reformed. The spirit of condemnation—this practice of giving one man credit as "good" and denouncing another as "evil"—condemning the "warrior" and praising the "peaceman"—condemning the soul of the "Spanish Inquisitor" and holding up the beautiful character of "William Penn"—will vanish when men come to apprehend and comprehend that the human spirit is compelled to act out its inherited character. It is beautiful to contemplate the character of the peaceful William Penn; but the inmost spirit of the Spanish Inquisitor is just as peace-loving and beautiful! Nay, do not refuse to be harmonially Democratic. When you have the happiness to obtain a broad view of humanity you will aid to prevent individual discord—not by condemnation, not by methods and measures which exasperate and excite and madden and mortify, but by lifting up, drawing out, and eliminating the divine "character" which is the inmost and the imperishable.

In the case of William Penn, or of any good and truth-loving person, is there not some manifestation of the *inmost* Character?

Most persons exhibit the character which they have derived from their immediate progenitors, first; and, in all their after-years, they show out the character which they acquired during the periods of childhood and adolescence; but very few there are, the inter-and-super-structures of whose character are transparent and plastic enough to reveal the form of the divine Image. There is now and then a temperamental conformation which affords an opportunity for the innermost to express and delineate itself by means of interlineation and open deeds, between the interstices of the acquired and inherited characters. Occasionally, we meet minds showing traits of the divine and celestial through the little chinks, so to speak, through the orifices and apertures and nooks of superficial character; and we rejoice exceedingly, in the midst of existing dissipation and discord and imperfection, that human nature can manifest goodness and truthfulness which are ever beautiful and admirable. Once I stood by a bank of plants which would bear flowers. By some freak of workmen the great door of a barn was thrown upon those rose-bearing plants; they were crushed to earth, and withered beneath the ponderous weight. Fortunately, however, there were *three or four knot-holes* in that door, and, in due course of season, *three or four flowers* came struggling up through those openings: and so presented themselves to the world crippled, deformed, yet beautiful. Now, do you not see what Society does? It throws itself, with its ponderous weight of formalities, upon the babe as soon as it is born. Then the Church and the State combine to mould and fashion the individual into their image and likeness. But, as in the comparison, there are some *holes in Society*—desperate and deadly holes also both in Church and State—through which man's native goodness and integrity come out into beautiful blooming! Also, through the characteristics inherited perhaps from mismated progenitors, somewhat of the divine bequeathment shines out: especially, when there exists an adequate cause to awaken and elicit it. Hence, in the lowest condition of man, there are some glimmerings of the Divine. Look within thee, O man, and behold the imperishable! The best Idea of thy divine progenitors is there; the inmost, the harmonial, and the everlasting. Thou art master of, and will ultimately conquer, that which was inherited from thy father and mother; also, everything acquired by contact with Society, the State, or the Church. Take courage, therefore, O man, and believe that, by coming together, shaking each other's hands, putting shoulder to shoulder and spirit to spirit, for the purpose of abolishing discordant characteristics, thou wilt receive heavenly assistance from the inhabitants of other Spheres.

Will you not state more in detail your impressions regarding the reformation of character?

Character, I reiterate, is that through which your spirit is forced to express itself. If you desire mental improvement, then improve your mental types and symbols. Obtain a knowledge of good works and deeds, as tools, with which to think; for all your thoughts will take the shape of your language; the same as water takes the shape of the drinking glass or containing vessels. Yes; your thoughts are fluid, and will take the shape of your words. Therefore, let the utilitarian furniture of your mind be put in order. This furniture consists of thoughts, and the words wherewith your mind declareth itself; a pure spirit seeketh a well-furnished residence. This is the first lesson of a harmonial reform of private character. Do this, by means of co-operative effort, and both your acquired and inherited characters will rapidly grow threadbare—permitting the immortal to bloom out full of fragrance. The superficial character, which good minds abhor, resembleth the rust on iron. Man is born into society. Society corrodes and oxydizes his surface; but glimmerings of the inward nature are occasionally seen through the exterior corroding. His neighbors chafe and irritate him, and thus certain temperaments find that they have self-power to rub this rust away. Such minds master one set of circumstances, then another yet more positive. Here beginneth a grand lesson of individual responsibility; the knowledge that you are a Power, not a circumstance. True, you are a circumstance at first, and you feel yourself helpless in the presence of surroundings. But one day you discover that a certain class of circumstances are not your masters, but, instead, that you have the power to surround and conquer! Yes; it is true, that influences and habits which are considered by an ignorant man to be his masters, are in reality not at all above the jurisdiction of his reason or will. Give a man confidence in himself, that he hath an inward character, and he will forthwith commence the work of reform and self-purification. Society and bad habits have superinduced rust upon thy mind. Begin now: rub it off by the friction of will. Oh, it giveth hope and gladness and strength to know that this *external character*, which does not declare the spirit, is like the stinging burr surrounding the concealed chestnut. The time cometh when the burr is sundered and falleth away, and the sweet meat of the chestnut is visible. But if the chestnut be carelessly handled, before the arrival of this time, the multitudinous thorns on the burr will inflict irritation and surfacial wounds. Thus, there are persons so coated-over and hedged in, by various acquirèd mental habits, that they severely wound those in contact with them; indeed, such temperaments may be compared to the sting and irritability produced by handling the thorns of a chestnut burr. The time certainly comes, I repeat, when this acquired character drops off! Man's external characteristics resemble the caterpillar which envelopes the butterfly. Hope for every one is based upon this fact: that all imperfections of both the external and the inherited characters are ultimately to be mastered and eradicated; so that not even a vestige of them shall remain to interfere with the future happiness of the immortal mind! Notwithstanding which each individual will differ everlastingly from every other individual. There is no *one* type proper to all mankind. You will be developėd, therefore, in the likeness and image of *your own interior character*, bequeathed ante-natally by Father-God and Mother-Nature!

QUESTIONS ON THE

BENEFITS AND PENALTIES OF INDIVIDUALISM.

I BEGIN with the affirmation that, by virtue of correspondential or analogical reasoning, the facts of mechanism may be seen reproduced in the operations of the human mind. In mechanical laws, we notice a *double* tendency; one from the outside to the internal—centripetalism; the other from the centre outwardly—centrifugalism: between these dual forces, all bodies revolve upon their respective axes. Even so, in the operations of the human mind, we observe two corresponding motions. While the soul manifests a tendency to fly from its own centre, it exhibits no less the contrary motion. In fact, the soul experiences the most *positive attraction* toward its own integral substance. Therefore, I would say: *man is organized for centralization.* He can not fly from this pivotal Innermost: on this rests the whole science of individualism. Individualism is the science of centralization; the law of mental mechanics; the doctrine of fidelity between orb and orbit; the philosophy of harmonial relations between centre and circumference.

If it be true that man's mind is more interested in itself than in others, is he not a selfish and egotistic being?

Let me consider. . . Although the method is somewhat invidious, yet it may be stated and adopted that man, in a certain sense, is a being of simple and compound selfishness: that is to say, whenever he acts, he acts from and to *his own* centre of revolution. He can do nothing, except through the centre of his *own* individual soul. When the mind exhibits a constant tendency toward the welfare of its own consciousness—regardless of the rights, and liberties, and individual welfare, of others—we then term it "selfishness," on the lowest plane of individualism. Such a mind is circumscribed, and needs expansion—needs to exercise more fidelity to the law of centrifugalism. It wabbles and hobbles around its orbit, like a wheel without relation or proportion.

Is it not natural for humanity to dislike and repel a purely selfish character?

Yes; a selfish person is universally detested by Humanity. This species of selfishness is the characteristic of undeveloped minds; a living sponge which absorbs every fluid or liquid near it; a maelstrom which draws to itself each contiguous object; a parsimonious desert which drinks greedily the April showers and morning dews, without returning so much as a blade of grass in gratitude—all these are more tolerable to contemplate than a "selfish" character. The inevitable cupidity of such selfishness—the violence it does to our sense of individual harmony—renders the condition transcendently repulsive.

According to your foregone definition, there must be a better selfishness: how would you describe it?

Yes; there is another form of selfishness, which is transcendently admirable. What is that form? It is the individualism of a human being manifested, like a fountain, from itself toward the circumference. Oh, there is grandeur in that! Pause, and contemplate a human soul extending its orbit to the boundaries of Humanity! The centre expands—in consequence of its generous exertions to spread its consciousness—over the whole circumference of interest. This is the highest form of selfishness; an identification of the individual with the whole. Some characters are so large and divine, that nothing less than the happiness of the universe can satisfy *their* selfishness.

Is it not natural for humanity to love and attract a purely benevolent character?

It is very natural. Before such natures we reverently bow—praying to realize their strong embrace—to be lifted up by their boundless love — to be sustained by the giant arms of such masterly minds. Some Jesus is born unto us; after his death we build altars, and bend in adoration to attributes so Godlike. Perhaps, however, in the hours wasted in yielding homage to another, we impair and measurably sacrifice our own individualism. In admiring the greatness and goodness of others, in adoration without aspiration, we debilitate and cripple the attributes of self-development. Here cometh the explanation which we seek: the reason why there are so few *individualized* men and women in the world. Men lose their best individuality and independence by an ignorant admiration of these manifestations in others.

In the English language there are two words, spelled and pronounced nearly alike, viz., "egotism" and "egoism" — will you explain the difference between them?

Yes; "egotism" is the term which I apply to persons who exhibit the first and lowest form of selfishness; but, to the last and best form of selfishness, the word "egoism" is strictly applicable. Egotism is a true label for minds who place themselves superciliously and pedantically first and foremost in a matter — who use the personal pronoun "I" in great abundance, as if everything and everybody were secondary and subordinated. On one occasion I received a letter from a person of this description, covering three sides of a common sheet, with no less than one hundred and sixteen "I's" in it — many of them emphasized — as if the writer stood between the earth and the sun, allowing the light of the latter to shine through his egotism as best it might! But, on the other hand, to the feeling of self-hood — to the relations realizable between individualism and the world without — we may apply the other word, "egoism," with the strictest propriety. Egoism is the truest form of individuality. The *egoist* is one who realizes the whole world through — and only through — the centre of his own being. The senses are channels leading to that centre. The centre is the seat of motion; the axis on which the soul revolves in its orbit. Egotism is the viper: egoism is the man. Between these may be found all forms and gradations of human character.

Has there not always existed a conflict between individual man and individual institutions ?

Yes; mankind have contended for supremacy on one side, and institutions have claimed exclusive control on the other. Institutions, although man-made and essentially arbitrary, have ever arrogated to themselves the right to rule the individual. And as it sometimes happens that the Individual openly ignores the right and supremacy of the Institution, so do we behold institutional attempts, by means of gibbet, rack, and fagot, to bring the traitor into subjection and perpetual dishonor. All political and ecclesiastical governments have been based upon this theory, viz.: *the innate disqualification of the individual for self-regulation*, and hence the necessity of institutional laws. When Jesus asserted *the supremacy of the individual*, by his own life and teachings, the Roman Government considered him a traitor and a conspirator; and so the old Romans maintained the affirmed dignity and alleged superiority of the Institution by forcibly putting him through the sepulchre into the World of Spirits.

Is it not true that Thomas Paine was also a conspirator ?

He was. When Thomas Paine asserted the supremacy of the people of America to the English Government, or to any government whatsoever, that country entertained the warmest hatred toward him, and would have gloried in his physical apprehension and destruction.

Was he thus sought out and destroyed ?

No; on the contrary, "The Rights of Man" prevailed over the wrongs of Government, over the prejudice of Tories; and Thomas Paine was read and honored by the lovers of Liberty. Having had his soul roused by a contemplation of the rights of man over and above institutional laws, he ventured subsequently to investigate and to direct his attention, endorsed by a manifest love of Justice, toward man's bondage to ecclesiastical organisms and religious dogmas. Like a man who respected his individuality, he made investigations into the *causes* of theological usurpation, and freely — perhaps too freely — declared to America his discoveries and his consequent opposition; but America now, and mainly for this reason, disliked and repelled him as cordially as before he was denounced and opposed by England. He desired simply to free the individual; but the ignorant supporters of institutions could reply only through denunciation and scorn. He realized and proclaimed the natural supremacy of man to all political and ecclesiastical organizations—his superiority to all churches and creeds—and hence, like a man thus illuminated (and not unlike the intrepid Jesus in the utterance of his honest convictions), he boldly and unqualifiedly presented his remonstrance to the world—accompanied with a collection of stupendous "Reasons," which (be it ever remembered) have been sneered at and despitefully used by the supporters of institutions, but never intelligently refuted or in any manner proved to be essentially unsound.

What would you propose to do in honor of Thomas Paine, for his defence of Human Rights?

Let me reflect. . . . We have already too many saints; else I would propose the immediate canonization of Thomas Paine. He may have said and committed a thousand foolish things, and so have all saints; may have, in his impatience, wounded the sickly-sentimental piety of honestly-prejudiced and impious persons; but, notwithstanding all, his noble defence of man's sovereignty—his unqualified announcement of the intrinsic inferiority of all institutions to man—covers a multitude of sins (or slanders), and renders him as worthy of a place in the "calendar of saints" as any humanitarian of past times. Saints of past times were appendages of institutions—were advocates of the supremacy of civil and religious laws, over the rights and liberties of Individual Man. But Thomas Paine, unlike saints, was a citizen of the world—an advocate of the sovereignty of the soul—and should therefore be called "Saint Thomas" instead of those blasphemous titles given him by the Church. And yet, I would not blaspheme nor willingly dishonor the memory of Thomas Paine: therefore, I refuse further to stigmatize his character by attaching the word "saint" to any portion of it. Yes, he was superior to a saint! Why so? Because he was a defender of the Rights of Man; while saints, on the contrary, are foes of individualism, and defenders of the faith. They endeavor to anathematize independent manhood in this life, and to fix its damnation throughout eternity.

Suppose Mankind should yield to the requirements of Institutions, what would follow?

The answer is plain. In proportion as minds yield individual supremacy to the Church or State, they give themselves up to the encroachments of slavery and to its multifarious degradations. Institutions combine and conspire against individual freedom; and men, so long accustomed to vassalage, yield themselves conscientiously to perpetuate the iniquity. For example: the political Institutions of America deemed it expedient to legislate and enforce a Fugitive-Slave Law. This law commands those in bondage to remain so, under the penalty of being captured and punished for every violation. And each man in the Free States is appointed by government as a sheriff, with power to arrest the flying fugitive, and consign him to the control and management of his master. But suppose I believe that a man's rights and a man's liberties, irrespective of complexion, are first, and foremost, and supreme; furthermore, suppose I believe the Church and State, and all other institutions, to be secondary and intrinsically *inferior* to the prerogatives of the individual; and suppose, also, that the Church preaches submission to civil laws, and that the State commands me to live and act in subordination to its decrees; I ask—"What must I do? Shall I sacrifice my soul on the altar of an institution?" Oh, Religion of Justice, forbid it! My course is plain before me: I would obey my soul's highest perceptions of Right, although the State might burn me with green fagots as Calvin did Servetus!

Would you not at this point receive some of the penalties of individualism?

Yes; but these penalties are positive benefits, and of high service. See! I stand in friendship with my own central consciousness! *I have helped a fugitive to gain individual freedom.* Therefore, before the omnipresent bar of my Father-God, I stand acquitted of all crime; and more, I am deeply and substantially rewarded for doing a deed of goodness for my brother!

What kind of reward is that which you thus receive?

My reward consisteth in the building up and confirmation of my *individualism*, which giveth me—

"Light and strength to bear
My portion of the weight of care
That crushes into dumb despair
One half the human race!"

And, besides, the benefits come out at another point: I am not individually lost in a mischievous institution; I am not destroyed, as a ship is swallowed, in the recognised maelstrom! Great men, and the so-called wise, around me, are supporters of organizations: they stand in the midst of evils, and have, therefore, no power to discern them; while I rest unperturbed on the firm basis of my own God-inherited interior spirit, worshipping Truth, and Justice, and Harmony, through the functions and portals of my *individual* existence.

But, in the midst of these internal benefits, do you not experience outward penalties?

Yes; the outward penalties, though negative and transitory, tread hard upon the heels of these permanent benefits. They occupy the battle-ground of my worldly relations. Instead of smiles, I meet sneers. Stones are given for bread. Old friends withdraw their friendship. They pity my fantastic zeal, and smile contemptuously. But I would join Paul, conferring "not with flesh or blood." They think and treat my family as unworthy of usual respect; although they may, from habits of duty, try to entertain philanthropic sentiments. In my business relations I am assailed at every assailable point. Old customers leave me very fast; new ones, even with less reputation, come very slow. At school, my cherished ones are pointed at. The orthodox minister's children—echoing what they hear at their home respecting me—hoot scornfully at mine. And thus my wife, with a conservative mind, is roused to the horrors of my unpopularity. She seriously prays for deliverance; perhaps, she contemplates divorce. Her relatives combine with her, and my prudential friends unite, to augment the opposition. Every other mail brings me advisory letters from very honorable uncles, and reproving messages from religious, time-serving, and respectable aunts. The minister frowns upon me: therefore, my church-going wife; therefore, my worldly children. Like Roger Williams, I must seek some spot of Liberty, or be for ever buried in the tomb of popular Institutions. Like the brave Huguenots, I must quit the presence of my foes, or be crushed beneath their overmastering weight. Like Madame Roland, I must respect my soul, and die; or, like Galileo, prudentially confess Truth to be an error, and live an ignominious life!

Suppose you do, from prudential reasons, live in harmony with prevailing Institutions: where will you go to find an instance of greater strength?

This question is hard to answer. If I am not true to my own centralization of consciousness—if I honor not my own orb and orbit—where can I expect to find what I fail to revere in myself? Shall I find it in Jesus, in John, or in Paul? If so, then must I also seek and find it, as they did, in the science of individualism. If I spend my time in acts of devotion to the memory of these individuals, then will I weaken or neglect *my own power* to be as they were. In the most interior closet of their own souls, these men prayed to the God whom they could realize. So also must I pray to that God whom I can realize. I must be strengthened in my personal progression; I must aim equally after political and religious emancipation; I must learn, as it were by heart, the Law of Liberty. In body and in soul I must develop to the fullness of the stature of a perfect Man!

Is there not a period, in the life of every one, when the soul is called to decide whether it will be a master or a slave?

Yes; every kind of situation, and all species of circumstances, bring the high and low alike to this experience: the mechanic, whether he will be a boss or a workman; the tradesman, whether he will be a merchant or a salesman; the student, whether he will be a public man or a private artisan; the printer, whether he will be an editor or "follow copy;" the husband, whether he shall assume the reins of family government; the wife, whether she will be a convenience or a companion.

In true individualism is there any necessary antagonism?

I think not. The motto is, "Let each one be all he can, for the benefit of the whole." It is true that individual currents may encounter and cross each other's paths—as the planets and the comets waltz through each other's orbits; but, with cultured persons, there is in this no infringement, no unwelcome or evil discord. Say to the torrent: "Stop in the midst of yon mountain; because, should you flow down as you wish, you will uproot the trees of the valley." The torrent will answer: "I must obey the law of my nature."

Does Mother-Nature wish every individual to remain true to himself?

Yes; although there is a constant divergence and a convergence—a perpetual centripetalism and a centrifugalism—in the daily operation of individual souls—yet, steadily does Mother-Nature defend each against every other, and maintain a sort of police regulation and jurisdiction in her every department. "Nothing is more marked," says a writer, "than the power by which individuals are guarded from individuals." This is a world "where every benefactor becomes easily a malefactor, merely by a continuation of his activity into places where it is not due." Thus, the pleasurable warmth of the body might be continued into a fever; or, the kindness of an unwise friend could be prolonged and extended out into cruelty. All things are blessings only as they come and go when needed.

Should a man guard his Individualism against the magnetical influence of Institutionalism?

Certainly. If I were to state this matter commercially, I would ask: "*Does it profit a man to sell his soul for popularity?*" If he shall gain the whole world, and lose his own soul (its individualism), how can he be profited? What shall a man give in exchange for his soul? In other words: "What is there in the world more valuable than *Manhood* to a Man, or *Womanhood* to a Woman?" The World answers, "Nothing!" And yet, behold the universal practice of distrusting and crucifying the Individual! Before the gods mankind bow—yielding adoration to mythological idols—to the dishonoring and degradation of his own individuality.

Man has been taught to distrust himself, and to extol the virtues of invisible beings: is this wrong?

All exaggeration, I reiterate, is injustice. Ignorant of his nature, and ignorant not less of the mass of idolatry predicated upon it, man habitually does an *injustice* to himself (in his religious systems), by encouraging the development of extravagant conceptions of divine personalities. The institution of the Trinity has well-nigh absorbed the individual Unity of man. Man can not afford to take from himself and give to gods. No: he is himself in need of all the veneration which he bestows on supposed divinities. He needs all the time and all the talents for purposes of personal development, which, with such imbecile prodigality, he consecrates to the wealthy Upper Circles of Love and Wisdom. The rights of men, in all systems of religion, are buried in the rights of God.

But man is really very insignificant: what is man, but a drop in the bucket?

True: but the ocean is composed of lesser oceans—as the heart of little hearts, and the brain of lesser brains. Does not this fact demonstrate the importance of the least to the existence of the greatest? Yea, I urge the proposition—that all thought which is expended in magnifying theological abstractions, is just so much subtracted from the valuation and welfare of human beings. You purloin from your own divinely-inherited character, and give to self-admiring gods, who have, consequently, no need of your generosity or adoration. Transitional and impractical minds frequently employ themselves, in profoundest seriousness, by grotesquely and uselessly magnifying the attributes and works of their favorite deities. These minds render the invisible so boundless and all-important, that Man is almost utterly lost sight of—is pronounced as insignificant—as an infinitesimal portion of the Infinite Whole—the soul to be swallowed up eventually by the great Ocean of Life whence all things flow. Yes, the fact can not be concealed, that men first create gods; that the process of creation subsequently changes hands; and, lastly, that gods make men. Innumerable religious errors, I repeat, have taken their rise from these false exaggerations. Absurdities, insufferably crude and barbarously despotic, can claim no other parentage.

What do you consider to be the most hurtful effect of these exaggerations?

The most prominent of all religious despotisms—growing out of human exaggerations of the divine, and consequent diminutions of the human—is, the concession to gods of all rights and all liberties, and the permission or granting to man a residuum of duties and obligations. Man, according to such religions, can never feel free of debt. He is a slave! His life is *permitted* or intrusted to him. He must work for the mythologic Master! This, in plain words, is a religious despotism. It neutralizes and absorbs the individualism of man. It seeks to impart propensities toward servility. It takes from him the proprietorship of *an inward power*, on which alone he can unfurl the banner of Liberty. Deplorably true is it that the individuality and sovereignty of men are almost irretrievably lost in these false exaggerations of the individuality and sovereignty of gods. Man first makes an all-absorbing Idol; then, in ten generations, he forgets that he made it; then he puts into tradition that it (the Idol) existed from all eternity; then he teaches, or pays men to teach, his convictions to his children; and, lastly, succeeds in establishing a superstitious theory of divine government. And why? Because his belief has crushed out almost all the individualism of his own spirit. By a harness of iron and traces of steel, the real creature is attached to the inquisitorial car of the fabulous Creator.

Did the doctrine of "duty" arise from the concession of rights to the gods?

Yes; the phantom of "Duty" stands ever near, with upraised lash, to whip the devotee through the countless vicissitudes of a rudimental existence. The Romanish system permits its popes, its bishops, its priests, and the catalogue of saints, to participate more or less in heavenly rights and liberties, which rights and liberties are denied to common men. But Protestantism, being an improvement, permits the universal diffusion of these rights. It teaches each man to consider himself a *centre* of political privileges; that he may exercise private conscience on questions of religion; that, in prayer, he may hold a private correspondence with Heaven; that, in the sphere of his own free will, he can and does maintain certain private moral business relations of "profit and loss" with the Divine Being. And yet, these two systems of religion are predicated upon equally false exaggerations of the gods—the Trinity.

How can you sustain this assertion?

By the fact that both systems, in considering human relations to God, are alike in diminishing man's individualism. In these conscientious variations, from the line of Truth, lie all the pernicious mistakes of theologians. The rights which they theologically concede to man, are not regarded as integral, but *permitted* only, by the system of government which God has seen fit to adopt for the regulation of his creatures. Free will and liberties are lent to man, if I may so say, as an experiment on the part of the gods—to see what he will do, and where he will go, by the use which he makes of them—whether to heaven, or to hell. Now, I affirm all this to be *the most unwholesome form of theology.* Man can never grow into true manhood under it; no more than can a southern slave grow *wealthy* by picking cotton during a long life for an indolent planter. I know of no religious system which conceives that *man has constitutional rights and integral liberties*—independent of all grants or privileges, lets or hindrances, of an arbitrary character. And, therefore, the Harmonial Philosophy which affirms man to be an organization of essences and elements—imparting rights and liberties of their own—is in direct antagonism to all systems of theology, and to all popular forms of religious worship. Hence it freely declareth itself to be the friend of Truth; the exponent and promoter of the interests of Humanity.

Are declarations of individualism daily multiplying?

Yes; and the influence of Institutions is daily diminishing. Man has gradually approached the centre of gravity; and the times are pregnant with promise, that each may become a law unto himself. In every department of society we *need more* individualism. There is now too much sameness; the monotony is irksome; we almost see the uniformity of imbecility. Farmers, for instance, should be more individualized. It is to some extent true that their position bestows upon them social independence. But is it not sad to behold the mental sameness throughout? The son laying stone-walls and digging ditches just as his father and grandfather did before him! The same old plan of haymaking. The barns and outhouses have no new departments. Cattle are kept through the seasons as they were a century ago. The treatment of lowlands is little better than when the first farmer began. And yet, we stand on the brink of a utilitarian improvement in the science of Agriculture. The river of Progress rolls majestically before the young farmer's vision; and now comes the question, "Who will be the Columbus of this new voyage?" The general success of all European farmers—the recent development of agricultural machinery—the spirit of progress exhibited by Western earth-workers—all, fixes a foundation for the realization of ambitious hopes in this direction.

Have we also promises of more individualism in the medical world?

Yes; and I will tell why it must come. Although the troop of candidates for the regular profession is large, absorbing some of our best young men, yet the confidence of the mass of the people is being daily *taken from drugs, and placed upon obedience to the Laws of Nature.* Hence, all manner of medical *individualism* is being, and must continue to be, developed. Men and women, independently, are entering the field of Medical Reform. Each reiterates this gospel: "Health consists in obedience to Physiological and Mental Laws." Clairvoyance has done much toward spreading man's faith in the philosophy of getting well under the influence of simple remedies. Therefore, men may cherish much hope that the Laws of Health will one day concern the world more than the astrological science of curing Disease.

Does individualism appear among editors of newspapers and conductors of periodicals?

I can not give the most desirable answer. Political antagonism has crushed hundreds of editors beneath the weight of party restrictions. Now-and-then, however, there cometh a man from the political institutions, who holds up his head, swings his own arms, thinks and writes his own thoughts, publishes his own "Chronotype," or mounts his own "Tribune," pronouncing "pro and con" on prevailing things and ideas, and at length is heard no more.

Do people in general appreciate the penalties of individualism?

No; the penalties of individual independence are unknown to those who have not had the womanhood or the manhood to make a declaration. Of course, by "independence," I am not understood to mean a burly, swaggering, defiant opposition to established customs; nor yet am I apprehended to mean a foolish, egotistic pride of being *unlike* others, which indicates a self-conceited and pugnacious character. No, nothing of this kind enters into my impressions of individual independence. But, instead, I mean a straightforward, manly, and womanly perseverance in honor of the Spiritual Right that lives and rules within—a strict obedience to the highest idea of Truth that resides in your own soul—regardless of all political institutions and ecclesiastical requisitions to the contrary. ☞ Why judge ye not of yourselves what is Right? ☜ Why not act as your soul, in its highest mood, bids you to act? The cost, or the penalty? That, I know, is heavy. But, mark the fact: *you can never respect your own nature on any less terms!* You can never honor your Father-God and Mother-Nature by a less expensive existence. Out of the heavens a voice speaks to each individual soul: "*Sell all thou hast, and follow Truth!*"

But will you tell us what is Truth?

Your deepest and highest conviction, *that* is your Truth; my deepest and highest conviction, *that* is mine. You can not, therefore, altogether follow me, nor I you; but each may revolve in his own orbit, to the other's benefit.

On this principle, who can help admiring the individualism of John Huss, the Bohemian reformer?

John Huss stood up against what he felt to be religious intolerance and error. He lived nearly a century before Martin Luther, opposed the doctrine of transubstantiation, and, in consequence, was physically *burned to death* by order of an institution called the Council of Constance. In your souls I behold reverence for the *Individual;* for the Council, abhorrence only.

Was not Martin Luther another instance of individual protest against the authority of institutions?

Yes; when Martin Luther was requested, by the nobility, and princes, and prelates of Germany, to defend his new doctrine, he responded in person; and before the Emperor, in the presence of a vast assemblage of opponents, he manfully asserted that noble Sovereignty of Individuality and Reason which Protestants now *deplore* in you and me! He concluded his defence by saying: "Let me, then, be refuted and convinced by the clearest arguments; otherwise I can not and will not recant: for it is neither safe nor expedient to act against conscience. Here I take my stand; I can do no otherwise, so help me God!" However much men feel to differ from Luther, one thing is certain—that his *individualism* challenges universal homage. It is with similar emotions that I think of Swedenborg and of John Wesley, of John Murray and of George Fox, of Charles Fourier and of Robert Owen, of William Ellery Channing, George Combe, and Theodore Parker.

What would you say of these men?

Of these men I might say many things. But it is their individualism which impresses me deepest; the *manifest superiority of their souls to Institutions!* No calm mind can withhold from these men feelings of respect, of veneration. And yet we may not, by being true to our own orbits, find ourselves in unison with them. But this is not worthy of a thought. Because, as I have said, individualism brings no inevitable antagonism; merely an honorable difference; conceding to each star (to each soul) a glory of its own.

Are there not other examples of individualism?

Yes; there are many more. How the soul kindles with the fires of hope, when, in the midst of Institutions, it contemplates the Individuality of such as William Lloyd Garrison and Wendell Phillips, of Lucretia Mott and Lucy Stone! What individualism do these exhibit! These typify a greater troop to emerge from Institutions. Thomas Carlyle, Henry Ward Beecher, and Ralph Waldo Emerson: how exalted above Institutions do these minds *sometimes* appear! Oh, I could almost consent to call these independent persons "saints"—but I forbear: yes, and my reason for forbearing is, that "saints" have, from the first, advocated Institutions (the despotism of arbitrary laws), in opposition to the Rights of Individual Man!

Will unimaginative and utilitarian minds practise individualism without first calculating the wordly penalties?

I think not. Merchants stop with the question of "profit

and loss:" how much *per annum* will it cost to tell the Truth in trade? Where is the man, in the vortex of business, who will follow Truth? Will the wine-merchant, even when convinced that his merchandise is bad for man, leave his occupation? Not at all. Why not? Because it costs too many dollars. Will the tobacconist, the flour-speculator, the stock-broker, the physician, the lawyer, or the clergyman, will any one of these, when persuaded that his occupation is wrong, leave the business, assert the soul's supremacy, and do something more congenial? I fear not: because the penalty is too severe. Oh, what shall a man give in exchange for his soul?

If you were to consider this question like a merchant, what would you say?

If I were to speak as a merchant, I would say, that it will never "pay" to resign or neglect the centristantial fact of the soul. Each man and each woman occupies an original position in the scale of life. There are intrinsically *no* "common people:" a Plato and a Paul, a Huss and a Howard, are human possibilities. These are bows of promise for you and I, and even more; they seem to say: "Be faithful, all ye children of earth, for greater works than these shall ye do!" The hearty Hibernian uttered this truth when he jovially exclaimed: "Mind yer eye (I), boys: for one man's good as another, and betther too." Perhaps, all men feel an inward prophecy of this fact.

Do you mean to teach that individualism is an innate inheritance?

Yes; each one is an eternal FACT—and to it, every other *fact* in the universe must eventually come. The exact point of time when each person "will be better," and do "greater works" than earthy ideal now prognosticates, will remain with the Law of progressive development to determine. But through the alembic of Reason—through the receptive vessels of man's consciousness—must flow every Truth, and every Fact, also, which a principle can possibly embrace. Each, therefore, should have his own Life—his own Liberty—his own Experience—his own Truth. To man's mind everything is subservient. The heavens above, the earth beneath, and profoundest principles, are all his own. To the Turk and Christian, to the Jew and Gentile, to the Serf and Emperor, to the Slave and Master—to each of these, all rights and all liberties will come at last. I know this in the depth of spirit ual wisdom. Most grateful do I feel for the power to realize the fact, that influences are now being exerted, on all sides, for the amelioration of our universal race and the establishment of individual Rights and Liberties.

What have sectarians said about rights and liberties?

The time hath been, as I have shown, and it is not gone by, when sectarians believed that none on earth had rights and liberties, save the pope, the king, the bishop, and priest. Our ancestors, especially those who lived prior to the protestation of Luther, held to these opinions. This doctrine is theocratic, is monocratic, is aristocratic, is—everything, but democratic and republican! All Christian institutions have somewhat to *unlearn* on this subject. By the Church system, man is still denied the ownership of any constitutional liberties. Free Agency is part of a religious Drama: an alleged scheme, on the part of gods, to escape the blame of being accessory to the torment of the wicked. Protestant clergymen, with few exceptions, assert the all-mightiness of God, and thus logically demonstrate that all rights remain with the gods—to man, *a category of duties* The gods command; and man should obey.

What is this but a Roman Catholic idea a little more tenderly stated?

It is the same thing. In essence, the two systems assert the same dogma, viz.: that *the people have no rights*, only duties—obligations to the gods, through obedience to the commandments of his vicegerents—to the dignitaries of the Church.

Need I further explain the restriction which all this imposes on individualism?

Yes; while there remains, in popular creeds and institutions, ideas so utterly hostile to the "Rights of Man," man can not enjoy individual liberties. The idea that the *gods are lawless*, because more powerful than we, is every way injurious. It serves to make man a weak, timid, superstitious, miserable slave! Suppose the mythological gods to be almighty—suppose they possess all powers: does might make Right? The true idea of Father-God is very different. He can not change. The Central Power of this Universe is eternally amenable—

as much as you and I—to the unchangeable Laws of Truth, Justice, Love, Wisdom, Liberty. This idea repudiates all arbitrary religion: and thus, unlike any theology, liberates the Individual.

Will you not utter a few practical additional words, by way of encouragement?

Yes; let all men take courage. The long midnight age of despotic combinations is fast departing. But, like a mighty saurian-lizzard of primeval origin, it will struggle desperately before it dies. You will be summoned to the field of battle. The individualism of man is to be resurrected. The *few* will profoundly respect and fight for it; while the *many* will side with institutionalism. But one Man will put ten thousand such to flight: and the victory will be sure and speedy, on the side of Humanity. It is impossible to make all, of any country, followers of any *one* man, except for a brief period. Why not? Because *no one* can feel and supply the wants of all—Each man comes into being with a code of immutable laws. These laws are righteous—adapted to the development of the whole man—and, some day, the *penalty* is heavy if he goes counter to their demands. These laws are more important to your welfare—are more divine—than all the external bibles, creeds, codes, or churches. Nay: do not doubt! In all soberness I tell you the simple Truth. Faithful obedience to these laws will develop each one's innate character differently, but harmoniously. Under these conditions, each *man* would become A MAN: and each *woman* A WOMAN—not the mere *things* of custom, as they now are—imitator of others less developed than themselves—fleeting reflections of the images of antiquity—automatic followers of some particular age or personage. The well-meaning utilitarian clergy of America think, commercially, that "it don't pay" to teach this modern doctrine of personal emancipation: *to teach a religion so inexpensive as individualism.* Hence they meet us, at the very threshold of this subject, with a "Thus said the Lord." But I say: "Thus saith Humanity." Humanity is not greater than Father-God, I grant; nevertheless, it is the broadest and truest exponent of His word and works.

QUESTIONS ON THE

BENEFITS AND PENALTIES OF INSTITUTIONALISM.

THE terrific conflict between man and institutions, has continued for ages. Individuals have at long intervals openly rebelled against institutional arrogance and despotism; but, the "rebels" were soon struck down and silenced by the inquisitorial aids of tyranny—prisons, dungeons, racks, fagots, and the guillotine. But the revolutionary spirit of these individual rebels lived after them. The spirit of Liberty never sleeps—never lies on the dungeon's floor. Ignorance may retard the progress of liberty; but Nature, in due time, is mighty for the Right. Men have yet a valuable lesson to learn—viz.: *that all penalties are benefits:* that, through discord we ascend to harmony.

What are the terms with which the world designates the friends and enemies of institutions?

Supporters of venerable institutions are called "Pharisees" and "conservatives;" opposers are called "radicals" and "fanatics." Men who lend their money and influence to sustain institutions, are termed "the friends of law and order:" the reformers of institutionalism, on the other hand, are stigmatized as "abandoned heretics and godless infidels." Friends of institutions are called "loyalists;" the friends of Human Rights are marked down in history as "conspirators." Institutions and Aristocracy were married long ago; the ceremony was solemnized by two Mosaic priests — the first is Pride, the second is Power. Individualism and Harmonialism are also married; they wedded each the other, in the presence of Nature's two prime ministers — the first is Reason, the second is Liberty. On the side of institutions you behold all kings, emperors, popes, priests, and orthodox clergymen; on the side of human Liberty you behold the slave, the serf, working men, working women, hewers of wood, drawers of water, fishermen, and minds who perform their own thinking. Institutionalism dwells in churches, in palaces, in opulent families; individualism, on the contrary, lives in honest heads and courageous hearts. Institutionalism goes to heaven by faith; individualism, by works. One serves theology and the gods; the other anthropology and mankind.

You said that institutionalism serves the gods: have gods any need of human gifts?

Far from it: must slaves work, from babyhood to the tomb, to make rich masters richer? The chief end of man, on earth, is to bless and elevate Humanity. To attempt to glorify the gods — the Trinity — would be an act of supererogation. Can man add anything to the glory of gods? Can man impart new splendor to the heavens? Nay: man should only attempt possibilities. He can add glory and splendor to his kind; this, then, is his field of action. Such would be Individualism; the religion of Manhood.

Is institutionalism father of churches and governments?

Yes; there are already hundreds of thousands of churches dedicated to the gods; but there are not ten consecrated to Mankind. Governments are made to defend the rich; and to subjugate the poor. In Louisville, Kentucky, a rich man's son was recently freed from the gallows, through the power of money; while almost every month we hear of "the dignity of the law" being vindicated by the formal strangulation of friendless persons for crimes far less aggravating. Institutions are made, by the strong, to maintain power. Individuals, therefore, have but one course to pursue — namely — *to rebel against Institutions, and take the penalties.*

Will you briefly reconsider the influence of institutions upon character?

Yes; the power of institutions, over the liberties and tertiary characteristics of individuals, is tremendous. Few can withstand the popularity of their despotism. Few can maintain manhood, and manifest their divine character, in the midst of a magnetism so energetic. To many persons, with certain predisposed secondary characters, the attractive power of popular institutions is irresistible. In fact, popularity to the majority of minds, is like some fair crystal river, in which melancholy pilgrims drown themselves. They lose themselves willingly in its enticing bosom. It looks smooth, the tide is popular, and in they plunge. The Niagara of Reformation is too fearful for the navigator of inland rivers. The roar of Revolution disturbs the opium-eater. He who unfortunately has been nursed by the hand-maid of Institutions, rocked in the cradle of Popularity, fed gruel with the silver-spoon of Aristocracy, and sung to sleep in the lap of Opulence, is not the man for Humanity. No! Humanity's man, on the contrary, is always born in a manger. He hath the blood of the people in him. He declareth that *institutions were made for man;* not man for institutions. Governments and religions are less than Man—because, from his mind they emanated. Therefore, all laws are really subject to the will of the world. Each man is a prophet, priest, and king.

Are you not opening mischievous liberties to individuals?

No one need fear the sovereignty of individualism; the right of each to act in accordance with his highest Intuitions. For, should one man transcend his boundaries, another will let him know it. We need to practise the gospel of self-government. The conservative may cry aloud for the safety and sanctity of Institutions. But heed him not! His voice cometh not from the open field, not from the mountain's top. Far from it. On the contrary, his cries proceedeth from the wilderness of crime and marshes of despotism, which are tenfold more dangerous than the everglades of Florida. Hark ye! American Republicanism will be transformed into Tyranny, unless individual man declareth himself independent of all political and ecclesiastical Institutions.

Do you not believe that American institutions, more than those of any other country, look toward Freedom?

American churchianity is too despotic; so, also, are American politics; and yet, it is true, that both, more than those of any other country, are looking toward Freedom. It is also true that independence of mind and speech, is not encouraged but generally denounced. Men think and speak as yet on sufferance. Yes; I urge the proposition, that the right to think and to speak freely is not yet established. On the Connecticut Statute-Book is a law against freely discussing, what I term the gods—usually called the "Trinity." The Hartford Bible Convention was, therefore, denounced as "illegal" by several conservatives. If the speakers at that memorable convention were not legally apprehended, "fined one hundred dollars, and sent to jail," the fact was owing to a spirit of toleration pervading the community; not to any real love of Liberty as a principle of human speech and action. That convention was permitted, suffered, tolerated; not defended and protected by the legal or religious institutions of America. Yea, I repeat it, we have no *absolute* Liberty among us. We demand something more than a patronizing spirit of *toleration:* because, there is no security for individual freedom under circumstances so superficial and temporary. According to our institutions, as I have already said, the wife is the husband's property. He owns her person, her garments, her children, her rights, her liberties. But woman, becoming more and more individualized, is now resolved to rebel against our institutions. Not only has she determined to assert her Rights, but she has resolved to step forward and *take* them. The Conservative says: "Woman has now as much liberty as man." But here is the mistake: her liberty is not real. The wife is tolerated or suffered *to do nearly as she pleases;* nevertheless, the laws of the institutions are against her individuality. Her liberty is not a matter of principle; it is secured mainly through affection, urbanity, and civility; it is but a defence of the weak by the strong.

Do you mean to affirm that in this, as in every other respect, our political institutions are antagonistic to individual freedom?

Verily; and the same is true of our American Church. It

was not wholly owing to the love of Liberty among priests that the church meddles not with political action. That is t say, the people are not politically free, because the priests love to have it so; far from it; they endorse individual liberty in legislation—first, because they make "a virtue of necessity" —second, because northern people, as a mass, have outgrown the absolute tyranny of institutionalism. It was not Love of Liberty that originally separated State and Church: it was the *anger* of Henry VIII. of England; because the Pope would not divorce him from his then wife, Catharine of Aragon. But good has come out of it! And yet, our political institutions would not contradict popular ecclesiastical enactments. The Church says that Masters and Servants are proper according to providential decrees; the State responds—"Amen." The Church says that Paul, *the Saint*, sent the slave back to his master; the State responds "Amen," and institutes a Fugitive Slave Law. The Church asserts that "the desires of the wife shall be unto her husband, *and that he shall rule over her;*" the State responds "Amen," and institutes legal provisions accordingly. But humanity is somewhat resurrected in this respect, and laws more liberal and just are gradually being developed. "To smother its grand adversary, Liberty (says that great political economist and faithful historian, Guizot), has ever been the first and last aim of the church. The overthrow of freedom is its mission and its hope. No man can read its history, the doings of its conventions, its laws and canons, without perceiving that in every act its aim has been to crush human liberty, under pretext of piety, and to found a tyrannical despotism civil and religious."

There is a political party, recently organized, called the "Know-Nothings"—composed chiefly of native-born American citizens: what are your impressions concerning it?

The paramount and governing principle, or policy, of this party, is, *opposition to all foreign influence*—directed principally against the Irish and Roman Catholics. It refuses to them the right to hold public positions as officers, or to make laws for the American people. Now, I am fully aware that the Papal power in America is daily developing into prodigious strength. And many political papers encourage the spread of this power by securing, or endeavoring to secure, the votes of the Irish population. The Whigs and Democrats, the Hards and Softs, the Doughfaces and Emptyheads, and other appropriately-named parties, studiously avoid every word that could be construed into opposition to Roman Catholicity—because, simply, the Irish vote is very important to the election of favorite candidates. I am also aware that the genius of the Catholic system, *its real animus*, is politically and ecclesiastically despotic. It is Institutionalism against Individualism. And yet, notwithstanding all this and much more, still worse, I could not consent to become a Know-Nothing. Why not? Because I can not oppose error with error. Native Americanism is a home despotism organized to put down a foreign despotism. It is, therefore, force, and prejudice, and tyranny, against tyranny, and prejudice, and force. Liberty, on the contrary, can prosper only by Liberty. If Native influence puts down Catholic influence by force, and if the American character is made to endorse it, who can tell when another party will not arise to put down the Harmonial Philosophy? In a country where the Principle of Liberty is not fully admitted and proclaimed, I feel insecure—yea, uncertain of the Rights of my Individualism. But you ask—

Do you not look at the consequences—the results of the spread and supremacy of Papal power in America?

With the question of consequences I have nothing to do—only with the Principle. Results can not be wrong when Right is pursued. The same political spirit that would persecute and prostrate Catholics in this country, might, in the next fifteen years, persecute and prostrate Harmonial Philosophers. How so? Because, although Roman Catholics and Harmonial Philosophers are absolutely *opposite to each other* in most questions, yet do they harmonize in their opposition to the Protestant systems of religious quackery; and they also agree to make the charge that American politics are fearfully destitute of the principles of distributive Justice and universal Liberty

What plan would you suggest whereby to prevent political and religious despotism?

The only certain plan whereby to prevent the establishment

of political and ecclesiastical despotism, is this: a universal education of our people to revere and to practise the principles of Absolute Individual Liberty. All faith in a miraculous, arbitrary, despotic Revelation, must be carefully removed, and placed upon Father-God and Mother-Nature. The inner Light, the religion of Justice in the soul of each, must become the rule of faith and practice. American Theology and Roman Catholicity would then die—never to breathe again, never to know a resurrection!

According to your definition, what is an Institution?

An Institution, according to our best definition, is an establishment appointed, prescribed, and founded, by *authority*—intended to be permanent. Thus, we speak of the established institutions of Moses or Lycurgus, or the laws of the Medes and Persians. The popular idea of an Institution is, an organized society, established by law, or by the authority of individuals, for the promotion of any given object, social, political, or religious. Hence, it can not but be seen that an Institution is somewhat like the Chinese Wall—a stupendous and systematic effort to keep individuals permanently within or without. The Individual is never encouraged to grow and expand, save to the circumference of the circle. *There* he must stop, or be called a conspirator, a rebel, and—take the penalties.

Will you point to some examples of institutional wrong?

Examples are too numerous. It was an Institution, under the direction of Herod the Great, which caused the slaughter of four thousand children within the precincts of Bethlehem. It was an Institution that presented and accomplished the diabolical deeds of cruelty termed the "Massacre of St. Bartholomew," when in one day more than forty-five thousand persons were slain in Paris and the provinces of France. Do you wonder still that I refused to prefix the word "saint" to the name of Thomas Paine? It was an Institution that established "the office of the Holy Inquisition," for the systematic extirpation of infidels, Jews, and other heretics. It was authorized by the Roman power, and put in practical operation in Italy, Spain, and Portugal. The indescribable tortures of the victims of that Holy (!) Institution—their piteous cries for help—come to us even unto this day, laden with admonitions—with portentous warnings—saying: "We beseech you, see to it, that you arise in wisdom against the despotism of Institutions!" It was an Institution that crucified the loving Nazarene. All Wars are outbirths of Institutions. Slavery of every description—social, political, religious—results from Institutions. There is a "peculiar Institution," consolidated into adamantine strength, under the heavens of the sunny South. There the sable brother has no right to his body, no right to his soul: his wife, his little ones, his sisters and brothers—all, belong to the Institution. And this Institution is the property of the few, who, owing to the mere accident of birth, carry the purse, and therefore the power. What an unutterable misfortune it is to be born within the precincts of such a political and spiritual pestilence!

What may be said of Russian Institutionalism?

It was an Institution which, amid millions of human beings, selected the Czar of Russia to act the part of Despot. The Muscovite Autocrat is himself an Individual. His moral organization, nevertheless, is fashioned by his circumstances. His conceptions of justice are huge and arbitrary; not fine, and springing from an idea of universal distribution of rights. An Emperor's tertiary character is cynical in some particulars. He sees no really *good* thing in man; because, owing to his usurpations, the openly or secretly *bad* is everywhere manifested. He is not certain of anything human; yet he treats his immediate associates with great respect.

Is the Russian Emperor inclined to religion?

Almost every Russian despot has been actuated by a peculiar reverence for the sacred institutions of God. He thinks the Greek Church to be the especial emporium of the designs of Deity. In this particular, the Despot is as conscientious and superstitious, too, as any orthodox clergyman in the United States. For he is fully "persuaded in his own mind" that he is doing God a genuine service, even when he entraps and subjugates other nations, to provide the Church with rich and numerous adherents. He considers himself as much an "agent" for the Almighty as any New-England teacher of the faith once delivered to the Saints. He firmly and conscientiously believes that he has a "mission" to fulfil. It is right and essential to order, in his opinion, that he should place himself at the head of Church and State.

Do Emperors usually possess strong heroic feelings?

The Russian ruler's love of country is strong, but his national pride is weaker far than his pride of power. His hereditary and acquired characters compel him to be a worshipper of power. In this respect, an Institutional Autocrat is morbidly ambitious. He prays to extend his dominions, his power and government. He studies hard to *out-general* the world. His firmness in this direction is unwavering and indomitable. He thinks strongly, steadily, indignantly. He can not consent to be weak enough to pardon an enemy; his love of power makes him unforgiving. His moral organization is so constituted, that *suspicion* of human nature is inevitable. He is enough superstitious to believe himself the *spiritual and legal head* of a God-made Institution: his nature, therefore, is unable to form a clear and steady belief in the intrinsic goodness of any Individual. This silent conviction—I might say skepticism—tends to render him cruel, despotic, absolute. To his acquired character, it sometimes seems that—

'Deception is the warp and thread of being;
The sky is fickle, and the elements
Are traitors all. The spider plots his living
In deceit; and in the air, the kingly birds
With cruel art on weaker ones descend,
And gorge their appetite. The beasts and fish,
Who have some lordly sway, turn land and sea
Into a stage for drama treacherous,
Whose plot the Almighty laid. Therefore do I
Stand up in Nature's centre, and my foot feels
Her heart beat, while I scheme."

When I view an Emperor altogether, with all his characteristics taken in combination, I see a man who is an *instrument*, or circumstance, in the hands of confederated diplomatists. Everything is done over his shoulder.

What effect does this produce upon him?

This flatters his love of power, and gives him a reputation

for great skill and courage, which he seldom really works to earn: hence, as an individual, he enjoys the position he occupies extremely well. The present Emperor's father, Nicholas, had so much pride in the sagacity and diplomacy of his public officers and chief nobles, that he affirmed them to be superior to the most civilized nations whom he spurned to copy or imitate in any particular. From strangers the Emperor would consent to learn or borrow seldom. There is something anomalous in the character of this Emperor. He is master—he knows it—all acknowledge it in his nation; but he *never claims* such absolute prerogative or control. Church and State are both beneath his governmental regulations. He makes the ecclesiastical patriarchs and bishops swear unequivocal allegiance and obedience to himself; yet, when meeting the higher clergy in public, he devoutly kisses the archbishop's hands, and displays other evidences of religious reverence and submission. With the populace this policy operates like magic. They behold the agents of God, organized and maintained at incalculable expense and ceremony, for the sake of the people. To all outward seeming, the Emperor aspires to be a conscientious Christian, a devout priest, a careful king—a despot from the force of religious necessity—a chief ruler among the nations.

What seems to be the religious belief of the Russian Emperor?

The Emperor is moved by the conviction that he is designed by God to spread the Muscovite government over territories of the heathen. Russia is moved by its chief toward the East. The idea of Heaven's decree—a religious duty, a sacred mission—acts upon him and his chief officers and ministers as powerfully as ever a superstition influenced any mind. "Eastern powers must become Russian!" This is the watchword. The Emperor is fully convinced that there can be no permanent power in a country where the people are permitted to act out their depraved private wills. He feels that Pope and King should exist only in one man, as religion and intellect meet in one organization. Actuated by his acquired skepticism in regard to the tendencies of human nature, he watches this focal concentration of ecclesiastical and political power as jealously as did Othello the virtue of Desdemona. And you can not persuade him, with his intellectual and moral organism, out of the idea that he should make war upon heathen nations, and convert them and their possessions to the saving ordinances and government of the Greek Church. He would be somewhat skilful in managing a conquest—bold, combative, courageous, hopeful, firm, and ambitious of power—and being, withal, so religious in his wars, though employing other motives as pretexts, you may be sure that he will spring his plans *when* and *where* they are least expected.

What effect does Russian Institutionalism exert upon the inhabitants?

Under the institutionalism of Russia, I can see no escape for the serfs. The Russian ministers, I think, are more fond of triumph and subjugation than the Emperor himself. They do much toward bringing about pretexts for making war upon the East; and the Czar gets all the praise and condemnation. He is master; his will is supreme. But his will coincides with the legislation or suggestion of his chief nobles and public officials; and yet it must be seen that the Emperor's own peculiar mind acts clearly enough in coloring and shaping all plans and decrees. He is a victim as well as King; a subject as well as Emperor. The nobles, as a class, are excessively proud. The serfs, as a class, are exceeding submissive. The Czar, as a man, is ambitious. All are superstitious, and actuated and bound together by absurd religious convictions. And there is no greater civilization possible in Russia—no more freedom to be expected in the empire of Nicholas—until Individualism is recognised, and some valuable education is bestowed upon the ignorant and stultified peasantry.

What is the heading of every despotic institution?

The programme of every despotic institution is headed with —"Believe, or be damned!" And the head and front of our offending is, a personal remonstrance. But how difficult to swim against the tides of popularity! The waves dash furiously against and roll over you. You must have a confidence in the Truth—else you will sink beneath the surface of Institutions, and become food for reptiles that crawl on their blood-stained foundations.

"Once we thought that Kings were holy,
Doing wrong by right divine;
That the Church was lord of conscience—
Arbiter of mine and thine;
That whatever priests commanded,
No one could reject, and live;
And that all who differed from them
It was error to forgive!"—

But now we declare ourselves a "free and independent" race of Brothers—EACH A LAW UNTO HIMSELF. Institutions shall not for ever bind us: and, when we say this, we speak for the oppressed African, the Italian, the Hungarian, the Russian serf—we speak for all the Nations!

Can you illustrate the influence of institutions upon character?

I have already done so. You probably remember a certain son of Erin who opposed the rigid Institutions of England, and yet advocated American Slavery. The freemen of the North were astonished. At home, he was the friend of Liberty; here, the supporter of Slavery. At home, he denounced the Institutions; hence, the Institutions deprived him of individual liberty. Here, a fugitive from British tyranny, he puts up a voice in favor of slavery. It were better had he remained the friend of Freedom. The North could not easily bear the sting which he added to its smarting, burning, twinging, black Cancer, in the South. And so it was that men condemned John Mitchel. Because of his apostacy, they wrote to render him infamous. But let us not forget that, from his early youth—yea, by hereditary descent and generative blood—he was a victim of Institutionalism. Perhaps, real Liberty he had not known—still feels not. Nevertheless, he manfully rebelled against certain political restrictions. But the grandeur of Individualism he could not, perhaps can not, realize. Therefore, while I fraternize with and compassionate John Mitchel, I all the more repudiate the Institutions of which he has been, and still is, a victim.

"Once we thought that sacred Freedom
Was a cursed and tainted thing—
Foe of peace, and law, and virtue,
Foe of magistrate and King;

That the vile and rampant passion
  Ever followed in her path —
Lust and Plunder, War and Rapine,
  Tears, and Anarchy, and Wrath !" —

But now we think that true individual freedom will for ever prevent all these evils. While Liberty is the "foe of magistrate and King," it is not less the friend of "peace and virtue;" and elevates — by its benign influence, so attractive and so strong — each of our common race. The Tyrants of the Old World still regard our Republic as an experiment. They prophesy that the people will one day overthrow the foundations of our government. But we are Progressive! That explains enough. We go from alteration to improvement; we wound, only to heal. Hence, with every American revolution comes development. An earthquake would result in better geographical conditions — in better atmospheric combinations. Let a people practically believe in Progression, and they will ascend from bad to better, "from evil educing good," as upon the rounds of a ladder.

But is there not a philosophy in Government?

Governments procreate and reproduce themselves; they come in the natural course of things. The first human government was like an acorn. When it was planted, out of human necessity, then began the historical series of Institutions which have marked the pathway of mankind. The last shall be as the first in quality, but infinitely superior in degree: even so every acorn reproduces its kind, and progresses by means of multiplication.

What was the first form of government?

The first government was Anarchy; that is, no government at all. This was the germ. The last will be even so — with this difference, that each individual at first was actuated by his passions; at last, each will move by the light of Reason. At first, each considered might as right; at last, each will esteem right as might. At first, the people worshipped the god of Wealth and Power; at last, they will venerate the god of Love and Wisdom. But the Individualism of Mankind will at last stand out even more absolutely against Institutions than at first. The Anarchy of the first days was Confusion; the Anarchy of the last days will be Harmony. The first form of government, being anarchical, forced every person to rely upon his own centre of strength. But the soul was then unable to practise Individualism upon a higher plane. Not Love, but Force, was manifested. The strong began to oppress the weak. Innumerable troubles arose among neighboring tribes; and so, from the bosom of Necessity, came another form of government.

What was the second form of government?

The second form was Patriarchal. Now, each tribe had its own Father, who was arbiter and absolute governor. But this form gradually changed into Theocracy.

What is a theocratic government?

A Theocracy means the government of a people by the supposed immediate direction of God. The Israelites furnish an example. The priest, however, really had everything his own way. He had but to say, "Thus saith the Lord"—and his commands, good or evil, were unhesitatingly obeyed.

What is the fourth form of government?

The fourth form is Monarchy. Monarchy is a government in which the supreme power is lodged in the hands of a single person.

What is the fifth form of government?

The fifth form is Republicanism. This is a form of government in which majorities rule. The sovereign power is lodged by the people in their representatives.

What is the sixth form of government?

The sixth form is Democracy. I am led to affirm that a real *democratic* form of government has never as yet been developed on earth. The government of Athens, in Greece, was an approach to it. Democracy is an institution in which the supreme power is lodged in the hands of the people. America is not a Democracy: it is Republican. Republicanism invests representatives with all the power of legislation: Democracy, on the other hand, is the power of the people to legislate for themselves. We aspire after a Democratic form of government. It is superior to Republicanism. It will secure the rights of Workingmen; the rights of Free-laborers; the rights of the Slave; the rights of Woman; the rights of Children. But even this form of government is *too formal* for Humanity. *The last shall be as the first.* The Anarchy of the first must come out at last in the Individualism of refined and civilized man. Hence, Progressives as we are, we declare ourselves openly in favor of no government. The people are governed too much. They will rebel. They will gradually become ungovernable. They will demand at each other's hands *absolute, supreme individual sovereignty*—which Patriarchalism, which Theocracy, which Monarchy, grants unreservedly to Fathers, to Kings, to Emperors, to Popes, to Tyrants.

What will be the seventh form of government?

The seventh form will be Autocracy. An Autocratic form of government is that in which a ruler, a sovereign, holds and exercises the powers of regulation *by inherent right*—subject to no restriction. THIS IS PERFECT INDIVIDUALISM!—independent or absolute power of self-government; supreme, uncontrolled, unlimited right of governing in a single person. Yes, each person will become an Autocrat. And each Autocrat will be a power, exercising equal justice, on principles set forth in the twelve commandments.

Do you realize how this doctrine seems to a timid conservative?

Yes; I am well aware that, to a timid conservative, and to those who breathe in the atmosphere of Institutionalism, all this bears the impress of Original Anarchy. They fear that Confusion will be worse confounded. Such minds would urge me to "beware of extreme radicalism." They would preach against Individualism, as Tyrants protest against Republicanism. But I tell you that Individualism will eventually develop out of Democracy—just as Republicanism was developed out of Monarchy—naturally, as blooming Summer comes out of rigid Winter.

But suppose the American Union were dissolved?

There is to-day no obvious ground upon which to rest such a supposition; and we will not spend our time in useless argumentation. Yet grant, for a moment, your supposition. What would be the result? My reply is, an immediate reorganization, with a no better Constitution.

How do you know this?

From the fact that neither the character nor the soul of the American people has *outgrown the form* of its present Institution. If a farmer should attempt to destroy poisonous weeds by cutting off their leaves—the roots still remaining firm in the earth—his efforts would result in disclosing to himself his own ignorance. The weeds would grow all the more abundantly. That is to say, our government is based upon an idea of justice. But this idea is found to be imperfect. Notwithstanding which, the government will remain strong, unshaken, unaltered, until the soul of this Nation outgrows its political fundamentals. When a higher idea of justice gets into the American people, then, and only then, will the Union decompose like a dead body: then, too, will the newer, the greater, and the juster soul, be clothed upon with a newer, a greater, and a juster Constitution. All this oratorical flourish about the dissolution of our Union is useful, because it moves the people, and compels many to look into the philosophy of government.

What good can you accomplish by teaching the doctrine of Individualism?

If I teach the doctrine of Autocracy—if I urge you to accept and *live out* the principles of Individualism—I do something toward elevating, and expanding, and universalizing the Soul of the American people; something, also, toward hastening the national *decomposition* of arbitrary forms of Institutionalism, as well as all phases of bondage and slavery. Most explicitly, however, I acknowledge a certain *transitional* good in Institutions. Although it is true that they have long opposed the growth of Humanity—have always said, "Believe, or be damned!"—yet, let us recall the principle that *all penalties are benefits.* The crushed rose emits a sweeter fragrance: even so is obstructed and arrested Liberty gaining strength and righteousness. There is a Father-God in the constitution of Mother-Nature, who bringeth *good* out of seeming evil—harmony from discord—so positively and surely, that even war is at last to benefit Humanity.

Can Individualism exist independently of all Association?

No; there is a degree of Institutionalism which is natural to man, in all stages of growth, and absolutely necessary to that growth—viz., the Institution of THE GREAT HARMONIUM, based upon the law of Spiritual Attraction; having *no bond of union except the Affinity of Love and the Unanimity of Wisdom.* Popular Institutions are made from outside influences—supported by legal enactments—infringing upon the liberties of large minorities. Humanitarian institutions, on the contrary, will resemble solar bodies—each revolving in its own orbit—at once an honor to Father-God and a happiness to all men. Benevolent, Attractive, Industrial, and Educational Associations, are, on this principle, desirable as transitional means of Individual development. Man was not made for forms, remember; but forms for man.

"The veriest coward upon earth
Is he who fears the world's opinion—
Who acts with reference to its will,
His conscience swayed by its dominion.

"Mind is not worth a feather's weight
That must with other minds be measured;
Self must direct, and self control,
And the account in heaven be treasured.

"Fear never sways a manly soul—
For honest hearts 't was ne'er intended:
They, only they, have cause to fear,
Whose motives have their God offended.

"'What will my neighbor say if I
Should this attempt, or that, or t' other?'
A neighbor is most sure a foe
If he prove not a helping brother.

"That man is brave who braves the world,
When o'er Life's sea his bark he steereth;
Who keeps that guiding star in view—
A conscience clear, which never veereth."

A PSYCHOMETRICAL EXAMINATION OF

WILLIAM LLOYD GARRISON.

For the world's sake, I propose to devote a few hours to the psychometrical examination of a certain notorious and celebrated character. Moved by this self-made proposition—coupled with a special desire to investigate for myself the intrinsic nature of the gentleman—I yesterday procured a lock of hair from the head of William Lloyd Garrison, the well-known editor of the "Liberator," a weekly paper devoted to the advocacy of unconditional freedom, with this motto—"Our Country is the World, our Countrymen are All Mankind"—published every Friday morning, in Boston, Massachusetts. With this hair I expect to throw my mind so clearly into clairvoyance, that, to examine this public man—to see him just as he is, and *not* as he or others may think he is—will be comparatively an easy matter. Of course there is sufficient skepticism, respecting this power to discern human character, to give both the friends and foes of this gentleman "the benefit of the doubt."

As yet, I have had no real opportunity to obtain a correct external knowledge of this indestructible Garrison.* I have met and passed friendly words with him on several occasions; but nothing has ever occurred, in any of these interviews, to

* This examination was made two years ago; since which I have spent several useful hours in his presence.

let me into the "real reality" of his constitution. With the public estimate of his character I am familiar. I have heard and read opinions of him at which my soul revolted; which caused me to wish never to meet with so wicked a man.

His friends have never given me any description of him. The only definite thing I ever received from any one respecting him was said to me by a very ardent friend of his, in these words: "I want you to know Garrison; I think you will like him; and I want him to know you." Now, in my opinion, the quickest way for me to arrive at this desirable knowledge, is to make an examination of his primary, secondary, and tertiary characteristics in the manner proposed; and, as he is to some extent, the property of the people, I will make my impressions publicly known as fast as I obtain them. I propose to investigate him *objectively*, *socially*, *intellectually*, *morally*, and as an *individual*, in relation to the world. Let us now proceed. The following were my

Impressions when viewing him objectively. His physical system is evenly balanced and well developed; it is neither too large nor too small; sufficiently full of strong, elastic, enduring, muscular fibre, associated with a nervous organization, which is naturally steady and firm, but very sensitive. His brain is composed of fine material, remarkably active and brilliant; giving, as whole, an organism very capable of withstanding the insidious operations of disease, the force of atmospherical changes; and will sustain for a long time, a vast quantity of carefully-graduated corporeal and mental labor. His personal presence has breadth, chastity, and manliness. When he walks, there goes a man with an object before him; with something ahead to be accomplished. When he stands in conversation, his manner is upright and downright; he is constitutionally graceful, precise, emphatic, earnest. When he teaches before an audience, there stands the same man with the same manners: you see him gesturing, without impetuosity, with his right arm, as if hammering his thoughts into the mental fabric of the people. His countenance is strikingly indicative of straightforward, unchangeable earnestness; shows an attachment to whatever is inherent, vital, genuine, glorious; to nothing unmanly or superficial. His mouth is indicative of kind feelings and moderate mirth; with a slight curve at either corner, signifying a tendency toward rebuking criticism. His eye is generous, serious, penetrative, thoughtful; it looks at and reads you, then turns playfully aside, as if nothing had occurred; while the mouth is earnestly but familiarly engaged in conversation with you or others. He appears like a person who is fond of personal refinements and quietude; fond of all the outward temperate comforts furnished by a rational civilization. With the superior portions of his head completely divested of hair—not from age, but through hereditary causes; with his somewhat prominent and well-defined features—though not sharp, irregular, or unbeautiful; with his face and neck carefully shaven and deprived thus of what was by nature designed as a useful ornament and the peculiar superscription of a man; with a simple cravat nicely adjusted; with gold spectacles, sitting with dignity before his expressive eyes; with his person neatly clad in a suit of black—and, with his manly form and becoming stature—there is a "certain something" about this William Lloyd Garrison, in his external appearance and unsuperficial department, whether standing or reposing, which positively attracts your attention and unequivocally challenges your respects. The following were my

Impressions when viewing him socially. In his family and among his friends he is peculiarly domestic and social. His love for wife and children is steady, truthful, heartfelt; but it is not sufficiently powerful to urge him a hair's-breadth from what he conceives to be the path of Right, in his relation to the brotherhood of man. Home has a genial—not a moulding—influence, upon his affections and disposition. He enjoys the *idea* of having a "local habitation" of his own; yet, the love of locality is temperate, and gains no real mastery over his higher attractions and purposes. He is far more playful with adults than children—more mental than physical, in either case; is never reserved or saturnine in company; and, although inclined to satire and irony, is seldom betrayed into their use in common conversation; but leans easily to a jest, or pun, and is (or may be) quick and fortunate at repartee

His private character is remarkable for its uniformity and simplicity; the artlessness and spontaneity of the child are invariably manifest; and through these winning attributes the strong, indomitable characteristics of a Man shine brilliantly forth upon his companions. The continuity of his social nature is likewise very remarkable; before wife and children, before friends and enemies, he is ever the same person. He is a stranger to "dignified or contemptuous silence," and not less to all feelings of a supercilious or exclusive nature. No one's opinions, no one's experiences, no one's ideas, no one's concerns, are without interest to him; and he will, when not engaged in elaborating or completing a thought then agitating his own mind, listen to the tale of the most humble and illiterate. To his friends he is warm and confiding; to his enemies he is frank and honorable; to both he will earnestly express his opposition to their errors, thinking of neither their approbation nor displeasure, when a *principle* is under debate; and yet he has quite a strong love of praise, and has no disposition, *per se*, to wound the feelings of any man. The following were my

Impressions when viewing him intellectually. His is a high order of intellect, but not the highest. It is more than usually well arranged and evenly balanced; superior, in this particular, to most public and literary men. It looks like a house put in order. The furniture is well chosen, and seems, without irrelevant ornament or useless display, most admirably adapted to the size and architecture of the dwelling. In his mind there are no useless materials. Each thought and every experience is made to subserve some present contingency and immediate purpose. This intellect is not diffusive and nebulous; it is a compact, transparent unit—a *one*ness. He does not reason very frequently from cause to effect—interiorly and analytically; but mostly from inward prompting, with external observation and a critical comparison of statistics, historical events, general circumstances, and contiguous or present facts. He is, therefore, a surface and transparent reasoner; and this enables him to render his ideas definitely to the people. He seldom reasons deep enough to reach the metaphysical and imaginative functions of the human mind. He is honest, and always *out and out.* Yet, he possesses the requisite mental power to dive beneath the surface, and searchingly too, if he should especially desire to do so.

When occasion challenges him, he can construct a logical, broad, manly, and tremendous argument. He is very vigilant, and guards his fundamental positions or outposts, like an accustomed warrior. Without oratorical embellishments or poetic flights, always compact and well joined, loaded to the brim with cannon-balls calculated to do the execution designed, his argumentations are clear and addressed to the highest as well as the most *practical* faculties of the human mind. And being consciously endowed with ever-available powers of intellect, capable of grasping great themes, he experiences no mental reserve or trepidation.

Memory of words and ideas is remarkably good. His recollection of music is not so perfect as of the sentiment; the former is remembered through the later by association. He is fond of poems with generous and universal themes; ordinary versification on sentimentalities is exceedingly distasteful. To him classic literature is replete with attractions; his literary tastes and powers are keen and pungent; he writes his ideas with pecular distinctness; and is disposed to be hypercritical, and captious even, in his own use of terms. In respect to the choice of words, he is naturally guarded and intellectually conscientious; they must signify literally what he thinks, or what others think, and nothing more. He is quick at discerning flaws in arguments; the premises and conclusions are mathematically adjusted in his mind; *and there can be no mistake or alteration in positions he thus assumes*, i. e. in his honest opinion. Yet, he is ever willing to investigate those assumptions afresh, and takes new views of them, when his judgment is convinced. Although disposed to irony, he seldom thinks or writes under its influence; and though no less disposed to sarcasm, he tempers his didactic thoughts and exegetical language with benevolence and a kind of imperious suavity. There is a nobility in this intelligence. It is strong, energetic, active, sensitive, cultivated, available, and self-sustaining. His intellectual integrity — that is, his self-justice in thinking or reasoning on any theme — is very extraordinary and peculiar to himself. His words are naturally not numerous, but by development and necessity, they flow out without much interruption; and with a conscientious precision. The following were my

Impressions when viewing him morally. Some minds are receptacles only; this is a source. Some are goblets and pitchers ready to receive and entertain; this is a fountain. In the moral department of this mind, I feel more at home. His love of JUSTICE AS A PRINCIPLE, *per se*, is sensitive, intense, powerful. I feel an imperial *right* to examine the relations between man and man. Enthroned above all other thoughts and deeper than all other sentiments, are — GOD, JUSTICE, LIBERTY. These standing and ruling thoughts never sleep; neither do they dream. The whole mind is moved from centre to circumference by them, as a world by the attractive laws of gravitation; they not only influence, but they mould, and give shape to all the elements of his hereditary and acquired character. Actuated and energized by these *sovereign* sentiments, he feels a *severe indignation* — a species of outrage committed upon his own soul — at the injustice done to the liberties of a fellow-being. His justice is severe and somewhat arbitrary; fortunately, it is pleasingly tempered by benevolence. But for this, he would be a second JOHN CALVIN — a person of an indomitable will — with a persecuting disposition. But with GOD, JUSTICE, and LIBERTY, so supreme to all personal or selfish sentiments — so paramount to all other thoughts and attractions — this mind esteems everything of a temporal or prudential nature as unimportant, and, to some extent, as wholly beneath his consideration, when compared with the universal adoption and practical application of these PRINCIPLES. Home, friends, health, reputation, fortune, and even existence itself — though these are dear and genial to his nature — are considered secondary to the enthronement of God, Justice, and Liberty, in the constitution of men and society.

When I let myself unrestrainedly into the inmost recesses of his character, I feel like speaking to a great audience upon a great theme The occasion is full of interest. I wish to see the people excited and deeply incensed against some gigantic wrong; willing to go to the rack or stake for the Truth's sake. I would willingly be burned to have the Idea—the inherent, vital, glorious, divine PRINCIPLE I advocate—survive me, and be accepted into the consciousness of my fellow-man. I must speak, great, earnest, manly, burning words. My soul must be felt. My theme thoroughly appreciated. If not, then I must away. But the mob must be addressed. Before and to the face of each man I must rebuke the wrong-thinking, the wrong-saying, the wrong-doing. Courage, hope, faith—the divine sense and strength of Right—possesses my whole soul. I feel like quoting passages of expressive, emphatic, hopeful, courageous poetry—I feel like using certain verses from the Old and New Testaments—to explain my inward, but far more *authoritative*, convictions. I must pay no deference to an opinion or institution which has only the prestige of antiquity to recommend it. If it suits not my conscience—my intellectual perception of the logical and absolute relations between premise and conclusion—then I must hesitate not to speak against it. But I must not confound my subjects. Where I speak, there all can speak—my platform is free as Truth makes free—which freedom and my honor are inseparable.

Thus, do I feel when I let my mind into the ruling emotions of William Lloyd Garrison.

His Cautiousness is large and very active, but his religious feelings, being so superior to selfishness of any ordinary kind, enables him to feel no fear. Hope, confidence in self, and courage, are large and active. He is self-supporting; and desires to lean on no man for anything. This mind and its subjects are *one* and indissoluble. He realizes no difference or distinction between itself and its principles—his life, soul, intellect, and they, are one; belong to each other. Hence this Garrison can not think of policies, prudentialisms, compromises, and middle positions; for nature can not be faithless to itself. His love of Father-God is powerful. He has a good appreciation of human nature. He is spiritually minded and intuitional; loves to pray in a practical manner, in the secret closet of his own heart; he believes in, and aspires toward divine principles, subjects, and personages. His mind has *constitutional or vital concentrativeness*—an adhesiveness and integrity to its own positions, motives, and purposes—which does not come from *firmness* or voluntary willingness to be steadfast. He can not be otherwise. In this particular his mind is extraordinarily organized. It would be phrenologically supposed that his "Firmness" is large enough to give rise to stubbornness and dogmatic obstinacy; which is not true. His is the firmness and stability of the oak; the integrity of nature to itself. It would also be supposed, phrenologically, that his "Combativeness" is large enough to lead him to destructive extremes; which is not true. His energy and dauntless courage come wholly from his religious and strong-feeling conscience, which, ignoring all creeds and constitutions, worships at the shrine of GOD, JUSTICE, LIBERTY.

He is jealous of honor. His sensitive and energetic conscience constrains him to discover Wrong and to condemn it, in the most practical or forcible terms, whether that wrong be manifested by rich or poor, church or state, friend or foe. Having no respect for middle positions or compromises, he can not, under any temptations or circumstances, "make friends with the mammon of unrighteousness;" and his out-spoken denunciations of Wrong would be very likely to give offence to opposite characters.

His conscience puts him wholly out of harmony with dominant institutions and constitutions. He finds the most unpopular side of almost every question endorsed by the best consciences, nearest to truth (or likely to be), and therefore more attractive and congenial to him than the common side which every grade of mankind accepts. That abuse which he may receive from the popular conscience, is esteemed by him as complimentary. To be approbated by the majority would startle him exceedingly, with the conviction that he could not be in the Right, *for Right is unpopular!* He takes side with the abused, despitefully treated, and persecuted; because his benevolence urges him to do so, while conscience compels to the work.

Mr. Garrison has no ambition to be either *conspicuous* before the world, or *martyrized* for the glory of principles—he would like it if it were otherwise—but he counts everything of his own as naught, as forming no welcome part of his existence and happiness, which is obtained at the sacrifice of human rights and liberties. His constitutional dignity is so strong, his estimate of personal honor so high and noble, that he can not allow himself to descend to the plane of evil-doers—can not condescend to return evil for evil—can not consent to do evil, however slight, that good may come; therefore he is, from the inmost principles of his character, a NON-RESISTANT. Yet, he will explain, resist, and denounce what he sees to be Wrong. He believes only in the opposition of arguments—in the resistance of a peaceful and manful spirituality—to the evils and wrongs of humankind. No war, no cruelty, no arbitrary punishment; no unequal distribution of liberties among the people. All manner of faithlessness or hypocrisy are to his mind unutterably detestable; so much so that they incline him toward the boldness and exemplification of the opposite extreme.

No man appeals more magnanimously to the high moral and manly feelings of the human mind. He speaks directly to them. Every word must make its legitimate impression. He arouses and cultivates your conscience; he makes you feel indignant and outraged at crimes committed against a brother-man. He is a lover of righteousness; and to obtain it, he fears not to fight the world with a two-edged sword. Finally, the following were my

Impressions when viewing him individually. I will now sum up the effects of this character upon the world. With his organization, William Lloyd Garrison is sure to be *cordially loved and appreciated by his friends, and thoroughly hated and misunderstood by his enemies.* The superficial public will *hate* him—because he so peremptorily ignores their prudentialisms. To the politician, he is "a *rebel*"—because he will not consent to sell his soul to gain the world. To the business or mercantile man, he is "a *fanatic*"—because he is strictly unworldly, self-sacrificing, and unselfish. To the slaveholder, he is "a troublesome *disunionist*"—because he rebukes him for his gigantic crimes, and his wrongs against humanity he unsparingly exposes. To the devotee of creeds, he is "a *blasphemer*"—because he can not be a conservative *except in what he feels and sees to be the Right,* irrespective of forms, external authority, or precedent. To the bible or *pen-and-ink* Christian, he is "an *infidel*"—because he believes only in the *spirit* of Religion, and subjects the letter to free and unrestricted criticism. To the world he is "a radical *Reformer*"—because he can not hold fellowship with the agents and doers of manifest injustice. To his absolute friends, he is "the most sterling and important MAN" of this century—because they know him to be, in every essential particular, just what this psychometrical examination declares—nothing extenuated nor ght set down in malice.

THE END.

www.ingramcontent.com/pod-product-compliance
Lightning Source LLC
LaVergne TN
LVHW020219110826
845151LV00003B/764

* 9 7 8 1 4 2 5 5 3 3 1 9 9 *